"Benjamin Shestakofsky takes us inside the world of Silicon Valley start-ups by centering venture capital's imprint on technology companies. This meticulous organizational ethnography examines the cultures of a globe-spanning firm whose workforce stretches from San Francisco and Las Vegas to the Philippines. A must-read for anyone interested in how technological innovations reproduce global and intersectional inequalities."

—Kimberly Kay Hoang, Professor of Sociology, University of Chicago, and author of *Spiderweb Capitalism: How Global Elites Exploit Frontier Markets* and *Dealing in Desire: Asian Ascendancy, Western Decline, and the Hidden Currencies of Global Sex Work*

"*Behind the Startup* stands to be a groundbreaking ethnography that will shift the conversation about technology, automation, and the future of work by refocusing our attention on the problem of venture capital. This book gave me a whole new way to understand how the gig economy works."

—Ben Snyder, Williams College

"*Behind the Startup* reveals the inner workings of a high-tech startup and exposes how venture capitalists' demands drive inequality among startup workers. Shestakofsky's thought-provoking insights draw from rich ethnographic data of both onshore and offshore sites. A phenomenal study and a must-read!"

—Megan Tobias Neely, Assistant Professor, Department of Organization, Copenhagen Business School

Behind the Startup

Behind the Startup

HOW VENTURE CAPITAL
SHAPES WORK, INNOVATION,
AND INEQUALITY

Benjamin Shestakofsky

UNIVERSITY OF CALIFORNIA PRESS

University of California Press
Oakland, California

© 2024 by Benjamin Shestakofsky

Library of Congress Cataloging-in-Publication Data

Names: Shestakofsky, Benjamin, author.
Title: Behind the startup : how venture capital shapes work, innovation,
    and inequality / Benjamin Shestakofsky.
Description: Oakland, California : University of California Press,
    [2024] | Includes bibliographical references and index.
Identifiers: LCCN 2023041548 (print) | LCCN 2023041549 (ebook) |
    ISBN 9780520395022 (cloth) | ISBN 9780520395039 (paperback) |
    ISBN 9780520395046 (epub)
Subjects: LCSH: Venture capital—California—San Francisco Bay Area—
    Case studies. | New business enterprises—California—San Francisco
    Bay Area—Finance.
Classification: LCC HG4751 .S53 2024 (print) | LCC HG4751 (ebook) |
    DDC 332/.04154097946—dc23/eng/20231113
LC record available at https://lccn.loc.gov/2023041548
LC ebook record available at https://lccn.loc.gov/2023041549

33 32 31 30 29 28 27 26 25 24
10 9 8 7 6 5 4 3 2 1

Contents

Preface

As soon as I open the door it's clear that this isn't a typical Friday at the AllDone office.[1] Exuberant pop music and excited chatter fill the former industrial warehouse that is now home to one of San Francisco's fast-growing tech startups. Rounding the short hallway into the main space, I find the team's twenty employees scattered in clusters around the office: some are chatting in the kitchen, others are standing by their desks. Two executives and the office manager are seated around a table, feverishly collating documents.

People get dressed up for occasions that really matter to them: weddings, funerals, proms, quinceañeras. At AllDone's San Francisco office, today marks one of those occasions. As I approach my desk, I notice that many of my colleagues have traded their usual casual startup garb for fancier attire. Carter, AllDone's president, is sporting a crisp, pink-checkered button-down shirt—he's more dressed up today than he was for the last board meeting—and Victoria, a recent marketing hire, is wearing a black dress and heels. I put my backpack down and Paul, a member of the marketing team, is already sauntering toward me with a broad smile on his face. "You pumped for quarterly review?"

AllDone is an early-stage tech startup that launched its website two years ago. The company runs a digital platform connecting buyers and sellers of local services—housecleaners, plumbers, math tutors, and everything in between—across the United States. Four times a year, business as usual stops at the AllDone office as the staff gather to assess their progress over the past three months, lay out their goals for the next quarter, and spend the night partying at a local bar or event space. At 2:00 p.m. this afternoon, staffers rearrange a long row of lunch tables so everyone can see a video projection screen for a series of presentations, during which anyone will be able to question the executives and managers representing each department. The group starts to calm down, and an expectant hush fills the room.

Peter, AllDone's CEO, begins the meeting by laying out the team's recent accomplishments. The good news is that user growth has "exploded" since the last quarterly review. The bad news, Peter adds, is that "we are not a sustainable enterprise." AllDone is quickly burning through the $4.5 million it raised just a few months ago in its first round of venture capital funding, and the company would have to more than double its revenue over the next six months to start breaking even. But generating more revenue would do more than help AllDone become a self-sustaining company: it would also make the firm more attractive to new investors. Peter displays a slide that reads: "Need to have a rock-solid revenue model before we raise money again." "With Series A," Peter elaborates, referring to a firm's first round of venture capital funding, "you're selling a dream" to investors. "With Series B," he continues, referring to a startup's second round of funding, "you're selling a spreadsheet. We still have a long way to go. No one's gonna drop eight figures [on a company] with uncertain revenue." The room is quiet as a couple of people shift in their seats.

Peter passes the slideshow clicker to Adam, AllDone's director of engineering, who diagnoses the problem. Adam displays graphs showing that, while AllDone's user base is growing, its revenue is plateauing. He says that AllDone has to do a better job of "monetizing" its service, and that his team will have to try out a lot of different strategies to reach the revenue goal. "Maybe the commission model gets us there. Maybe it's some combination [of models] for different services." When Martin takes over to report on the marketing department, he echoes Adam's emphasis on experimentation, explaining that his team will be testing out a variety of ways to attract more users to the platform.

Soon Josh, AllDone's product manager, begins his presentation. He puts up a slide stating that one of the central criteria for deciding which features to develop will be to "Send signals to investors and the broader community." Josh explains that the team needs to ask itself, "What will a Series B investor want to see? What would they be scared to see?" He announces that the product team will be reorganizing its production process, rearranging people into small groups that will focus on particular aspects of the product so each can be held "accountable" for moving key metrics up.

Employees pepper each of the presenters with questions, propose ideas, and engage in spirited debate. Finally, nearly three hours after it began, the meeting draws to a close. AllDone's three cofounders deliver closing remarks emphasizing how excited they are about where the company is heading. Martin has the final word. He tells the group that a friend had recently connected him with a venture capital investor who specializes in marketplace platforms like AllDone. The investor said that his firm was watching AllDone. "You guys are sitting on top of a gold mine," he told Martin. "If you can just crack the nut, you'll be the next Amazon."

· · · · ·

We're frequently told that innovative technologies are changing how we live and work. With the tap of a finger, you can instantly hire someone to drive you home from a bar, deliver your groceries, or assemble your furniture. Over the past few years, researchers and journalists have interviewed members of this burgeoning workforce, studied their posts on online forums, and analyzed the design of the apps they use to make a living.[2] Some have even signed up to perform tasks on digital platforms to experience this new world of work firsthand.[3] Drawing on the voices of so-called "gig workers," their analyses reveal that the conveniences associated with an on-demand economy come at a cost: most workers lack the benefits and protections available to traditional employees, and many quickly discover that their livelihoods are subject to the whims of anonymous and unforgiving algorithms.

This picture of an economy increasingly mediated by digital platforms, however, is incomplete. The algorithmic infrastructures that connect consumers with workers are themselves designed, built, and maintained by the people whose labor sustains platform companies. What happens inside the firms whose technologies are changing the world usually remains inscrutable to those of us on the outside, as much of a "black box" as the algorithms that power their products.[4] Yet there is widespread agreement that their activities are playing a central role in shaping our future. This book is about the people behind one such platform—about the lofty aspirations and pragmatic decisions that structured the experiences of its workforce and of the millions of people who used its software.

I was able to witness the scene recounted above because I spent nineteen months working at AllDone while simultaneously conducting sociological research on the organization. Few scholars have been permitted to observe the inner workings of a tech startup for so long. From my unique vantage point alongside the company's employees, I was able to see the connections and communications between people across the entire firm— and to feel the cycles of excitement and disappointment that are endemic to startup life.

To have any hope of becoming "the next Amazon," tech startups like AllDone must constantly evolve to beat out the competition and attract venture capital funding—money they can then deploy to fuel successive cycles of ever-greater expansion and investment. But the imperative to realize rapid growth at all costs presented AllDone with an ever-shifting array of problems: How could a tiny team of software engineers run a nationwide market for local services? How would a company with a miniscule marketing budget reach new users? And how would AllDone deal with the disillusionment of existing users who were upset with how the platform was constantly changing?

AllDone's architects addressed problems not just by building software, but also by finding new ways to combine the technological capacities of algorithmic systems with the capabilities of low-wage workers. AllDone eventually achieved its vaunted status as one of Silicon Valley's "unicorns"—a tech startup valued at over $1 billion—by building a web of connections that linked software developers in San Francisco with information-processing workers in the Philippines and customer support agents in Las Vegas.

Being part of a high-velocity, high-risk startup meant different things to differently positioned workers. Some enjoyed the thrill that came with orchestrating change, while others struggled to keep up with the platform's dynamic rules and systems. A handful reaped massive rewards as the company grew, but many found that the enterprise to which they'd devoted themselves no longer had a place for them. Although startup founders frequently tout their products' potential to "make the world a better place," AllDone's story highlights how the lion's share of the gains generated by Silicon Valley companies are siphoned into the pockets of a small cadre of elite investors and entrepreneurs—and how technological innovation in our contemporary economy relies on and reproduces long-standing inequalities of gender, class, race, and nation.

This book examines how the capital market that supports technological innovation is reshaping the world in its image. I situate the development of new technologies within the business model that drives innovation in Silicon Valley. I show how venture capitalists compel tech startups to pursue rapid growth and continual experimentation as they try to generate windfall profits for investors. Looking at the organizational processes behind a company's algorithmic systems reveals the role of capital in structuring our technological future. At the same time, investigating how investors' interests shape technological development in our contemporary economy can also open our eyes to alternative models for funding innovation that could lead to different outcomes for workers and societies.

The chapters that follow could in one sense be read as a time capsule from the early 2010s, when I conducted my fieldwork. At that time, the denizens of Silicon Valley were rarely forced to confront the elitism of the tech world or its negative social consequences. Today, technologists are subjected to far more public scrutiny. Nevertheless, the issues illuminated in the pages that follow—including the lack of diversity in the upper ranks of the tech industry, its questionable labor practices, and its wildly unequal distribution of rewards—have not receded, nor have startups become any less relevant to our economy and our everyday lives. Indeed, the amount of investment capital plowed into new tech companies has continued to break records. Between 2012 and 2022, the number of startups receiving funding each year doubled, and in 2021, more venture-backed firms went public than ever before.[5]

Like most companies of its ilk, AllDone was run by privileged white men, and I leveraged my own social status as a white male affiliated with an elite university to gain entrée into the firm. Fieldworkers endeavor to see the world through the eyes of the people we study. We use ethnographic description to communicate those perspectives to our readers, while doing our best to minimize normative judgment. My goal is not to lionize some individuals or to condemn others. Rather, my aim is to uncover the broader structural forces that influenced the activities of the people I observed. By telling AllDone's story, I hope to help people better understand how startups work, what this means for us all, and how we might imagine something better.

Introduction

In 2006, *Time Magazine* famously named "You" its Person of the Year, claiming that the rise of the internet was "a story about community and collaboration on a scale never seen before. . . . It's about the many wresting power from the few and helping one another for nothing and how that will not only change the world, but also change the way the world changes."[1] The free flow of information, it was said, would revolutionize how people communicated and collaborated. Durable social hierarchies would be replaced by decentralized networks. A revival of democratic discourse would return power to the people, toppling dictatorships and challenging political corruption around the globe. And corporate gatekeepers would no longer hold the key to employment—anyone, anywhere, could turn their passion or free time into a job by using the internet to instantly connect with customers or find an audience.

Silicon Valley had assumed its place near the center of the economic universe, and an explosion of tech startups were the stars in its firmament. During the dot-com boom, companies like Yahoo!, eBay, and Netscape combined emerging technologies with ambitious ideas to develop products beloved by millions, while generating massive wealth in the process. People flocked to the San Francisco Bay Area to find jobs, investors poured money into new ventures, and startups went public on the stock market at a record rate. In the five-year span between March 1995 and March 2000, the tech-centered NASDAQ composite more than quintupled in value, signaling the rise of a "new" economy powered by innovation.[2] The high-tech hype came crashing down to earth at the dawn of the new millennium, after the stock market collapsed under the weight of a glut of unproven and unprofitable companies. But techno-optimism quickly came roaring back as a new wave of startups emerged, embodying the hope that visionary founders and the companies they led would change the world for the better.

Over the last few years, however, dreams about our technological future have turned into nightmares. Today it is commonly understood that even as Silicon Valley has overcome technical bottlenecks, it has simultaneously created massive social problems. The old corporate elite has indeed been unseated, but it has not been replaced by empowered citizens. Instead, the plucky and idealistic upstarts of yesterday have become today's formidably entrenched tech titans. Google, a company once guided by computer scientists whose missionary motto was "don't be evil," mines and exploits personal data from almost every aspect of our lives for profit. Instead of giving rise to democratic resurgence and resilience, Facebook has facilitated the global weaponization and spread of misinformation, contributing to the breakdown of the public sphere, vaccine skepticism, and even genocide in Myanmar. Uber flouted longstanding laws and regulations as it sought to conquer the personal transportation sector, worsening urban traffic congestion and pollution while building a business worth tens of billions of dollars on the backs of its poorly compensated, precarious workforce. And this is only a small sample of the critiques leveled at just three once-revered tech companies.[3] What went wrong? Why do startups that promise to change the world for the better create so many problems as they grow?

As the public's infatuation with tech startups has faded, scholars and commentators have produced scores of texts attempting to explain what happened. One set of critiques focuses on the design of the software itself. These accounts show how social disparities and biases get baked into the data that powers algorithmic systems, and how those systems can end up producing unfair and discriminatory outcomes.[4] Another has explored

the role of toxic founders and CEOs, producing entertaining yet horri-
fying profiles of the leaders of companies like Theranos, WeWork, and
Uber.[5] A third set of critiques views the rise of AI, algorithms, big data,
and metrics as coincident with a shift in the structure of capitalism and
processes of capital accumulation.[6] But the leading theories of "platform
capitalism" are pitched at a high level of abstraction, distanced from the
organizational processes, investment patterns, and actors who make—and
are affected by—technology choices. Their explanations rarely specify the
mechanisms through which financial actors' interests, activities, and man-
dates come to define the shape of innovation.[7]

This book builds on these structural approaches to understanding tech
companies by bringing readers inside the day-to-day operations of a successful startup. I was fortunate to gain incredible access to a company
I refer to as AllDone—which ran a platform connecting buyers and sellers
of hundreds of local services like landscaping, wedding photography,
and piano lessons—just as it was beginning its ascent. After entering the
field as a participant-observer conducting research while simultaneously
working for AllDone as an intern, I quickly worked my way into a middle-
management role that afforded me a comprehensive and in-depth view of
the entire operation, from the activities of top executives to the bottom of
the org chart. From this vantage point I witnessed the early stages of the
platform's growth, when an entrepreneurial idea began to make a real impact in the world. My insider access afforded me a unique perspective into
how startups generate social problems.[8]

What I saw was not a case of algorithms run amok. In fact, many of
AllDone's core algorithmic processes were performed not by computers,
but by human workers laboring on a digital assembly line. Nor was it the
story of a solitary genius confidently executing his vision to lead a fledgling firm into new stratospheres of success. AllDone's three cofounders
relied on over 225 people distributed across three locations to keep its
product functioning as the company lurched from crisis to crisis.

Instead, I saw how investors' logics structured everyday life inside a
fast-growing venture. The need to scale as quickly as possible presented
managers with a series of organizational problems. The decisions managers made—and consequently the experiences of AllDone's workforce
and its users—were driven by the need to optimize everything to meet

the expectations of the financiers who could fuel AllDone's growth. Each problem was addressed by reconfiguring the relationship between the company's technology and its workforce. But the costs and benefits of involvement in an ever-changing organization were unequally distributed across AllDone's three work teams in San Francisco, the Philippines, and Las Vegas. The *internal* instability generated by venture capital was then pushed out onto hundreds of thousands of *external* participants—the sellers of local services who used AllDone's platform to find work. Frequent changes to AllDone's rules and payment models caused significant disruptions in users' lives and livelihoods.

In this book I argue that it's time for us to center capital in our investigations of innovation and its impact on societies. A robust account of what tech startups do must include not only how their products affect their users, but also the institutions and incentives driving software development. Technologies are typically produced inside organizations, and organizations exist within institutional ecologies that shape the expectations and possibilities for action.[9] The structure of capital thus shapes and constrains what the people who inhabit organizations do. Instead of taking capitalism for granted as the static background against which technological change plays out, we need to interrogate the motives, goals, and perspectives of the actors who drive the outcomes we observe. What do investors want? How do they go about accomplishing their aims? And how do these imperatives structure the landscape of technological change at this particular moment in history, in the age of algorithms and AI?

HOW TO GET RICH IN TECH

This book examines the dynamics and consequences of *venture capitalism*.[10] Venture capital is what turns today's startups into tomorrow's Big Tech. The structure of the venture capital financing model incentivizes startups to make specific types of choices that come with pervasive downstream effects, constraining the direction of technological development and channeling idealistic visions of a better future for all into a narrow set of outcomes that disproportionately benefit a small number of powerful stakeholders.

Firms adopting the venture capitalism paradigm are founded with the goal of rapidly and precipitously inflating the company's valuation, allowing owners of equity in the startup to achieve a massively profitable "exit" via a lucrative corporate acquisition or initial public stock offering (IPO). Contrasting venture capitalism with traditional entrepreneurship illuminates its core principles.

Imagine an entrepreneur named Michelle who applies for a bank loan to start a limousine service in her city. Michelle's marketing is targeted toward members of her community. To beat out the competition, she focuses on keeping her customers happy by providing high-quality service at a competitive price. Michelle's goal is to establish positive cash flow and steadily build a profitable business. This will allow her to repay the principal and interest on her loan and provide for her family while contributing to the local economy. If she is wildly successful, she may eventually be able to expand her operations into additional locations across the country. In this model, Michelle makes money by convincing her customers to pay more for her service than it costs her to offer that service. Her small business is valuable, in other words, because it generates profit.

Venture capitalism describes a different—and in many ways peculiar—system for creating enterprises. Instead of seeking a traditional bank loan, an entrepreneur might trade an ownership stake in her new company for money she needs to grow her business. Venture capital investors fund startups that they believe have the potential to yield enormous returns, banking on the fact that, in the future, someone else may be willing to pay far more for equity in the company than they initially paid.[11]

Like other investor-owned companies, such as publicly traded corporations, venture-backed startups are not just capitalist organizations that produce and sell goods or services. They also represent a financial asset: a particular type of investment for a particular type of financial actor that imposes a particular logic on its portfolio of firms. As economic sociologist Jens Beckert notes, "credit has a disciplinary effect: it pressures the debtor to act in ways conducive to repaying the loan."[12] Similarly, the venture capital business model is predicated on the expectation that the companies venture capitalists fund will generate profits for investors—in this case, by dramatically increasing their valuation as quickly as possible.

The "general partners" of venture capital firms—also known as "venture capitalists" or "VCs"—are investors who create and manage venture capital funds. Venture capital funds are largely comprised of substantial outlays from "limited partners" such as public and private pension funds, university endowments and foundations, insurance companies, and wealthy families and individuals. General partners often invest some of their own money in the funds they manage as well. Venture capital funds are designed to liquidate their assets and distribute returns to investors within a limited time horizon—typically ten years, but sometimes more or fewer.[13]

Changes in public policy during the late 1970s set the stage for the VC industry's explosive growth. In 1978, the federal tax rate on capital gains was slashed from 49 to 28 percent. A year later, a Department of Labor ruling allowed private pension managers to include riskier investments in their portfolios. In the early 1980s, American VC funds collectively raised between $100 and $200 million per year; by the decade's end, the annual total had reached $4 billion.[14] As the Great Recession of 2007–2009 receded from view, wealthy investors shifted their portfolios from mortgages and credit default swaps to companies founded by hoodie-clad programmers. By 2021, US venture capital firms were investing an annual sum of $311 billion. Globally, venture capitalists plowed $621 billion into nearly thirty-five thousand deals—almost six times as much money as investors sank into dot-coms during the boom in 2000. Over nine hundred startups were valued at over $1 billion, compared to just eighty in 2015.[15] The list of organizations and people with a stake in the venture capital system stretches far beyond a small cadre of professional investors: because venture capital funds have become a standard component of the portfolios of institutional investors, their profits and losses can affect millions of people who invest in public and private employee retirement funds.[16]

Like other financial institutions, venture capital leverages corporations' dependence on external funds to advance its own interests.[17] Venture capital firms build portfolios of high-risk and potentially high-reward startups. VCs expect that most of their investments will either result in losses or yield little to no profit. One or two out of every ten, however, will ideally be incredible successes.[18] A single successful startup can multiply in value by a factor of tens, hundreds, or even thousands, potentially generating billions of dollars in profits for financiers. For example, Sequoia Capital's initial $585,000 investment in Airbnb was worth $4 billion following the company's initial public offering in 2020, representing a 7,000-times gain; its total investment of $260 million across multiple rounds of funding yielded $11.76 billion.[19] The small fraction of highly successful startups that participate in the most lucrative acquisitions and IPOs cover investors' losses and generate the vast majority of returns.

Competition for venture capital funding can be fierce: VCs commonly claim that they receive hundreds or even thousands of pitches from entrepreneurs for every startup they choose to fund. In exchange for their services, general partners extract substantial fees from limited partners, including an annual management fee of 1.5 to 3 percent of funds committed and 20 to 35 percent of the fund's returns over a predefined benchmark. (A "two and twenty" model is most common.) Given these high fees and the risk involved, investors expect substantial profits: top VC funds may net investors an annual return of over 20 percent.[20] In comparison, during the 2010s, annual economic growth in the United States typically hovered around 2 percent.[21]

To help offset the risks they assume when investing in new companies, venture capitalists take an active role in the startups they fund. The lead investor of each VC deal is typically awarded a seat on the startup's board of directors. From this position, investors monitor the firm's performance and participate in corporate governance, pushing each of the companies in their portfolio to attempt to become one of its rare successes. Board members' voting rights afford them direct input into the company's decision-making processes. They use this authority to protect their investments and ensure that the company acts in ways that will maximize the financial interests of their limited partners. Board members control the firm's most important decisions, including when and how to change corporate strategy, when to raise additional funds, and whether to replace the company's executive team. It is also common for VCs to be directly involved in recruiting executive-level managers for growing firms.[22] Consequently, when entrepreneurs accept VC funding, they cede a significant degree of control over the firm's strategy to investors who favor risk-taking over efficiency and emphasize relentless innovation geared toward rapid— and even arguably reckless—growth.[23]

The case of Uber, one of the most influential venture-backed startups the world has ever seen, illustrates how the model works. In 2008, Garrett Camp had an idea for a new digital platform that could revolutionize the personal transportation industry by allowing customers to instantly summon a private car using a smartphone app. Instead of securing a bank loan to jumpstart their business, as did Michelle in the hypothetical example above, Camp and cofounder Travis Kalanick sought funding from venture capital investors who took a bet on a risky proposition and proffered millions of dollars in exchange for an ownership stake in the fledgling startup.

Because Uber's cofounders and investors dreamed of someday selling the company for billions of dollars, their primary commitment was to "scale"—creating a product that could accommodate an ever-expanding network of users who would come to rely on the platform's services. Uber publicly launched its app in 2011 in San Francisco. In 2014, Uber had a presence in one hundred cities around the globe; a mere two years later, it was in five hundred cities. By the beginning of 2016, Uber had facilitated a total of one billion trips; within another year, that figure had increased to five billion, and a year after that it stood at ten billion.[24] The company's aggressive expansion was fueled by venture capital investors who were eager to share in Uber's success: VCs repeatedly pumped millions—and then billions—of dollars into the fast-growing firm.[25] When Uber held its initial public stock offering in 2019, the company was valued at $69 billion, with its top five shareholders (three investment funds and two cofounders) owning stock worth a combined $27.1 billion.[26]

Yet, for all its successes, one curious fact about Uber demands our attention: at the time of this writing, the company had yet to log a year in which its revenue outpaced its losses. In fact, it has famously lost billions of dollars per year, with no clear path to profitability. And Uber is not alone. During the first three quarters of 2018, a record 83 percent of US IPOs were of companies that had been unprofitable at the time of their listing, the highest proportion since recordkeeping began in 1980.[27] According to one recent analysis, over half of the publicly traded companies that VCs once valued at over $1 billion have registered more than $500 million in cumulative losses.[28] For many startup founders, building a sustainable, efficiently run business is a distant goal. Their more immediate motivation is to turn their ideas into blockbuster deals by achieving scale at all costs—hence the common refrain of "growth first, profits later." On this front, founders' interests are aligned with those of venture capital funds, which generate profits not from a company's operating revenue, but instead when the firms in which they invest appreciate in value.

In sum, venture capitalism describes a system for funding new enterprises aimed at scaling rapidly and precipitously. Whether or not a VC-backed firm makes more money than it takes in is largely irrelevant from the perspective of its investors; what is most important is its ability to cultivate the perception that it can push its funders toward a massively profitable exit that leaves other parties—either a larger corporation or the public markets—holding the bag.

This book is about venture capital's imprint on technology companies—not about venture capitalists themselves. Their story has already been told by journalists, scholars, and industry insiders.[29] Instead, *Behind the Startup* proceeds like the film *Jaws*, in which the powerful figure of the shark remains largely unseen, and the audience comes to know it through people's responses to it.[30] Venture capital produces imaginaries and incentives that nudge individuals and narrow their choices. This book offers an intimate look at the evolution of a tech startup to uncover both the social processes that drive the VC system and its consequences for entrepreneurs, workers, and societies. Readers will see what VC's influence does to an organization as it mobilizes different groups to co-construct its power.

FUNDING INNOVATION

Innovation—or "the profitable combination of new or existing knowledge, resources, and/or technologies"—is one of the key drivers of capitalist economies.[31] New tech companies are inherently uncertain propositions. Startups typically develop novel and unproven applications of technologies and are often founded without a product in hand or evidence that there will be a market for that product. At multiple stages of their development, entrepreneurs need money to commercialize their ideas and fuel their companies' operations. Enter venture capitalism, with its insatiable appetite for high-risk, high-reward investments. VC firms provide funding to nascent innovation-based enterprises—as well as advice, access to a network of resources, and reputational benefits—in exchange for equity in the startups they fund.

If the goal of venture capitalism is pursuing scale to rapidly inflate a startup's valuation, it employs distinctive techniques in support of that goal. These practices have been most succinctly described by Facebook's longtime motto: "Move fast and break things." This approach to innovation rewards a willingness to experiment over proven results. A startup's software engineers often release product features rapidly and with relatively minimal testing, then track user engagement to continually repair and refine them through iterative, data-driven processes.[32] Relentless experimentation helps nascent tech companies figure out exactly what their product is, how it will work, and where they can find a market for that product. As early-stage startups struggle to define themselves, nothing is nailed down and everything is up for grabs. Those that outlast the competition and secure a quasi-monopolistic position in the market can achieve massive gains for investors as their valuations skyrocket.[33]

Just as venture capitalism prescribes a startup's goals and techniques, it also advances a particular set of ideas about how business should be done, and about the moral status of the startup in our world. Founders and investors typically buy into an ethos of "techno-solutionism," which holds that technology can solve even the world's most intractable social problems. Failure is good, provided that it's framed as the outcome of an "experiment" that yields experiences and data to inform the development of future product features or ventures.[34] The ideal worker is someone who takes on an "entrepreneurial" mindset and eagerly embraces risk in a fast, flexible, and ever-changing work environment—regardless of her eventual share of the rewards.[35] The "disruption" of existing markets—and the destruction of industries, jobs, and livelihoods associated with the old ways of doing things—are justified on the grounds that innovation represents progress toward a better world for all.[36] By combining unbelievable wealth with the assurance that entrepreneurs can get rich while doing good, the promise of venture capitalism has captured the imagination of countless people around the globe.

The world of the venture capitalist is defined by "radical uncertainty."[37] The VC's job is, as noted investor Brook Byers has said, "to see the future," or to anticipate which founders and enterprises stand the best chance of success in creating and marketing a product that may be without precedent.[38] Prominent VCs like Peter Thiel cultivate public personas that position them as oracles of our technological future, near-messianic decision-makers uniquely skilled at selecting and supporting the groundbreaking visionaries whose ideas will change the world.

In the United States, the links between capital, innovation, and ideological justifications of "disruption" have been reinforced by structural shifts in corporate governance. In the decades following World War II, the research and development arms of large corporations churned out inventions that changed the world, such as the transistor (AT&T Bell Labs), the personal computer (IBM), and ethernet technology for local area networks (Xerox Palo Alto Research Center). In response to pressure from investors to increase shareholder value during the 1980s, large corporations began to reduce their investments in internal research. New businesses founded by entrepreneurs became the source of an increasing proportion of new high-tech hardware and software applications—and those businesses were increasingly backed by venture capital.[39] The first modern VC firm in the United States, American Research and Development Corporation, was founded by academic, business, and political elites in Boston in 1946 in an effort to fund regional growth. In 1959, Draper, Gaither and Anderson became the first venture capital limited partnership founded in Silicon Valley.[40]

Half a century later, Silicon Valley has emerged as the undisputed geographic locus of the tech world.[41] The Valley boasts an unparalleled institutional ecosystem designed to help entrepreneurs bring new technologies to market, encompassing accounting, executive search, law firms, investment banks and venture capital firms, commercial and industrial real estate brokers, and research universities and startup accelerators, among others. Today, Silicon Valley-based startups reap more venture capital funding than the region's four closest US competitors (Massachusetts, Southern California, New York, and Texas) combined.[42]

By 2018, the five most valuable companies in the world were Apple, Amazon, Alphabet (Google's parent company), Microsoft, and Facebook— all tech companies, and all supported in their early years by venture capital.[43] Today, tech entrepreneurs take for granted that the road to success is paved with VC funding; that a startup must engage in relentless experimentation to grow its business and inflate its valuation as quickly as possible; and that innovation is a force for good, no matter how many lives and livelihoods are "disrupted" along the way.

FINANCIALIZATION AND WORK

Venture capitalism is a manifestation of structural changes that increasingly shifted power into the hands of the financial sector, which began to cement its influence over the economy following the crisis of the 1970s. Amid increased competition, rampant inflation, and rising energy costs, American corporations' profit margins began to stagnate.[44] Powerful actors responded to this threat by mobilizing for changes in corporate governance and public policy to reinvigorate profits—a social movement of the elite aimed at reinventing the corporation.

The owners of large firms—their shareholders—increasingly held executives accountable for the slowed growth in profits. Investors advocated for the "shareholder value" conception of the firm, according to which the sole purpose of publicly held US corporations is to maximize the price of a company's shares on the stock market, thereby increasing the returns to owners. Shareholders organized to increase pressure on executives, incentivizing them to make decisions that would be perceived as prioritizing investors' interests.[45]

The so-called "shareholder revolution" changed the nature of the game that corporations were playing. Previously, executives had been focused on increasing sales to maintain their companies' growth and stability, reinvesting gains in developing products and workers. At the same time, they attended to their responsibilities to an array of stakeholders, including their customers, employees, and the communities in which they operated. General Electric's 1953 shareholder report touted how the company worked "in the balanced best interests of all," describing how much the company paid in salaries, benefits, and taxes before mentioning that it had returned a modest 3.9 percent of sales to investors.[46] Today, executives must commit to pleasing shareholders who view the corporation not as a social institution but as a bundle of assets.[47] It has become less important for companies to focus on balancing their books and more important that they increase the firm's market value every quarter, regardless of the instability that may result from their actions. Companies are designed to redistribute resources upward and risk downward. Managers are duty-bound to maximize the returns delivered to investors; considerations of the social value they create or the harms they inflict on workers and societies are secondary.[48]

As the criteria for being considered a successful company changed, firms altered how they operated. Corporate reorganizations became more common, and companies adopted more cost-cutting technologies and employment practices such as layoffs, outsourcing, and scaling back compensation and fringe benefits. At the same time, ostensibly nonfinancial firms, like General Electric and General Motors, increasingly pursued financial activities like mortgage lending as a means of generating profits.[49]

As companies found new ways to trim costs and boost revenue, executives began to siphon off a far greater share of corporate profits to investors. In the 1970s, publicly traded US companies paid their shareholders about one-third of their earnings via dividend payments. A 1982 rule change at the Securities and Exchange Commission allowed corporations to buy shares of their own stock, rewarding investors with inflated share prices by reducing the supply of company stock on the market. Since then, stock buybacks have come to consume most of the earnings of S&P 500 companies. By the late 1980s, publicly traded corporations were distributing *more than 100 percent* of their profits to shareholders via dividends and stock buybacks, either by drawing down savings or selling off assets to pay investors more than the companies had earned.[50] This has left corporations with less money to invest in opening new plants and stores or training and compensating workers. During the 2010s, publicly traded corporations spent over $3.8 trillion on their own stocks—more than every other type of investor (e.g., mutual funds, pension funds, foreign investors, and individuals) combined.[51]

These developments were indicators of the trend toward financialization—what economist Gerald A. Epstein has described as "the increasing role of financial motives, financial markets, financial instruments, financial actors, and financial institutions in the operations of domestic and international economies."[52] Deregulation of the banking sector during the

1980s, the concentration of the financial industry, and the introduction of innovative financial products further contributed to the dominance of financial actors and activities in the US economy.[53]

The rise of venture capital funds as a mainstream investment option for wealthy individuals and institutions is among the most visible manifestations of this trend. VC investment decisions are premised upon the belief that, at some point in the future—through the sale of shares to another investor during a subsequent round of VC funding, corporate acquisition, or initial public stock offering—another party may be willing to pay a substantially higher price for a comparable ownership stake in the firm. In this sense, venture capital is no different from financial activities in other segments of the finance industry. In the words of one investment banker, "at the end of the day, with any investment product, you might say, you're looking for somebody else to pay you more for it."[54]

Yet there are also aspects of venture capitalism that are not adequately accounted for by theories that specify how finance capital affects organizational structures and practices. Capitalism is a system characterized by "dynamic disequilibrium," so it's no surprise that even after tech startups grow into publicly traded corporations, they continue to innovate as they compete for attention and dollars.[55] But venture-backed startups represent a supercharged version of financialization that takes its core logics to extremes. VC investments are far more speculative than investments in publicly traded firms, and VCs invest with the knowledge that most of the firms they fund will not survive. Startups maximize flexibility not to wring more efficiency out of existing operations, but instead to facilitate constant experimentation aimed at rapid and precipitous growth. Startup workers build companies on quicksand; if organizations are to survive while developing untested products in fast-changing environments, everything must be subject to change.

The consequences of the rise of finance have been far-reaching, particularly for workers. In an increasingly financialized economy, workplaces and work are increasingly structured to serve the interests of investors, often at the expense of employees. Before the shareholder revolution, firms typically hired additional workers to cover new roles and responsibilities associated with growth. Now, however, companies (and their investors) prioritize organizational flexibility. In practical terms, this means that the corporate workforce has become increasingly bifurcated. Organizations typically invest in a smaller "core" of well-compensated employees and maintain arms-length relationships with a greater share of (often outsourced, subcontracted, or part-time) "peripheral" workers, many of whom possess less specialized skills, receive lower wages, and enjoy fewer of the legal protections associated with full-time employment. Workers with previously secure jobs have found themselves exposed to more insecurity in the labor market. The availability of middle-class union jobs for people holding only a high school degree has plummeted.[56] Median employment tenure has shrunk, as has the percentage of employees receiving fringe benefits like medical coverage and defined benefit retirement plans. Meanwhile, protections like unemployment and health insurance remain tied to full-time employment, failing to reflect the rise of nonstandard employment arrangements.[57]

These changes in the relationship between workers and employers have contributed to a staggering rise in income inequality. Between 1980 and 2014, the top 1 percent of earners in the United States saw their share of the national income double, from about 10 to 20 percent. Workers in the financial sector have been among those driving this phenomenon: the increasing profitability of financial institutions has allowed its workforce to claim a wage premium of 50 percent over workers in other industries.[58] Yet, for workers in the bottom three-quarters of the income distribution, wages have been stagnant. The increasing importance of financial activities in corporations has decreased the relative value of workers involved in productive activities; along with the declining power of organized labor, this has left workers with less leverage to advocate for their own interests within firms.[59] In short, workers' cut of the national income has decreased even as productivity has risen, signaling a redistribution of income from workers to managers, executives, and investors.[60]

In venture-backed startups, where stock options are commonly included in privileged employees' compensation packages, some workers may find themselves in a unique position, inhabiting the role of employee while simultaneously sharing investors' dreams of a massive payout. Yet, unlike investors, startup workers—who may log long hours in precarious jobs while in some cases even being asked to forego their salaries—find that their fortunes are tied to *particular* companies or industries, leaving them with fewer opportunities to diversify their risk portfolios.[61] Founders value organizational flexibility both because they genuinely do not know what the future will hold for their startups, and because they know that investors would be wary of companies that make long-term commitments to specific people and processes.

This dynamic makes startup cultures ideal sites in which to observe how the financialization of the economy is transforming workplaces and workers' subjectivities. Sociologists have long endeavored to situate labor relations within their social contexts to understand the cultural dimensions of work. Managers and workers participate in organizational cultures that endow tasks with meanings and values, which in turn matter for how workers are motivated, how tasks are executed, and how workplace technologies are deployed.[62] Venture capitalism invites workers to dwell in fantasies of how being a part of a startup could transform their lives. *Behind the Startup* thus attends not only to fluidity in the organization of production at AllDone, but also to how startup workers' livelihoods and emotions are linked to the imaginaries invoked by venture capital and the organizational flux that it instigates.[63]

LAG, DRAG, AND THE CULTURE OF STARTUPS

Behind the Startup examines how a Silicon Valley company that I call All-Done navigated the pressures imposed by its quest for scale. By offering readers a firsthand look at the dilemmas managers faced, the decisions they made, and how their perceptions of problems and solutions were informed by the imperatives of investors, I show how the institution of venture capital shapes processes of technological innovation and workplace cultures. Venture capital creates organizational problems that must be addressed not only through technology development, but also through the continual reorganization of labor in and around technological systems.

In making this argument, I am informed by and building on scholarship that cuts across the fields of the sociology of work, economic sociology, management and organization studies, science and technology studies, and critical data studies. Through analysis of the case of AllDone, I develop theory about the dynamics of venture capital–backed firms.

Tech startups' activities are set in motion by *valuation lag*—a temporal and imaginative gap between a venture capital firm's investment in a company and its ability to realize returns. At each phase of an entrepreneurial firm's development, the demands of investors systematically generate organizational problems, which I call *drags*. Imagine a spacecraft lifting off from a launchpad. If the rocket fails to achieve enough velocity to escape the atmosphere, it will eventually plummet back down to Earth. Similarly, startups must continually accelerate their growth, overcoming roadblocks that threaten their ability to meet the ever-rising performance benchmarks imposed by VCs. A drag is thus an organizational problem that must be solved in order for the company to meet investors' expectations.

I use the terms *lag* and *drag* because investment is by its very nature future oriented.[64] The venture capital business model pressures startups to forge a path into an imagined future of immense and rapid expansion. Yet the realities of organizational life at any given moment inevitably trail behind investors' and executives' projections. Managers must find ways to catch up—to bring reality in line with the dream and to ensure a path to substantial payouts.

Startup workers inhabit the accelerated temporality of finance capital.[65] Moving fast is imperative as entrepreneurs strive to simultaneously build their company, grow their user base, and gather successive rounds of funding while outpacing the competition in emergent and fluid markets. Advice for startup founders reveals an obsession with dynamism. According to one prominent VC, in a fast-growing startup, "the need for change never stops"; or, as a founder puts it, "In startups, if you take your foot off the pedal, the default mode is reverse, not neutral."[66] The problem of speed lies at the heart of the VC-backed firm, whose leaders are haunted by the ever-present worry that they are falling behind. Startups race to fix whatever is putting drag on the rocket, trying to alter its trajectory to meet the future state that founders and investors envision rather than the state it is currently moving toward. Yet, as startups evolve, their leaders and employees frequently discover that the technology isn't quite where it needs to be, that users aren't quite ready for the changes they've designed, and indeed that nothing seems to work the way it's supposed to work.

How do startups overcome the barriers that threaten to impede their progress? In media appearances and pitches to investors, executives often suggest that their companies' ingenious technology will allow them to grow their businesses and seamlessly accommodate exponential increases in users. In reality, however, achieving scale at a breakneck pace is rarely so simple.

At AllDone, the demand for expansion through ceaseless experimentation generated interdependent work practices and divergent experiences of organizational change across the company's three work teams. For software developers in the San Francisco office, it was fun and exciting to tinker with the product. By pushing the numbers up, they hoped to push the company and themselves toward an imagined future of winning big and cashing out. Meanwhile, workers in the Philippines handled routinized information-processing tasks, supporting or standing in for software to allow AllDone's engineers to stay focused on innovation. They developed a culture of familial love that reflected—and helped to reproduce—the relative stability of their jobs. The fact that AllDone's product and even its business model were always shifting created major challenges for frontline workers in Las Vegas. They felt traumatized by AllDone's irate customers and frustrated that the engineers didn't seem to care about their input or the emotional pain they were experiencing.

Rather than examining full-time employees and far-flung contractors in isolation from one another, this book considers a tech company as a globalized system comprised of computing and human labor. This perspective allows us to observe how startups displace pressures emerging from investors' demands onto particular subunits at particular times. As they labor within a fast-changing organization, different groups of workers affix different meanings to their work and their place within the company's technological systems and hierarchies of value.

In high-tech workplaces like AllDone, the direct coercion of workers has increasingly been replaced by managerial strategies designed to elicit their consent, cooperation, and investment in work. Culture has consequently taken on a more important role as a means of workplace control.[67] Members of each of AllDone's three work teams relied on different appeals to authority—collaborative (San Francisco), hierarchical (Philippines), and charismatic (Las Vegas)—to orient workers toward a common goal of achieving massive growth at all costs. Comparing AllDone's three work teams allows us to see how workers' experiences with technological change are filtered through the organizational strategies that managers enact to meet investors' expectations.

The processes through which investors' imperatives are translated into organizational practice are messy and unpredictable. What is consistent, however, is that tech companies rely on various forms of human labor—much of it poorly compensated and hidden from users—to overcome organizational drag and help new technologies fulfill their promise.[68] Successfully addressing a source of drag generates returns for owners of equity in the firm by creating measurable progress toward the achievement of organizational goals. Once procedures are in place to address a particular drag and the startup acquires additional funding, investors then establish new targets that guide the subsequent phase of organizational development and the generation of new sources of value. Each new drag is layered atop the existing organizational infrastructure, creating a stratified foundation upon which new processes are developed and new value is created.

In sum, I demonstrate that, at the level of the firm, venture capitalism systematically presents startups with a series of obstacles that must be overcome in order to preserve the possibility of profits. The resolution of each problem, however, generates further hurdles as a firm grows—success in one moment begets escalated expectations in the next, and practices that supported previous stages of growth may themselves give rise to new and bigger problems. In other words, venture capitalism persistently generates novel contradictions inside small firms that are trying to accomplish big things as quickly as possible.[69] Rarely do we look at these contradictions from the point of view of the workers who must navigate them. Centering capital thus gives us a new perspective on tech startups by locating investors' needs at the root of both technology design and its social consequences for entrepreneurs, workers, and users.[70]

INTRODUCING ALLDONE:
INSIDE AN EARLY-STAGE STARTUP

In this book, I draw on data gathered during nineteen months of participant-observation research conducted at AllDone (a pseudonym), a tech startup operating on the frontiers of the digital economy. AllDone aimed to transform local service markets by using technology to more efficiently connect buyers and sellers. AllDone had launched its nationwide, online marketplace in early 2010. The company was one of many aiming to build an "Amazon for local services," a platform that would make it as easy to find and hire providers of local services online as it is to buy products. Its listings included more than six hundred service categories, ranging from home improvement (e.g., plumbers and electricians), to event services (e.g., DJs and caterers), to guitar teachers, locksmiths, and many others.

AllDone's users were buyers and sellers of local services. Buyers who visited AllDone from a computer or mobile device were presented with a text box in which they could enter the type of service they were looking for. Buyers would then fill out a short form, answering three or more questions about the details of the job. For example, a buyer seeking a landscaper would first be prompted to select items from the following list that best described the type of services she needed: mowing, trimming, and edging; de-weeding and weed prevention; leaf raking/cleanup; seeding; fertilizer application; mulching; insect control; aeration; or other. Then, she would choose from a list of five options to specify the approximate size of her lawn. Next, she would indicate how often she needed this service: one time, once a week, every other week, two to three times a month, as needed, or other. The buyer would then be provided with a text box in which she could write any other relevant details about the job. Finally, the buyer would select from a menu to indicate when she needed these services: flexible, in the next few days, as soon as possible, on a particular date, or other. After the buyer clicked the "Submit" button, she would be provided with a message informing her to expect quotes from local AllDone sellers to arrive in her e-mail inbox within twenty-four hours.

Sellers used AllDone's service to connect with potential buyers of their services. On AllDone's platform, sellers competed with one another to win customers' business. Upon signing up with AllDone, each seller established a profile page describing the services she offered, accompanied by one or more photographs and reviews of her services. Whenever a buyer submitted a request for services, AllDone would distribute the request to sellers in the buyer's area who might be capable of performing the job.

Sellers would receive an e-mail or text message informing them that they could review the request. Sellers who were available and interested in the job could pay AllDone a fee to send a quote to the buyer, including a price estimate, information on what was included in their price, and a pitch describing why they were qualified for the job. Sellers typically paid between two and fifteen dollars to send each quote, with prices varying depending on their geographic area and the type of services they offered.[71] Buyers and sellers managed any subsequent communication, provision of service, and payment; AllDone assumed no formal responsibility for the outcome of market activities.

AllDone provides an ideal setting in which to examine how venture capitalists' agendas influence technological design, as well as the consequences for the workers associated with a startup. The company was part of a new wave of Silicon Valley firms using software to transform traditional local service markets. Like Uber, Airbnb, and a host of other digital platform providers, AllDone aggregated a vast array of local markets into one centralized online clearinghouse. These platforms are designed to make it easier for buyers and sellers to locate and transact with one another, while also providing an opportunity for companies to extract fees from users and profit from their brokerage positions.

Like many tech companies, including Google and Microsoft, AllDone's workforce was populated by both full-time employees who received generous employment benefits and long-term contractors who did not.[72] At AllDone, the numerical imbalance between these two categories of workers was particularly stark: during the period of my research, less than 9 percent of AllDone's workforce was classified as full-time employees.

The organization was comprised of three work teams. For most of my tenure with the company, the San Francisco office was home to about twenty full-time employees in engineering, design, marketing, business, and operations divisions. A remote, work-from-home team of two hundred people across the Philippines typically handled routinized data-processing tasks. And a remote, work-from-home team of ten in the Las Vegas area interacted with AllDone users via telephone. Members of the two remote teams generally held full-time, open-ended independent contractor positions, which meant that they did not receive the range of benefits—including health insurance, stock options, paid vacation, and reimbursement for education and training expenses—offered to full-time employees in San Francisco.

Each of AllDone's three work sites was demographically distinct. All San Francisco staffers were educated at selective or elite colleges, almost all were in their twenties, and all but two were male. Most members of AllDone Philippines were college-educated and between twenty and forty years old, and over two-thirds were women. AllDone Las Vegas's staff was almost exclusively female; most were middle-aged, and some did not have college degrees. Filipino contractors were recruited, hired, and supervised via oDesk, a digital platform designed to connect employers with freelancers from around the globe who can complete projects online. Las Vegas–based workers were recruited using local job postings on Craigslist and then supervised via oDesk. Although members of the teams in the Philippines and Las Vegas were officially designated as contractors who were paid via an intermediary firm (oDesk), managers in San Francisco viewed remote workers as full-time members of their teams. Workers, too, understood their roles with AllDone as "online jobs" of indefinite duration.

AllDone experienced rapid growth during the course of my fieldwork. By the time I left the company, over 250,000 sellers had signed up with AllDone, with 25,000 sellers submitting at least one quote to a buyer per month. Each month, AllDone was acquiring 4,000 new sellers and sending sellers over 100,000 consumer requests. When I began my research, AllDone had just raised $4.5 million in its first round of venture capital funding; at that point, the terms of the deal presumed that the company was worth $17 million. Shortly before my fieldwork ended, the company raised a second round of funding totaling $12.5 million, at a valuation of $40 million. At that time, nobody knew that years later the firm would become one of the startup world's rare successes, with a valuation exceeding $3 billion.[73]

A friend helped me gain research access to AllDone by introducing me to Martin—a former high school classmate and one of the company's cofounders—via e-mail. Martin agreed to meet with me, and following our conversation offered me an unpaid internship. I would come to the office one day per week and assist Martin with marketing tasks in exchange for research access. As I became more involved in various projects, my role at AllDone quickly evolved into a part-time, paid position that later turned into a full-time role as AllDone's director of customer support and operations manager.

Organizational ethnographers often "learn by doing," engaging in the same activities as the individuals they study and working alongside them in the group's own space and time. This strategy can allow fieldworkers to obtain a firsthand perspective on what people do and how they make sense of their work. It is rare for researchers to gain prolonged access to the inner workings of tech startups, which may be protective of both trade secrets and their reputations.[74] The fact that I had previous work experience in a startup may have helped me convince AllDone's leaders that my time studying and working for the company could be mutually beneficial. But there were drawbacks to my position as well. The methodological appendix contains an expanded discussion of how I gained access to AllDone, how I gathered and analyzed data, and the opportunities and challenges associated with my role in the field.

Spending more than a year and a half conducting sustained and systematic participant-observation research within a tech startup allowed me to observe the evolving relationships between workers and innovative software systems. I employ internal comparison—examining each of All-Done's work teams in relation to the others—to analyze how differently positioned workers understood their place within a fast-changing company. My work responsibilities within the organization—where, among other roles, I served as a broker of information between each of the company's three teams—placed me in arguably the most advantageous structural position within the firm to understand the workings of and relations between all three groups simultaneously. Whereas most studies of work and technological change examine how the introduction of new machinery affects the organization and execution of work, I investigate how configurations of software and workers were repeatedly transformed.[75] These transformations were linked to the organization's efforts to adapt to shifting pressures from competitors, users, and, most importantly, investors.

This study provides a unique perspective from which to develop theory about the intersection of finance capital, technological change, and organizational structures and cultures. Although no single firm is representative of all other companies, examining the dynamics of work and technology within a venture-backed startup is advantageous. As a fieldworker, I could directly observe the logic of finance capital as it played out in an accelerated fashion within a particular organizational setting.[76] This approach allows me to analyze how the macro-level economic forces of financialization condition the micro level of everyday organizational activities.[77]

OVERVIEW OF THE BOOK

In the coming pages, I detail how pressure from investors required All-Done's managers to constantly experiment with product features, business models, organizational design, and labor practices. AllDone quickly inflated its valuation by pairing automation with low-wage labor. I show how the fledgling startup recruited different kinds of workers to solve the problems that must be overcome for investors to generate profits. Furthermore, members of each of AllDone's work teams experienced and understood the organization's chaotic dynamism in different yet interrelated ways.

The book is split into four parts, each of which is centered on a particular organizational problem presented by the expectations of venture capital investors, and how actors inside AllDone dealt with it. These four parts of the book proceed in chronological order. At the same time, they move across geographic locations to track the work team or teams tasked with "fixing" the lag or drag that defined each period of AllDone's development.[78]

Parts 1 through 3 of the book each contain two chapters. The first of each chapter pair examines how AllDone's workforce and technologies were organized to solve the primary problem that the firm faced during a specific phase in its development. The second chapter in each part investigates the subjective dimensions of organizational life, or how workers made sense of and communicated about what they did—which I refer to as "organizational culture." Taken together, each chapter pair provides a window into how members of each team contributed to and experienced the company's evolution.

Part 1 introduces AllDone's San Francisco headquarters, where the startup's product was designed and built. Here, I show how AllDone resolved the problem of *valuation lag* by combining labor processes that emphasized experimentation with symbolic practices that encouraged speculation. These strategies allowed the company to secure resources and enhanced the firm's perceived value to investors. AllDone's dynamism was a source of excitement for San Francisco–based staffers, as engrossing challenges, observable successes, and workers' financial stake in the company reinforced their belief that the startup and its employees could be destined for greatness.

Part 2 traces the first phase of my research, when AllDone's executives hoped to take advantage of the firm's first round of venture capital funding by increasing demand for the product. To overcome the problems of *technical drag* associated with the limitations of automation, AllDone employed information-processing workers located across the Philippines to support or stand in for software by performing repetitive tasks. AllDone Philippines' rhetoric of love, family, and gratitude reflected the relative stability of their jobs and work functions, helping to foster trust and affective attachments while simultaneously obscuring massive inequalities between contractors in the Philippines and managers in San Francisco.

In part 3, I describe the second period of research, when executives shifted their focus toward generating a sustainable revenue stream that would ensure the company's longevity and attract a second round of VC funding. Phone support workers distributed across the Las Vegas area addressed the problem of *trust drag* by managing the company's ties with disgruntled users and helping them adjust to modifications to the platform's rules and features. These workers struggled to keep up with frequent product changes orchestrated by developers in the San Francisco office while simultaneously managing the mounting dissatisfaction of AllDone's users, resulting in a workplace suffused with anxiety, frustration, and resentment.

Part 4 covers the final phase of research, when AllDone secured a second round of venture capital funding. Investors' new expectations for how the firm should be run highlighted the challenges of *organizational drag* as the company transitioned from an early-stage startup into a more mature enterprise. Across all three work teams, new leaders were hired to rationalize and professionalize the company's operations by implementing bureaucratic procedures, routines, and authority structures. Workers became increasingly disenchanted as the practices, values, and attachments they had come to take for granted were revealed to be temporary fixtures of an ever-changing organization. As AllDone flourished, venture capitalism's exploitative logic became increasingly clear to workers who had invested their lives in the startup dream. Some became disillusioned as they saw the fruits of their labor accruing largely to investors and executives. Others discovered that the company no longer had a place for them, and were unable to share in the success they had helped to create.

In the concluding chapter, I discuss how societies might promote new ways of organizing innovation that can distribute its benefits more broadly. For all the claims emanating from Silicon Valley about how its technological innovations will "change the world," the story of AllDone highlights how venture capitalism is designed to reproduce a vastly unequal status quo. Millions of people are involved in building, supporting, and using the products developed by venture-backed startups. These companies mobilize and manipulate the needs and desires of the many to deliver massive returns to a few of their wealthiest stakeholders. Many of the social ills that we attribute to technological change can be more accurately attributed not to the properties of technologies themselves, but instead to how innovation has become an avenue for a particular mode of capitalist speculation. If we want our future to look different than our current trajectory, we must first change how new technologies are funded.

PART I San Francisco

LAUNCHING THE ROCKET SHIP

1 Orchestrating Change

AllDone emerged from a shared ambition that eventually grew into an idea, an organization, a platform, and a business valued at over $3 billion. Four friends in their mid-twenties—all white men and recent college graduates, three from Ivy League institutions—dreamed of teaming up to start a company. Two had previously worked together to launch a political advocacy organization. One was the son of a highly successful tech entrepreneur. Over the course of a year during the late 2000s, they held weekly conference calls to identify the biggest possible business opportunities and how they could use technology to capitalize on them.

They recognized that, although companies like Amazon and eBay had achieved tremendous success by establishing online marketplaces on which people could buy and sell goods, the market for local services remained far more fragmented. In other words, it was easy to buy a book online, but much more complicated to hire a house cleaner. The major players—websites such as Craigslist and Yelp—offered antiquated user interfaces or limited sets of features. Given that local service markets in the United States accounted for between $400 and $800 billion of annual economic activity, the four friends surmised that the first company that managed to simplify the hiring process and achieve widespread popularity could become the next Amazon.[1]

When AllDone's cofounders landed on their potentially multibillion-dollar idea, they lacked the money they needed to build the business. Like many tech entrepreneurs, they first turned to the "informal risk capital market" for seed money to get their company off the ground.[2] After gathering $500,000 from family members and another entrepreneur-turned-investor, the cofounders moved into a townhouse in San Francisco where they lived and worked together. They recruited a couple of software developers to join them. In early 2010, AllDone's website went live and connected its first buyers with sellers. Later that year, AllDone took in $1.2 million from a group of "angel investors"—wealthy individuals (many successful entrepreneurs in their own right) who invested in the company in exchange for an ownership stake.[3]

Over the following year, the dream inched closer toward becoming a reality. The product was still rudimentary, but AllDone was gaining some traction in growing its user base, with thousands of buyers submitting requests to find sellers each month. AllDone's staff grew to include a handful of software engineers and designers. The team moved out of the townhouse and into a loft office in San Francisco's SoMa (South of Market) neighborhood, which was becoming a hub for local startups. Some attention from the tech press soon followed, and executives set up meetings with major players in Silicon Valley. AllDone's cofounders had reason to hope that their company was on the path toward converting its potential into real value.

But it wasn't enough. Two years after AllDone was founded, the startup's expenses still far outpaced its revenue, and it was running out of money. Members of the small, eight-person team were asked to forego their salaries in exchange for additional stock option grants (seven agreed to do so).[4] And the cofounders again faced the necessity of seeking funding, this time targeting a $10 million infusion of venture capital. They pitched their enterprise to over forty investment firms but were rejected by each. The cofounders began to talk about how they would let go of their team if no sources of funding emerged. One of them announced that he was leaving the company. The dream was on life support.

Six weeks from insolvency, AllDone finally managed to secure its first major round of funding. At $4.5 million, their haul from a local VC firm called Hayes was smaller than they had originally anticipated. But the remaining cofounders were relieved and elated that the company was back on track. As the funding registered in AllDone's bank account, it was clear that the organization was embarking on an exciting new chapter in its journey. What was less clear to everyone involved in the enterprise was how it would convert its promise into a business that was actually worth the money that Hayes had invested—let alone the billion-dollar valuation they hoped to eventually achieve.

AllDone is a classic example of a startup company whose continued existence depended on access to venture capital. Management scholars have developed an extensive body of research addressing how VCs make investment decisions and how entrepreneurs obtain venture funding.[5] Yet in-depth accounts of how the requirements of VC investors structure the everyday experiences of startup workers remain rare. This chapter investigates how the logic of venture capital was set in motion at AllDone.

Venture-backed startups confront a problem I call *valuation lag*—a temporal and imaginative gap between a venture capital firm's investment in a startup and the company's ability to deliver returns. Managers at AllDone orchestrated continual experimentation to try to demonstrate that they could close the gap between potential and reality. By relentlessly seeking out new ways to boost key performance metrics—such as attracting more active users to the platform and extracting more revenue from them—AllDone staffers hoped to rapidly increase the perceived value of the firm to investors. AllDone's San Francisco staff addressed valuation lag by employing a combination of material and symbolic practices. Materially, employees engaged in *engineering work*, continually building and rebuilding the organization and its product to identify ways to maximize the firm's value. Symbolically, managers promoted an organizational *culture of speculative optimism* to project AllDone's legitimacy to actors inside and outside of the company amid conditions of uncertainty (see chapter 2).

The firm's dynamism was a source of excitement for San Francisco-based staffers, as engrossing challenges, the company's growth, and workers' financial stake in the enterprise reinforced the belief that AllDone and its employees could be destined for greatness. The timing of my arrival at AllDone—just three weeks after the firm announced its first round of VC funding—allowed me to witness firsthand how organizational activities were oriented around aligning the realities on the ground with investors' lofty expectations. The benefits of AllDone's newfound fortune and the pressures that accompanied it would define the company's trajectory for years to come.

VALUATION LAG AND ORGANIZATIONAL DYNAMICS

AllDone's cofounders dreamed of building a product that would reshape local service markets and yield fabulous wealth. But their pursuit of innovation required access to other people's money. Organizational theorists Jeffrey Pfeffer and Gerald Salancik argue that if we want to understand why organizations do the things they do, we must first understand the environments in which they operate.[6] For a startup that has yet to develop a viable business model, that context is an overwhelming need to attract investors to keep the lights on.

Most startups fail, and a company's quest to turn its vision into reality is defined by the existential uncertainty it faces.[7] Developing a new business in an unsettled field presents entrepreneurs with an unending series of unanticipated challenges and possibilities. Unable to make substantial investments in research or long-term strategic planning, new ventures typically pursue a strategy of "opportunistic adaptation," developing ad hoc responses to unexpected problems as they arise and experimenting with a multitude of new initiatives whose outcomes are uncertain. Means and ends may continually interact and shift as problems and resources are encountered and reframed. Startups must always be prepared to "pivot" to the next idea if what they're doing isn't working. Because the environments in which they operate are unstable and unpredictable, organizations and products that remain "permanently beta"—or perpetually "under construction"—will be better positioned to outlast those that are rigid or inflexible.[8]

But entrepreneurial ventures like AllDone also need to acquire resources—such as capital, employees, and know-how—to survive. When the external resources an organization needs are both scarce and crucial to its survival, it must cede a greater degree of discretion and control over its own activities to the parties that furnish those resources. The founders of new companies experience these pressures acutely when they seek to acquire money from investors. Venture capitalists' financial resources give them substantial power over the firms they fund.[9]

Silicon Valley VCs guide successful entrepreneurs through successive stages of development and funding. Because rapid growth tends to generate expenses that outpace a company's sales, venture-backed startups are funded in "rounds." Given that smaller and newer firms are far more likely to fail than larger and more established businesses, investors in the earliest rounds typically receive more favorable terms, having risked their money when the company's prospects were most uncertain.[10]

A venture-backed startup's progression through these stages of funding is akin to the movement of the spiral groove on a screw.[11] Trace the groove up the screw with your finger and you'll find that, on the horizontal plane, you are moving in a circle. Each revolution around the circle represents a stage of a successful startup's development, in which entrepreneurs (a) seek funding from investors, (b) secure funding, and (c) invest newly obtained resources in projects that they anticipate will produce (d) outcomes that will help the company restart the cycle by attracting its next round of funding (figure 1). For example, a tech startup might seek funding to recruit software engineers who can build new product features. A successful round of fundraising would allow the company to invest in hiring, and subsequently to release product updates designed to generate additional user growth or revenue. These outcomes could then be used as evidence of the company's potential in subsequent pitches to investors, restarting the cycle as the startup pursues funding to facilitate another round of expansion. When each new round of funding is secured, previous investors and shareholders may have the opportunity to sell a portion of their stake in the company to the new investors at a higher valuation.

As a successful startup completes circle after circle, its valuation ideally climbs higher and higher, represented by its progression up the vertical plane of the spiral. Attracting new rounds of funding and continuing to scale gives startups the momentum they need to increase their valuation and maintain their upward trajectory.

The work of venture capital firms is defined by uncertainty. VCs must evaluate the potential of businesses that have just started to put their ideas

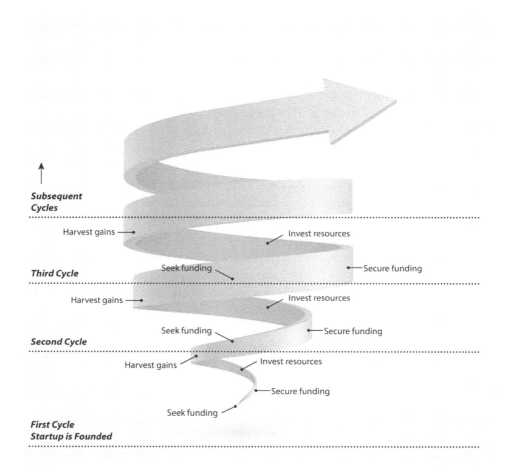

Figure 1. Progression of VC-backed startups through funding cycles

into practice. What's more, tech startups tend to operate in emerging or fast-changing markets in which information about the best pathways to success remains limited. Venture capital firms' investment decisions are thus informed by "fictional expectations"—imaginaries that allow them to organize their profit-seeking activities amid conditions of uncertainty, in which the outcomes of their actions are unpredictable and ultimately in-calculable.[12] VCs may invest in a company when they believe there is a

reasonable possibility that a nascent business will realize an imagined future in which its valuation increases rapidly and exponentially. Fictional
expectations thus create the valuation lag that startups must address if
they hope to attract additional funding.

Through their ownership of equity in the firm, a startup's founders and
employees are likewise enrolled in the imaginary of precipitous expansion. The organization's primary goal is to undertake the crucial task of
addressing valuation lag by closing the gap between expectation and reality. In the tech industry, the ambitions of entrepreneurs and VCs are
typically aligned: both aim to either sell the firm to the highest corporate
bidder, or, better yet, to sell shares in the firm on the public market via an
initial public stock offering (IPO), generating massive returns for those
who hold equity. When a startup's founders accept VC funding, they are
committing to the goal of "cashing out." Although the founders' ownership stake in the company they launched will progressively decline with
each new round of funding (often to between 3 and 10 percent by the time
a startup has an IPO), their equity in a successful firm can still be worth
millions—and, in some cases, billions.[13]

Just like the VCs who would become their partners, AllDone's cofounders stood to reap colossal rewards if they managed to convince successive
rounds of investors to provide the resources the company needed to su-
percharge its growth. The alignment of entrepreneurs' goals with those
of investors was vividly illustrated by a daily log kept, and later shared,
by one of AllDone's cofounders. The journal tracked both his own subjective sense of happiness and his predictions of AllDone's potential market
value. When charted on a graph, the two figures largely moved up and
down together.

Entrepreneurs' continued access to resources is predicated on their
capacity to bring the company's performance into alignment with investors' expectations.[14] Valuation lag—the gap between funders' investment in a company and the company's ability to generate returns on that
investment—thus set AllDone's organizational practices in motion. All-
Done engaged in relentless innovation to inflate the perceived value of
the firm at a time when the company's product and market remained
in flux. As AllDone's CEO once put it, echoing a popular trope among
tech entrepreneurs, managers and employees were "building the airplane

mid-flight." AllDone had raised funds by launching its product and cultivating expectations that it could dominate its market faster than its competitors. However, even as the company was trying to grow, it remained
unclear what the product it was building would ultimately look like. To
achieve scale when the firm's environment, content, and value remained
uncertain required relentless experimentation.

DATA DASHBOARDS AND ENGINEERING WORK

AllDone's San Francisco office—a former industrial warehouse with concrete floors, lofted ceilings, and an open floor plan—was where the imperatives of the venture capital cycle were translated into the labor of
innovation. Nobody had ever successfully created a nationwide, online
marketplace for local services, so there was no clear template to work from
as AllDone's staffers sought to address an unending series of problems and
opportunities. But while the lack of a template presented a technological
challenge, it also created a market opportunity. Being the first to bring
a product to market is particularly important in the platform economy,
where companies' fortunes hinge on their ability to attract an ever-greater
number of users to maximize network effects and profits.[15]

AllDone San Francisco's twenty employees—whose average age at the
time I entered the field was twenty-eight—were split into software engineering, product design, business development, marketing, and operations divisions. Although they enacted a diverse range of labor processes,
most San Francisco staffers performed *engineering work*. I use this term
loosely to refer to the efforts of employees who shared a common charge to
create change by designing and building products or processes.[16] When a
software engineer developed a new product feature; when a user-interface
designer altered the appearance of a webpage; when a marketer penned
new ad copy to try out on Facebook or Google; when an operations manager wrote instructions for remote workers to enact a new process—all of
these are examples of engineering work.

Employees envisioned AllDone's platform as a complex and interdependent web of buyers and sellers, which they frequently referred to as
an "ecosystem." Team members continually monitored Vision, an online

		05-01	04-01	03-01	02-01	01-01	12-01
Traffic	Search	157,427	533,504	510,475	422,354	363,600	279,415
Login	Users	46,808	112,550	106,960	96,286	95,548	79,641
Services	Created	2,761	9,957	12,150	12,730	14,711	11,282
Requests	Created	8,110	26,498	23,559	18,611	15,131	11,705
Revenue	Lead	21,755.6	76,508.0	67,168.1	52,178.0	46,482.9	26,160.4
	Commission	36	430	1,014	603.6	727.8	1,615.2
	Subscription	8,854.6	33,938.0	27,917.5	15,665.0	12,996.3	6,520.7
	Total	30,646.2	110,876.0	96,099.6	68,446.6	60,207.0	34,296.3
Bids	Fixed	3,772	13,896	12,645	10,319	9,286	5,809
	Commission	0	0	3,807	4,088	3,393	3,801
	Subscription	9,115	27,848	15,804	7,559	4,529	2,014
	Free User Invite	2,172	6,963	7,204	6,521	5,506	4,234
	Free Low Invites	2,291	7,718	1,045	0	0	0
	Free First Lead	839	4,512	7,600	9,938	11,662	9,338

Figure 2. A monthly overview report from Vision

administrative dashboard that tracked every user action taken on the platform in real time.[17] Each type of data could be aggregated into detailed reports revealing trends on an hourly, daily, weekly, monthly, quarterly, or yearly basis. Software developers tracked key metrics that provided insight into the size and health of the user population: for example, how many unique visitors were entering AllDone via web search, how many buyers submitted requests, and how many quotes sellers sent to buyers. Figure 2 depicts one of the numerous reports on AllDone's metrics that was generated by Vision.

Members of the product team (comprised of AllDone San Francisco's product manager, software engineers, and user interface designers) generally prided themselves on what they viewed as a rigorous, data-driven ethos of experimentation. "At AllDone, *everything* is an experiment," a junior engineer explained in a blog post. "We believe that the most difficult questions can be answered with data. This belief pervades everything we do."[18]

This position was reinforced by the company's leadership. One Friday night around 8 p.m. I had parked myself at the office's long lunch table to finish some work. Adam, AllDone's director of engineering, grabbed some food from the fridge, microwaved it, and took a seat near mine. He cracked open an Amstel and we started chatting about a presentation on statistics that Vince, a software engineer, had delivered earlier in the day.

> The biggest contributor to AllDone's accomplishments thus far, Adam says, has been the fact that the engineering team is "skeptical." That's why he didn't like hearing Frank [a user interface designer] talking today about how the "early results" of the experiment he's working on look good. "There *are* no early results!" Adam insists, not hiding his disdain. 'We have to assume that we don't know *anything* until we get the final, statistically significant results."[19]

Adam attributed AllDone's success to a near-absolute fealty to statistical logics. According to Adam, it simply wasn't worth assessing a project until abundant data about its performance were available. AllDone's ethos of experimentation was so deep-seated that it became a source of frustration for some product designers, who believed that the company's "data-driven" philosophy devalued their specialized knowledge and aesthetic judgment. Some complained that management would almost always prefer a design change that boosted key metrics, even if it detracted from a more elegant and user-friendly interface.[20]

If AllDone housed an ecosystem of buyers and sellers, members of the product team were AllDone's experimental population biologists: their task was to engineer the company's online environment to get key user metrics moving "up and to the right" when plotted on a graph tracking change over time. Engineers, designers, and marketers constantly theorized and tested new techniques to create statistically significant increases in important user metrics. Although they might occasionally conduct surveys of users, read incoming e-mails from users seeking support with new features, or invite a handful of people to the office for user testing or open-ended conversations, qualitative feedback was not the primary driver of product changes. Individual users' stories were viewed as providing only anecdotal evidence. Instead, employees continually conducted "A/B tests"—in which a portion of users were exposed to an experimental treatment, while others were assigned to a control group—to determine which changes would increase user engagement.[21] It was common for developers to be running two dozen experiments at any given time. Successful changes would then be rolled out across the entire user population.

One Monday evening around 7:15 p.m., Josh, AllDone's product manager, rolled a chair up to the workstation where Adam was sitting. Adam began telling Josh about a recent experiment he'd implemented, which was designed to boost the important metric of quotes submitted by sellers. A higher volume of seller quotes was good for buyers, who would have more choices when selecting a seller; good for the sellers who were able to win more jobs (though not for those who consistently lost out to competitors); and good for the company, which derived its revenue from charging sellers to get in touch with potential buyers. One of the myriad possible ways to increase quote volume was to increase the number of sellers who acted on the e-mails AllDone sent them when a buyer in their area submitted a relevant request. Adam had hypothesized that the text in the subject line of these automated e-mails could affect the number of sellers who opened the message. He devised an experiment that would allow him to A/B test a variety of subject lines to determine which was most likely to lead sellers to open an incoming message, and then to send a quote to the buyer. Each A/B test exposed one group of users to the "treatment" ("A")—a new e-mail subject line—and another to the "control" ("B")—the original subject line.

Adam pulls up a report from Vision on his screen and begins to tell Josh about the results of the subject line test. He explains that the version that performed best was "New message from [Buyer Name]," and that he wants to implement this new subject line across the entire population of sellers. Josh says he's worried that users might be confused by the change, or that they might find the winning subject line "unfriendly" or "robotic." He adds that the change could increase seller activity in the short term, but end up eroding sellers' trust in AllDone in the long term.

> Adam pushes back against Josh's reluctance to make the change. "We have to trick them into clicking for their own good," he argues. Even if sellers are initially confused by the change, or if the subject lines don't leave them with a warm feeling, Adam says it's important to "entice" them to open the e-mail, because the result will be more sellers competing for and winning jobs. Even if the new subject line might come across as "sketchy," he says, it could lead to a 20 percent increase in revenue.

Adam had used the data aggregated by Vision to discover which e-mail subject line resulted in the highest proportion of opened messages and submitted quotes. Although user metrics were typically the primary consideration in implementing changes to the product, secondary considerations could also come into play. Josh expressed his concern that the new, generic text would leave users with the impression that AllDone was a cold, distant, or "unfriendly" company. But in this instance, as in most others, it was ultimately the numbers that won out: the company made the change. Vision's technological toolkit thus informed and reflected the continual transformation of AllDone's product, shaping how San Francisco staffers understood and engaged with the user population.

Vision's reports were integral to AllDone San Francisco's engineering work. The data provided by the dashboard simultaneously reflected and informed developers' conceptions of the problems that needed to be solved, spurred the formulation of new features, and allowed members of the product team to systematically assess the efficacy of their experiments on the user population. Developers occasionally devised months-long, iterative tests of large-scale features, such as alternative payment models. Much more common, however, was constant tinkering with the user interface and experience. If designers changed the positioning of the "submit" button on the buyer request form, made it bigger, or altered its color, would more buyers complete their requests? If AllDone offered sellers a 50 percent discount on their first quote submission, would those sellers be more likely to become active users? At times it seemed that the list of potential experiments that could be run at any given moment was limited only by developers' imaginations. As AllDone's executives once wrote in a pitch to a potential corporate suitor: "We test almost every public-facing change made to our site on this [Vision] platform. We have learned over the years that even seemingly minor changes we think are not worth testing can make huge differences (both positively and negatively)—so as a general rule we test everything."

Members of AllDone San Francisco's product team enjoyed considerable autonomy in formulating and executing experiments. Executives set the rules of the game, or the primary goals the team would pursue (e.g., increase the volume of buyer requests, sellers' quotes, or revenue). Team leaders then decided which projects would be undertaken to meet those objectives, prioritizing those anticipated to leverage AllDone's limited resources to make the greatest possible impact. Employees were granted significant latitude to devise, implement, and assess the results of their projects.

Staffers made educated guesses as to how effective their experiments might be, but the results were ultimately difficult to predict. Because All-Done was a nascent startup experiencing rapid growth in a developing field, its conditions of operation were continually in flux, and developers had little historical data upon which to base their speculations. Managers encouraged staff to try out new ideas, and they accepted the frequent failure of carefully formulated tests.

AllDone's strategic focus on experimentation and rapid growth, paired with Vision's visual interface, helped to make software development an engrossing experience. Vision's dynamic displays allowed workers to track their progress toward conquering an endless array of challenges while also providing them with continual feedback. At the same time, the results of their experiments were often unpredictable, attributable to a combination of skill and chance. These game-like aspects of the work helped to keep software developers focused on pushing the numbers ever higher.[22]

One Thursday night around 8:20 p.m. I overheard Adam, the director of engineering, talking to Peter, the CEO, about an e-mail marketing campaign that the company would soon be launching. "It's hard to comprehend the magnitude of change it will make," Adam said. "It could be amazing. Or maybe [users] don't care. It could make a game-changing difference, or do nothing at all." In one instance, engineers had doubled weekly revenue figures by making a seemingly minor alteration to the algorithm that determined which sellers would receive each buyer request.[23] In another case, AllDone increased its revenue by 50 percent after engineers discovered that changing the titles of webpages that frequently appeared at the top of potential buyers' web search results dramatically increased the number who clicked on AllDone's links. Developing a feature that made it easier for sellers to respond to buyers by allowing them to reuse the last quote they had submitted boosted quote rates by over 20 percent. New experiments held the promise of substantially increasing important metrics, but the result of any given test was unknowable until it had been executed.

Mysteries also abounded in the relationship between actions taken by AllDone and the Google search engine algorithms upon which the company relied for the bulk of its traffic, which are shrouded in secrecy to prevent web developers from gaming the system. At a meeting introducing new staffers to Vision, Josh, the product manager, said that the product team watched incoming traffic from search with a "laser eye." However, he continued, "Google is a black box." Sometimes AllDone's developers would make changes to the website to try to boost its search rankings, and a while later they would see a bump in traffic, but they would never know exactly what had caused it. In these instances, uncertainty was introduced not by AllDone users' responses to change, but by the machinations of a third party upon which the company was dependent for resources.

Engineering work was not always glamorous. Software developers could spend hours reviewing and debugging code. For nontechnical employees, engineering work consisted of devising and documenting procedures for completing a project, outsourcing the execution to someone else, and taking on the next challenge. Workers who handled marketing or operations might spend days immersed in a series of spreadsheets, or hours writing instructions in painstaking detail for remote workers in the Philippines to perform a particular routinized task, such as screening out inappropriate reviews of sellers written by buyers (see chapter 3).

As an employee myself, I found designing and optimizing algorithms (in my case, written in English rather than computer code) to be surprisingly gratifying. Even when the work was tedious, the context in which it arose was stimulating: I was continually confronted with new problems to solve and trusted to formulate solutions on the fly. Regardless of their particular job function, members of AllDone San Francisco were directing processes that could help to propel the company toward a lucrative corporate acquisition or IPO—which, employees were told (and often told each other), could ultimately alter the course of their lives and change the world (see chapter 2).

SEEING LIKE A VC

At the same time that Vision oriented employees' activities and attention around key user metrics, it also aligned their view of the firm with the expectations of venture capitalists. Executives told the San Francisco staff that AllDone's investors (some of whom were also seated on the company's board of directors) frequently monitored Vision to check on the company's progress and inform their recommendations for corporate strategy.

Every three months, before AllDone's San Francisco employees gathered for their quarterly review, four or five clean-shaven white men who appeared to be in their late thirties or forties—some sporting the fleece vests that are famously popular among the Silicon Valley VC set—would appear at the office for a board meeting. The group would spend the morning in a conference room being briefed by AllDone's executives and weighing in on their plans. According to summaries of these meetings shared by leadership, board members' feedback focused heavily on strategic matters, including interpreting trends in user metrics and discussing which additional metrics should be measured. Board members also advised the company's leaders on important issues, such as where the product team should focus its efforts to boost growth, how AllDone should communicate with its users, what partnerships to pursue with other firms, and when to seek new rounds of VC funding.

In addition to informing AllDone's prior investors of the company's progress, executives could also use the metrics displayed in Vision to attract attention from new investors. During the quarterly review meeting described in the preface, Peter explained that, when AllDone had sought its first round of VC funding, it was "selling a dream" to potential investors. In contrast, when the company tried to raise its next round of funding, it would be "selling a spreadsheet." In other words, later-stage investors were only interested in firms with a demonstrated track record of precipitous growth.

Because the figures displayed in Vision were the same numbers that would appear in the "spreadsheet" that AllDone would present to potential investors, Vision helped employees "see like a VC," integrating the imperatives of venture capital into their everyday awareness and work practices.[24] Metrics were not valued at AllDone simply because they carried with them a veneer of objectivity, scientific rationality, or moral rectitude.[25] Instead, executives and employees were acutely aware that investors' decisions would depend in large part upon the figures that appeared in the Vision dashboard.[26]

The logic of venture capital investment—according to which VCs fill their portfolios with firms that have the potential to become "home runs" and reject those apparently fated to be mere "singles"—exerted a powerful influence over AllDone's everyday organizational practices. Recall again the all-staff meeting detailed in the preface, when Josh, AllDone's product manager, displayed a slide explaining that the projects developers worked on would be selected in part to "send signals to investors and the broader community." When making development decisions, Josh stated that the product team would need to ask itself, "What will a Series B investor want to see? What would they be scared to see?" He also said that the team would be reorganized into smaller groups so that each could be held "accountable" for boosting key metrics.

Decisions pertaining to which innovations would be pursued, which ideas would be ignored, and even how the product team was structured were explicitly made with investors' preference for high-risk, high-reward projects in mind. One Friday evening around 8:30 p.m., Bill (a software engineer) and Adam (the director of engineering) were standing near their desks, sipping drinks from the office beer fridge and discussing what Bill should work on the following week.

> Bill says he wants to test some new features to give sellers more "ownership over their profiles" on the platform. Bill contends that the changes he's envisioning would make sellers more satisfied with their experience on AllDone, and he speculates that these new features could increase the volume of incoming users referred by sellers. "With minimal effort on our part, they could be more involved in the marketing effort."

> Adam shakes his head and responds with skepticism. "AllDone is employing seventeen people [in San Francisco] and nine contractors [in Las Vegas], and it still loses a lot of money. We need a storyline that's compelling from an investment perspective. I don't think the seller [profile] thing is. Search and search-engine marketing is where traffic comes from, not referrals. Direct marketing is how companies make money at scale."

Bill wanted to try out some incremental enhancements to the product. He assumed that turning users into advocates for the company by improving their experience on the platform would be a good way to achieve growth. Adam rejected this logic, arguing that Bill's proposal was not "a storyline that's compelling from an investment perspective." The engineering team's priority should instead, he argued, be to pursue projects with the potential to "make money at scale," or to achieve the rapid and precipitous expansion that investors favor. The conversation continued:

> Adam compares AllDone to a competitor that "has been around [for] eleven years. They're not a [widely known] consumer brand, but they make hundreds of millions of dollars a year. I think even if AllDone fails, we can still make 20 or 30 million a year. You and I could buy a boat or something [by cashing in our stock options]."
>
> Bill smiles and responds, "I'd be OK with that."
>
> "I wouldn't," Adam quickly replies. "I want AllDone to be a transcendental consumer brand. I want AllDone to be like Amazon." Bill backtracks and agrees that this is what he really wants, too. Adam says that although he doesn't know if that level of success is possible for AllDone, it could happen "if we're lucky enough to raise" another round of funding as a next step.

Echoing the logic of venture capital, Adam stated that turning AllDone into a business making tens of millions of dollars a year—and cashing out his stock options for tens of thousands of dollars—would constitute a "failure."[27] Like AllDone's investors, his goal was to build "a transcendental consumer brand" on the order of Amazon. Bill had not convinced Adam that his proposed test was worth two days of his labor. Refining sellers' profile pages was seen as a waste of time because it was unlikely to immediately produce the kinds of results that investors wanted to see.

Although investor control could be overt, it did not have to be direct to be effective. Following their quarterly meetings, board members typically wouldn't be seen again in the office for another three months. But executives and managers were intimately familiar with the expectations that prevailed across the private capital market more generally. The VC business model indirectly disciplined AllDone's leaders to pursue an organizational strategy that would be favorable to investors' interests. Managers like Adam—and, subsequently, employees like Bill—were conditioned to think like VCs. Everyday life in the San Francisco office was in many ways driven by the logic of venture capital.

. . . . .

Imagined futures motivate the strategies pursued by VC-backed startups, setting in motion a host of organizational processes, roles, agendas, and allocations of resources animated by an investment logic that prioritizes fast and precipitous growth.[28] Like the venture capital investors who had funded AllDone, the company's San Francisco–based managers and employees acted as if a successful IPO or acquisition would materialize, if only they could bring their innovations to scale quickly enough. AllDone's San Francisco team was dedicated to addressing valuation lag—bridging the gap between the company's potential worth and its present realities.

Studies of organizational life are replete with tales of "decoupling," in which actors cultivate legitimacy by creating the *appearance* that they are conforming to external expectations while failing to do so in practice.[29] This was not the case at AllDone, where the pressure to catch up with the myth of the company's potential was immense. The logic of venture capital was performed in organizational decision-making and shaped employees' labor processes. This imperative set the activities of AllDone's San Francisco-based workforce into motion: employees engaged in engineering work, continually revamping, tinkering with, and tweaking the product. They hoped that, by orchestrating relentless change, they could discover new ways to push key metrics ever higher and bring the company closer to an imagined future of extraordinary success. They were instructed to follow wherever the data led them—and the numbers that mattered were those that were relevant to investors.

As the prominent venture capitalist Marc Andreesen has commented, from the perspective of an entrepreneur, trying to launch a startup is "absolutely terrifying. Everything is against you."[30] Only a small fraction of startups receives any VC funding, and even those that do are likely to fail. Entrepreneurs and startup workers labor in a fog of uncertainty, unsure of how long their ventures will last or what it will take to succeed. In the midst of existential doubt, metrics can serve as a source of reassurance and meaning.[31]

The case of AllDone shows how a process that may *appear* to be chaotic and ever-changing—building a product when nothing is nailed down and everything is up for grabs—can in fact be meticulously structured and ordered, rigorously designed to generate the outcomes favored by investors. Software engineers faithfully applied an approximation of the scientific method to the problem of growth. Innovation was not limited to the invention of groundbreaking new software. The systematic revision of minute aspects of product features, user interfaces, and even e-mail subject lines was an integral component of software developers' efforts.

The consequences of AllDone San Francisco's engineering work would ripple throughout the organization, transmitting VC pressure downward onto the company's remote workforce and its users. San Francisco–based staffers were able to keep their eyes locked on the future because team members located in the Philippines and Las Vegas were available to deal with the present. Members of AllDone's remote teams helped engineers enact experiments, performed a shifting array of experimentally validated processes, and attempted to manage users' emotional responses to change. As I will show in subsequent chapters, contractors in the Philippines and Las Vegas enabled AllDone's rapid growth by absorbing the frictions that arose due to the uneven development of relations between humans and technology. The costs of innovation were borne not by investors, but by low-wage workers. San Franscisco employees' attentiveness to metrics, rather than to the experiences of individual users, was also a frequent source of frustration for AllDone Las Vegas's phone support agents.

First, however, we will return to AllDone's San Francisco office to dig deeper into the experiences of these privileged employees as they participated in venture capitalism. Engineering work formed the basis of the team's shop-floor culture, where the meaning of work developed in relation to employees' continual efforts to push the numbers up and inflate investors' assessments of AllDone's value.

2 Dreaming of the Future

Chloe, AllDone's office manager (official job title: "director of happiness"), has rented out a private event space above a bar in San Francisco's Duboce Triangle neighborhood, near the center of the city and just a couple of miles from the office. It's a Friday night, and the entire team has shuttled over via Uber and light rail to celebrate following an all-staff quarterly review meeting. I approach a bouncer outside the entrance and state the "password" that Chloe distributed to the staff, and he directs me up a staircase.

As I reach the top, I find myself near the center of a long and narrow, dimly lit room with dark wood paneling along the walls and a bar staffed by two bartenders serving up free beer, wine, and cocktails. Chloe has strung up ribbons peppered with tiny clothespins on the far wall between two windows, where she's clipping and hanging photos that people are taking on an Instamax camera. There are two tables along one side of the room brimming with fruit, vegetables and dips, a make-your-own pulled-pork sliders station, bruschetta, and skewers of chicken and vegetables. The mix of Top Forty songs that can often be heard in the office is playing off a Spotify account on a computer hooked up to speakers behind the bar. Later, the space will be packed with employees and invited partners and friends, but for now only members of AllDone San Francisco's twenty-person staff are gathered in small groups, talking loudly and animatedly to be heard above the din.

Around 9 p.m., someone turns the music off, and I notice the thumping of bass through the floor from the bar one story below us. In a booming voice, Martin, one of AllDone's cofounders, declares, "It's time for toasts!" and corrals everyone together in the center of the room. I'm standing by the corner of the bar and notice that both of the bartenders have stopped pouring drinks and are also facing toward Martin, seemingly waiting to see what will happen next.

Martin's face lights up as he steps into the center of the circle. He begins to speak slowly and deliberately, stretching his arms out and loping around in wide arcs. He says he's "never felt better about AllDone" and its future. Some people chuckle, and someone shouts out that that's what Martin always says—this comment evokes more laughter. Then James, a software engineer, steps in and delivers a toast thanking everyone for making these "two amazingly memorable years" for him in San Francisco. He says it's been exactly what he was hoping for when he moved here after college. Josh, the product manager, is next. He thanks the team for tackling the toughest challenges together. Their intelligence, grit, and determination, he says, are why he loves working for AllDone. Katrina, a user interface designer, then toasts Josh for the grace with which he handles software development problems. Each speech is punctuated with a resounding "Cheers!" and the clinking of glasses. James steps forward again and delivers yet another brief toast. And then Martin returns to the center of the circle, declaring that "we're making our mark—that's why we're here, to leave one of the biggest marks in the history of technology." This statement elicits the biggest roars so far. I realize that we've all been holding our glasses up for a few minutes now, and some folks are clearly more than a little tipsy. The toasts continue.

Leaders of new ventures, particularly those that have yet to deliver on their promises, must perform cultural work to establish their legitimacy in the eyes of potential stakeholders.[1] Venture-backed startups like AllDone typically begin to seek funding long before they've created a viable product or garnered a large and loyal customer base. Most lack a blueprint for success: they may not yet know exactly how their product will work or how customers will respond to it. Under such conditions, projecting an image of competence and confidence can be crucial to a firm's success. The endless toasts weren't just a sign of fondness driven by drink, but an assertion of AllDone's potential and worth.

How did AllDone's founders and employees mobilize symbols, narratives, and emotions to convince others—and themselves—that they were launching a successful venture? In this chapter, I describe the particular manifestation of the Silicon Valley ethos that I observed in AllDone's San Francisco office: what I call an organizational *culture of speculative optimism*. A startup's capacity to inspire confidence in its future is a necessary condition for success. AllDone San Francisco's culture of speculative optimism bolstered the firm's external and internal legitimacy, helping the company attract needed resources—including venture capital investments and motivated employees.

BUILDING LEGITIMACY IN
AN UNCERTAIN ENVIRONMENT

An entrepreneur differentiates her new venture from others by emphasizing its novel qualities, yet she must simultaneously attempt to overcome the "liability of newness": young organizations are more likely to fail than established firms because they are perceived as less legitimate, must rely on unfamiliar outside parties for resources, and often find themselves unable to outcompete market leaders.[2] For startups experiencing valuation lag, it is particularly important to pair the material practices of innovation with symbolic work aimed at building current and potential stakeholders' confidence. As sociologists Paul DiMaggio and Walter Powell have argued, industrial conditions of uncertainty often give rise to imitation. Firms in unsettled fields model themselves on organizations and organizational forms that are widely recognized as successful.[3] In other words, entrepreneurs can benefit from emphasizing the ways in which their ventures are similar to other startups that have already made it big, as AllDoners did when they compared themselves to Amazon.

Silicon Valley workplaces generally conform to the tech industry's institutionalized rules of legitimacy.[4] Google's campus in Mountain View,

California, spawned countless imitators of its open offices, comfortable and whimsical common spaces, and amenities like free meals for employees. A single managerial decision can thus have both intrinsic and symbolic dimensions.[5] When a company's founder installs a keg refrigerator in a corner of the office and wears T-shirts and hoodies to work, he is signaling that his company sprang from the same mold as previous startup unicorns.

For founders and executives, presenting convincing displays of a startup's prospects is a crucial precondition for acquiring resources and generating wealth. As founders seek to address valuation lag, they find that investors' confidence in their companies' future potential matters far more than the value they have created in the present.[6] Entrepreneurs attempt to manage investors' collective beliefs about the company, building current and potential stakeholders' faith in an enterprise that has yet to demonstrate its worth by presenting an image of success and promoting excitement about the startup's future.

At a happy hour nearly five months after I'd begun my fieldwork, I listened as Peter, AllDone's CEO, explained the importance of engaging in exactly this kind of cultural work:

> We're seated on low, round, leather-upholstered stools around a long table next to an exposed brick wall. Folks are passing around plates of appetizers, and almost everyone has a drink on the table in front of them. Peter is seated to my left, Josh [the product manager] is to my right, and Carter [AllDone's president] is to Josh's right. They start to ask me about how my research at AllDone is shaping up so far. At one point I explain to Peter my observation that tech startups seem to have to convince people that they're successful before they can actually demonstrate it.
>
> Peter's eyes light up as he expands on the point. He says that leading a startup forces founders to embody a tension. 'On the one hand, you have to have—and express—complete confidence in what you're doing. You have to know that you *will* succeed, and you have to convey the "inevitability" of your success to others. On the other hand, you have to be honest with yourself and your employees that *nothing* is working, and that you have to make change after change to get where you need to be.'

Entrepreneurs are deeply aware that they must convincingly perform their self-assurance. Founders calibrate their emotional displays to build external parties' confidence in their startups. As economic geographer

Daniel Cockayne notes, entrepreneurs "perform their own human capital, demonstrating both their personal capacities for production and their affective attachments to their work" when expressing unfailing enthusiasm for their roles and their faith in their ventures.[7]

Like a startup's founders, its employees, too, find that laboring in organizations is not simply a matter of engaging in productive physical or mental activity. Work also requires individuals to learn the proper affective tone for their social setting. Employees regulate their emotional expression to match the expectations that accord to their role. Workers engage in "surface acting" when they manage their outer expressions— which may conflict with their inner feelings. But they may also engage in "deep acting" when they try to control their own thoughts and feelings so that they match external expectations for emotional display, as Peter describes in the passage above when he says that, as a startup founder, 'you have to know that you *will* succeed' in order to create convincing performances. When people engage in deep acting that matches what sociologist Arlie Hochschild calls a workplace's "feeling rules," it can be difficult to say where the "true" self ends and mere emotional display begins.[8]

In VC-backed firms, stock options link the interests of the workers who receive them with those of VCs and entrepreneurs, bolstering employee commitment to the organizations for which they labor. In practice, this means that the speculative logic of finance capital can pervade the upper echelons of the shop floor.[9] The promise of stock options incentivizes even mid-level workers to engage in emotional displays aimed at bolstering the legitimacy of the companies in which they hold a financial stake. In this context, hiring a "director of happiness" focused on keeping employees in a positive mindset makes sense as a concrete investment in the founders' ability to cash out.

The combination of autonomy in the labor process, uncertain outcomes, and intermittent feedback, combined with the potential windfall of stock options, created engrossing work for AllDone's San Francisco–based employees. These practices formed the material basis of an organizational culture of speculative optimism in which workers continually gushed over the company's prospects. AllDone's managers and employees participated in rituals that bolstered collective belief in the enterprise's potential—and in the possibility of massive payouts—by producing feelings of collective exuberance and solidarity.[10] Such practices endowed experiences of work with status and an affective charge that created symbolic benefits for the firm, its employees, and its investors.

WORKING AT ALLDONE HEADQUARTERS

When I first set foot in AllDone's San Francisco office, the tech industry driving the city's economy was booming. Privileged young people from across the country were flocking to the Bay Area in pursuit of wealth, fun, and the promise of building technologies that would "change the world." The news was not yet saturated with negative headlines about how algorithms, digital platforms, and tech monopolies threaten to undermine democracy, labor rights, and human freedom. In the popular imagination, the tech scene was still largely a site of wonder.

The appearance, layout, and amenities of AllDone's office reflected the design conventions of its time and place. The space was a repurposed industrial loft with concrete floors and rectangular wooden pillars stretching up to the ceiling two stories above. Employee workstations were located on large, shared tables arrayed across the office in asymmetrical configurations. The only natural light came from small, opaque, street-facing windows and murky skylights, but the office's elevated ceiling—along with bright white and exposed brick walls, an open floor plan, and comfortable couches—made it an inviting space with a decidedly noncorporate, "do-it-yourself" feel.

My initial impressions of AllDone headquarters were shaped by the abundance of food. The office's focal point was its kitchen, where Amy, AllDone's full-time chef, could usually be found preparing meals or snacks for the staff. Amy was an Ivy League-educated white woman in her late twenties who after college trained in French cuisine at the famed Le Cordon Bleu Institute. Free meals were on offer throughout each workday: employees dipped into well-stocked refrigerators and pantries to make their own breakfasts; Amy prepared a fresh lunch that AllDoners would eat together while gathered around a row of tables; and after lunch she made dinner for employees to fetch from the refrigerator in the evening.

Throughout the day, the clatter of computer keyboards was frequently complemented by the authoritative *chop-chop-chop* of a chef's knife. Enticing odors emerged from the kitchen and wafted across the office, tempting even those behind closed conference room doors to emerge for a lunch of cumin-seared fish tacos, a blueberry shake for dessert, or chocolate chip meringues as an afternoon pick-me-up. Gabriela, a middle-aged immigrant from Mexico, appeared in the office every day after lunch to clean up after the team. All employees were welcome to invite guests—typically professional connections and friends, occasionally partners and family members—to lunches or to Wednesday night "family dinners," when Amy would stay late to prepare an elaborate meal. Food was served at 7:30 p.m. on Wednesday nights; after dinner, many staffers stayed at the office until 10 p.m., and sometimes far beyond, for an evening of drinking, conversation, ping-pong and foosball matches, and for some, a little extra work. AllDone San Francisco's beer-brewing club also convened following Wednesday night dinners to craft home-brews in the office kitchen.

Free meals were among the many perks enjoyed by AllDone's San Francisco–based employees. New hires were invited to customize their workspaces with their preferred equipment at the company's expense (connecting one's company-issued laptop to a pair of massive computer monitors was a particularly popular choice). Staffers also enjoyed a great deal of control over their time, including flexible work hours, opportunities to work from home when necessary, and a liberal "unlimited" vacation policy. Each month a few employees took advantage of a benefit that reimbursed them up to $150 for using AllDone to hire a local service provider. Funding was also available for those who wished to pursue work-related educational opportunities. Chloe, the office manager, coordinated monthly chair massage sessions and occasional morning yoga classes in the office.

In addition to competitive salaries (most in the high five- to low six-figure range), full-time employees received allocations of stock options that varied according to their role and hire date. One quarter of each employee's stock option grant would be "vested," or granted to them, on an annual basis after each of their first four years with the company. Once their stock options had vested, employees would be entitled to purchase AllDone stock at a particular price, with the understanding that they would be able to sell the stock at a later date if the startup raised additional rounds of VC funding, was acquired by another company, or participated in an initial public stock offering. The higher the valuation of the firm at the time stock was sold, the greater the profit it would yield.

In general, the size of stock-option grants offered to new employees decreased as the company matured, and employees whose roles management viewed as more valuable (e.g., software engineer) received far more than those whose work was valued less (e.g., office manager). AllDone's cofounders owned substantial portions of the company. Early on, when AllDone was struggling to acquire its first round of venture capital funding, some software engineers accepted an offer to temporarily trade their salaries for additional stock options; one early hire was able to accrue a 1 percent stake in the company. Most employees held far less. I was told that my own stock option grant, if fully vested over four years, would be worth $1 million if the company were to achieve a $1 billion valuation.[11] The compensation and perks offered to AllDone San Francisco employees were aimed at helping the company attract and retain a talented workforce devoted to building an innovative product that would capture the attention, money, and imagination of customers and investors for years to come.

RIDING THE ROCKET SHIP

Organizational cultures—what management scholar Edgar Schein describes as "pattern[s] of shared basic assumptions" that posit "the correct way to perceive, think, and feel in relation to problems"—can guide the sentiments and activities of organizational members as they pursue shared goals.[12] Many corporations (and perhaps most famously, tech companies) develop and disseminate explicit statements delineating their company's "culture."[13] Organizations may describe their culture by outlining the types of behaviors that are rewarded, how employees should relate to each other and their supervisors, how they should conceptualize the meaning of their work, or how they should feel about their membership in the group.

At the time of my fieldwork, AllDone's San Francisco team—which grew from eight to twenty employees while I was conducting research—had not yet codified its workplace culture. There was no official document detailing what it meant to be a member of AllDone San Francisco, nor was there any list of "values" that employees or managers could reference to guide or justify their actions and emotions. However, an informal yet clearly observable culture had already emerged, characterized by shared rhetoric, rituals, and feeling rules.

While most fieldworkers' first days of research are filled with personal experiences of exhilaration that come with gaining access to and learning about a novel social setting, I also observed a palpable sense of excitement among my new colleagues, most of whom had been there long enough for the novelty to have worn off. Some of this, surely, was attributable to employees' relief at surviving the company's recent near-death experience. The injection of venture capital funding—which had come just three weeks before my arrival—had fundamentally altered AllDone's outlook. Conversations at the lunch table and around the office buzzed with upbeat speculation about the venture's prospects and potential value. Employees logged in to Vision and watched the company's user base grow larger every week.

The office itself also bore evidence of the firm's trajectory, as the eight-person staff that I had joined was expanding rapidly. During my initial stint as a low-status intern coming to the office one day per week, I would repeatedly arrive to my desk in the morning only to find that a new full-time employee had taken over my space and that I would have to set up my computer at a different table. In my first month in the office, a new team member came on board each week; within a few more months, there were twenty employees in the San Francisco office.

Managers and employees frequently mobilized the metaphor of the "rocket ship" to represent the company's progress and prospects—just like the numbers on the Vision dashboard, team members were all hurtling upward together. Carter, one of AllDone's cofounders, captured this ethos in an e-mail that he sent to San Francisco employees:

> Few people in the world have an admission ticket to ride a rocket ship like the one we're sitting on. Most of us will never get another ticket like this; I doubt I will. As [CEO] Peter likes to say, if we build our vision AllDone will touch each of us for the rest of our lives. It will transform us each personally— not just financially and socially—but it will stretch our skills, what we

thought we could personally accomplish, and be something that is with us
even decades from today.

Here Carter emphasizes the singular nature of AllDone's situation, highlighting not just the riches and fame that could follow from cashing in
stock options in a successful acquisition or IPO, but also existential benefits. He figures AllDone as a project that could alter employees' life
trajectories and permanently endow their lives with new and exciting
capabilities and sources of meaning.

   This sort of speech, in which executives circulated messages that displayed their mounting excitement about the startup's potential, was common at AllDone. In one all-office meeting, Carter told of an early backer
who had lamented, 'I'm afraid I'm going to regret not having invested
more' in AllDone. In another e-mail to the San Francisco staff, Carter recounted a meeting with Jeff, the founder of another company that hosted
a platform for local service providers. According to Jeff, his firm generated $12 million in annual revenue from its listings in just one major
US city.

> Think about that: $12mm in revenue from *one city* with less traffic than we
> get now. Think about how much revenue we'll generate when we have that
> kind of penetration and monetization in every city. And every country. Just
> billions and billions of dollars of revenue . . . and millions and millions of
> jobs created for our sellers . . . and thousands and thousands of employees at
> AllDone.
>
> We have the opportunity of a lifetime . . . few people get a shot at something
> like this. Let's make this happen baby!

In these and other examples, executives promoted the idea of AllDone's
limitless potential not only to investors, but to their employees as well.

   Managers established AllDone's culture of speculative optimism
through rhetoric and collective rituals. Upon being hired, employees received an introductory e-mail stressing not only the high standards to
which the company held employees, but also the expectations that employees should have for the company's success. "Our first guiding principle
at AllDone," it stated, was "**Play to win**: We're a professional sports team,
not a family. We're not here to have a good season. We're here to win the

Super Bowl.""[14] Employees were joining a team whose purpose was to become the champion of the startup world.

The office's feeling rules, or norms of emotional expression on the job,
were also practiced and reinforced from the bottom-up. Katrina, a user interface designer, penned personal notes to each member of the staff a few
weeks after she joined the team. Mine read:

> I'm burning to tell you how excited I am to be here, and how thrilled I am to
> work with you in the coming months! I've never been so fired up about suc-
> ceeding, and I need to let you know I'm giving you & AD my all. Let's share
> ideas, let's be open, let's launch this baby into space!

Regardless of whether Katrina was engaged in "surface acting" or "deep
acting," her vivid expression of enthusiasm clearly demonstrated her understanding of AllDone San Francisco's feeling rules, involving an almost
romantic notion of passion for one's work that could result in the inflation
of AllDone's value.[15]

Four times a year, the San Francisco staff spent an afternoon reporting
on each division's progress and goals. Quarterly review meetings represented opportunities for ritualized proclamations establishing the company's tantalizing prospects for success, as at the conclusion of the first
review meeting I attended:

> After we take a group photo outside and wander back into the office, Peter
> [AllDone's CEO] herds us into the large conference room to tell us that he's
> so excited. Nobody's ever done what we're doing before. We have the right
> people to do it, and the money to do it, so now it's our hard work and cre-
> ativity that will push us over the top. We have only ourselves to blame if we
> don't succeed.

AllDone's glory was not inevitable—but it was, according to Peter, there
for employees to seize. Carter then projected an administrative webpage
on the wall that listed about two dozen buyer requests submitted to All-
Done. 'Look at all these requests placed in the last fifteen minutes. Each of
these [service categories] is a company in its own right,' he said, meaning
that one could imagine a separate, successful business that would connect
buyers and sellers of dog walking, piano tuning, house cleaning, and each
of the hundreds of services offered on AllDone's platform. 'We're going to
be a juggernaut, doing them all.'

Quarterly review meetings concluded with a ritual of collective speculation. Each employee recorded his or her predictions for the following
quarter's growth in a dozen metrics (e.g., traffic, new seller signups, and
other forms of user engagement). Executives announced whose prediction
from the last quarter had proven most accurate, with the winner garner-
ing applause from the assembled group. These predictions were themselves a topic of discussion and competition throughout the quarter, with
staffers comparing their guesses to the company's actual performance. Although employee forecasts almost always projected growth in key metrics,
they exhibited variation in their degree of positivity. (For example, Martin's irrational exuberance became a running joke in the office.)

Each quarterly review meeting was followed by a party for employees
and their friends, usually held in an upscale bar or event space that was
rented out for the occasion. These events featured custom cocktails, copi-
ous hors d'oeuvres, and activities such as photo booths, karaoke, and car-
nival games. As described at the beginning of this chapter, at some point
during each quarterly celebration, someone would turn off the music so
AllDone's cofounders and employees could deliver a series of toasts that
often touched on how the company was poised to transform employees'
lives and change the world. Executives frequently cited the positive impact that AllDone's success was already having around the globe. They
claimed that by making it easier for buyers and sellers of local services
to connect with one another, AllDone was supporting the growth of the
small businesses that are the backbone of the US economy, while also providing employment opportunities that improved the lives of workers in the
Philippines (see chapter 4).

Managers also institutionalized AllDone's culture of speculative optimism in smaller and more frequent rituals. The staff would gather every
Friday afternoon for "demos," slowly wending their way through the office
to visit every employee's desk, where each person would show off something he or she had been working on over the past week. Every demonstration usually elicited "ooohs," "ahhhs," or congratulatory comments.
These meetings often concluded with seemingly spontaneous applause
and scattered pronouncements that it had been a "great week." Executives
also frequently sent all-staff e-mails marking new records or milestones
in metrics (e.g., matching more buyers and sellers in a week than ever
before). Progress reports often concluded with statements like "we're just

getting started," or hailing "the beginning of something very exciting," or the hashtag "Day1" (a term popularized by Amazon CEO Jeff Bezos, which conveys a similar meaning).

Optimistic projections of data and excitement about the future were part of the fabric of everyday conversation around the office. Staffers frequently indulged in sharing what one employee dubbed "speculation porn" when imagining how much a forthcoming project might boost user activity. For example, Friday demos were typically followed by boisterous, informal conversations about the potential impact of new projects. Many of these discussions centered on Vision, where employees could find detailed, real-time evidence of their future success (see chapter 1). Although my own work roles rarely required me to log into Vision, I found it easy to stay apprised of the company's progress by listening to impromptu discussions—involving nearly every team member at one time or another—regarding the results of recent experiments and up-to-the-minute trends in traffic, engagement, or revenue.

WATCHING OTHERS

News and events emerging from AllDone's external environment also fed the office's culture of speculation. During my first visit to the office, the lunch table was abuzz with talk of recent startup acquisitions.

> 'Did you see the Yammer today?' Martin asks the gang, referring to the company's internal social network. Someone has posted a news story about Amazon's recent purchase of an online education startup. This came on the heels of a recent announcement that one of AllDone's direct competitors had been bought by a major retail chain. Adam says it's great that companies in AllDone's "space" [market] are being acquired. That means there's a lot of interest, so AllDone could start to get offers. Plus, he noted, AllDone is already bringing in revenue—he predicts that by the end of the year they'll have netted $1 million. If they're making money and there's a lot of action in their space, Adam concludes, AllDone could even be in a position to receive and *turn down* offers.

Adam would later refer to the competitor's acquisition as "the best thing that could have happened to AllDone." During another conversation, he cited a local startup as an example of how 'it could happen really fast' for AllDone: 'Airbnb raised $10 million and then in like a year it was massive; now it's over a billion-dollar company. And they're in a similar space to us.'

Staffers appeared to enjoy these discussions of AllDone's prospects. One night, when AllDone was on the cusp of receiving its first acquisition offer (which it would decline), Adam, Vince, and I ended up staying at the office until almost midnight drinking beers, tossing around a Nerf football, discussing AllDone's potential valuation, and imagining how AllDone would change if an acquisition were to occur. By the end of the night, Adam declared, "We should be talking about this stuff all the time. It's fun!"

The possibility that AllDone could join the ranks of Silicon Valley's tech titans was never far from some employees' minds:

> I need to make a Skype call, so I walk over to Adam's desk to ask if he knows the password for our office's account. He looks up, tells me where I can find the password, and then adds, "eight billion." I am mystified by the number—not realizing that he was referring to how much Microsoft had recently paid to acquire Skype—until he follows up a moment later, remarking, "that could be us." If we could just get buyers to come back to our platform a few times per month, he says, half joking, "we could buy Twitter."

Just around the corner from AllDone's office was another startup that, on the heels of Facebook's recent $1 billion acquisition of Instagram, had been haled by a major news outlet as "the next big thing." During an in-office happy hour teeming with close to a hundred guests, Carter asked me if I wanted to hear some "startup gossip" about yet another company that was throwing its own party nearby:

> Carter tells me it's recently been valued at $4 billion, making its twenty-five-year-old CEO worth half a billion dollars. Carter says that a friend of his runs a staffing agency that typically places "hot girls" in executive assistant positions. At a recent party, his friend sent one of her "girls" over to chat up this newly wealthy CEO. The CEO ended up asking her out on a date to the movies. She was underwhelmed by the idea, but assented, only to discover that he had rented out the entire theater for their date. She was apparently impressed, in spite of herself. "That could be you someday," I suggest, probing for Carter's judgment of the CEO's actions. Carter demurs, saying he'd be happy to just have a party like the one we were having now, but on a boat—and, he adds, he'd bet someone in this room right now already owns one.

Carter's story underscores the fact that all around them, the young (mostly) men of AllDone San Francisco could find examples of people like them who had struck it rich in tech, become important figures in the scene, and put their money to use in the service of extravagant lifestyles that included what they perceived to be exciting sexual conquests and social events. At the same time, his story highlights the kind of casual sexism that pervades Silicon Valley, where women's opportunities for advancement are often limited by their objectification in the eyes of the men who lead the industry.[16]

SHOWING OFF

Managers in AllDone's San Francisco office also mobilized displays of the company's opulence and potential to attract new recruits. When I first arrived at the office, AllDone had just raised its first round of venture capital funding, and executives were planning to spend most of the money on hiring software engineers and product designers. In a thriving tech industry, rapidly expanding firms like AllDone confronted a tight labor market for technical workers. In light of the intense competition for top talent, a significant portion of everyday work life around the AllDone office—and even of employees' social lives outside of the office—involved recruiting job applicants.[17] The office was not only a place for work; it was also a site for engaging members of the local tech scene in what managers called "social recruiting" activities.

At the time of my fieldwork, AllDone's San Francisco office featured a gendered division of labor consistent with prior accounts of occupational segregation in the tech industry. Whereas men hold the vast majority of prestigious and highly remunerative technical jobs, women tend to work in marketing, public relations, and roles that involve "enabling" or "coordinating" the activities of others, which typically pay less than technical work.[18] For most of my time at AllDone, four women had a consistent presence in the office. Three of them—the office manager, Chloe; the chef, Amy; and the part-time cleaner, Gabriela—worked to facilitate the productivity and sociality of the rest of the team. Of those three, only Chloe was a full-time employee. The fourth woman was Katrina, a product designer.

Chloe, a twenty-two-year-old recent college graduate, was hired shortly after I began my fieldwork as the company's "director of happiness." Information scholar Silvia Lindtner calls similarly positioned women in tech startups "happiness workers" who are tasked with "providing a particular kind of affect and emotional support structure that ma[k]e the work of the (mostly male) tech entrepreneurs not only bearable but pleasurable."[19] In addition to her role as office manager, Chloe planned and executed in-office events and offsite celebrations for the San Francisco staff and those whom they wished to impress, packaging and exhibiting AllDone's upward trajectory for both internal and external audiences. Chloe repurposed the office for frequent social gatherings like informal "tech talks" in which AllDone's software engineers would share insights with their counterparts at other companies, a trivia night for tech workers, and a party for alumni of Martin's technical high school.

The company's promise—ratified by the investors whose money paid for the parties—was on display to anyone who entered the office. Chloe hired caterers and bartenders to staff the kitchen during events. Commercial-grade, glass-doored refrigerators showcased a selection of beers, and a shelf was always brimming with liquor bottles. Visitors noticed that employees' desks were equipped with state-of-the-art computers, multiple massive monitors, and expensive furnishings. At one party, I overheard a guest remark to her friend, "Dude, you know those chairs cost like eight hundred dollars? They're Aerons."

Executives believed that AllDone's outward displays of opulence would improve the company's standing among potential recruits. One Friday evening a month after I started my fieldwork, I attended a "happy hour" at the AllDone office. Over a hundred partygoers were mingling around the workspace, their voices rising above the din of indie pop music blasting from speakers beneath somebody's desk. People sipped beers and margaritas as they talked; some were sprawled out on couches. I imagined that if not for the desks threaded around the perimeter of the room, the setting may just as well have been a trendy San Francisco loft party. At one point during the evening, Carter told me that the event was "recruiting gold." It had been scheduled to end at 8:00 p.m., and it was already 8:15, so I asked if he was going to ask people to leave. "No," he replied. "Alcohol is cheap." To Carter, the cost of booze was nothing compared to the value added by

a good recruit. AllDone's office doubled as a social space designed to se-
duce young talent, impressing upon them the excitement and privilege
that came with being part of a fast-growing enterprise that had venture
capital funding to spend on showing off its success.

Every member of the San Francisco staff was asked to engage in "social
recruiting" activities, which involved both bringing recruits into the office
for social events and trying to connect with potential hires outside the
office or online. Company leaders urged staffers to invite friends and acquaintances who worked in the tech sector to join them for a meal in the
office. Employees often referred to the food cooked by Amy, AllDone's office chef, as "recruit bait." One day I sat down for lunch next to Carter, who
was sitting across from a twentysomething Asian-American man clad in a
tight, powder-blue graphic tee. Carter introduced me to Tony, who worked
for an LGBT travel website, and wryly explained to us both why Tony had
been invited to lunch: "You get him in with food and then hit him with the
recruiting pitch." I attended an event at another startup office where I met
a young software engineer named Carlo. After I told Carlo I was working
at AllDone, he asked, "That's the company with the chef, right?" He told
me that Bill, one of AllDone's software engineers, had repeatedly invited
him to the office for lunch. Carlo had declined because he viewed informal
lunch meetings at AllDone as "actually a way to ensnare" new recruits, and
he was planning on leaving the industry to attend graduate school. Bill
had also written a blog post extolling AllDone's "food culture," and many
employees posted images of meals that Amy prepared on social media.
On most days, at least one guest was present at lunch, as well as at the
office's weekly Wednesday-night dinners. AllDone moreover incentivized
employees to mobilize their social networks for the purposes of recruiting
by offering a $5,000 bonus for each referral that led to a new hire.

In addition to drawing employees' friends into the office, AllDone's
leaders also asked staffers to perform social recruiting activities outside
of work hours. In an all-office e-mail, Carter implored his colleagues to
always be looking for recruitment opportunities:

> We need to go faster. We need to be more aggressive about asking friends for
> introductions to engineers. (Side note: Last weekend I was at a club for a
> friend's birthday, and while my friends danced, I spent an hour at the bar
> talking to a guy because he mentioned he was a front end engineer at Meebo.)

Many employees reported back to colleagues about meeting friends and acquaintances for meals, coffee, or cocktails outside of work to pitch job openings at AllDone. Some promoted displays of AllDone's success by sharing images and news from the office on their personal social media accounts. And staffers also sought out recruits by setting up tables at software engineering conventions around the Bay Area to entice job applicants. They took breaks from writing code to write blog posts about the work they were doing at AllDone. Some software engineers frequently came to work and left the office wearing an AllDone T-shirt or hoodie. These and other public displays suggested that many employees considered AllDone to be a "cool" place to work. Showing off the office, AllDone's brand, and the company's success reflected positively on their status while likely allowing them to enjoy being the object of others' envy.[20]

Although "network hiring" is common among small and less formalized companies, drawing on workers' existing social ties to drive recruitment efforts often contributes to elitism and the reproduction of a homogeneous workforce.[21] At the same time, the "performative informality" of startup offices—where appeals to "having fun" are pervasive—can obscure the perpetuation of hierarchies and exclusion.[22] One Friday evening around 8 p.m., Adam and I were chatting and drinking beers while seated at AllDone's lunch tables. The conversation turned to the sexism that pervades Silicon Valley.[23] In staff surveys, both male and female employees had cited the office's gender dynamics and the prevalence of traditionally masculine activities (e.g., beer brewing, foosball, participating in a startup dodgeball tournament) as items in need of improvement.

Adam felt strongly that the AllDone office should be an inclusive space—I had seen him call out colleagues when they made comments that he believed could contribute to an unwelcome environment for women. "In this industry," he said, "in Silicon Valley, we have to be really sensitive about this because it's a male-dominated field where women are made to feel uncomfortable." Still, when it came to hiring, Adam felt that the company couldn't yet afford to widen its recruitment net, as he told me during a conversation following one Wednesday-night dinner.

'I don't like that phrase, "bro culture,"' Adam says. He doesn't think it applies to AllDone. 'We're open to everybody.'

'Yeah, well . . .' I reply, rolling my eyes.

'Hey,' Adam interjects, 'we *are* open to everyone.'

I note that AllDone has only two women working as full-time employees, adding that if a company really wants to get serious about diversifying its workforce, 'sometimes you just gotta decide that your next hire will be a woman.'

'We don't do that,' Adam says. 'We look for the best people, and it's great if they're women. Look, Google can hire fifty recruiters to look for qualified women and entice them to work there. We can't compete with that.'

In an industry in which women were underrepresented, AllDone's leadership believed that their small startup lacked the resources they would need to locate "the best" female recruits and convince them to work for their company.[24] AllDone's workforce was overwhelmingly white and male. Relying on employees' existing social networks for recruiting made it more likely that this would remain unchanged.[25]

DREAMS AND DISTANCE COEXIST

My conversations with colleagues in AllDone's San Francisco office, as well as many more that I overheard, confirmed my sense that most employees harbored the startup dream: That through a steady march to a successful initial public stock offering or the firm's acquisition by a larger company, their jobs could make them millionaires. At times, employees openly fantasized about the lifestyles that AllDone's triumphs would enable: a house, a boat, parties, a chauffeur, or hired help to handle household chores. For some, this imagined future affected real-life financial decision-making: Adam maintained that he would wait until he knew the disposition of his AllDone stock before purchasing a home. As Carter once explained to me, a startup is 'like a lottery ticket. . . . I mean, with AllDone, I just think, what if I made a billion dollars? What would I do with it?'

The excitement surrounding potential payouts was not limited to the cofounders and software developers who held the largest allocations of stock options. During one quarterly review celebration, I was seated at a dark leather bench at a swanky bar that AllDone had rented out for the occasion:

> Chloe [AllDone's office manager] plops down onto the bench next to me. She is beaming as she cries out, 'I'm gonna get rich!'
>
> 'From AllDone?' I ask.
>
> 'I have way less stock options than the rest of you, but I think I am,' she replies with a mischievous smile. 'Peter said we're gonna be huge!'

For employees up and down the org chart, holding a stake in a high-growth company made dwelling in the everyday gyrations of its data tantalizing and fun.

Given the existence of extensive research suggesting that well compensated tech workers are prone to stress and anxiety caused by long work hours, demanding performance standards, high cognitive loads, and feelings of employment insecurity, I was surprised to encounter such unfettered, relentless optimism in AllDone's San Francisco office.[26] During the course of my fieldwork, I rarely encountered obvious manifestations of strain among AllDone's San Francisco workforce. Although the feeling rules implicitly prescribed by the team's culture of speculative optimism may have predisposed employees to exude positivity, there are other reasons why workers' experiences may have diverged from those described in many prior accounts of tech work. The fact that the company had received an injection of VC funding shortly before my arrival certainly affected employees' sense of the value of their work and fed the dream of a lavish payout. Most employees—overwhelmingly young and without children—spent much of their leisure time with colleagues, likely reducing the tension between team members' work- and non-work lives. And last but hardly least, employees expressed confidence that their skills would be in demand in the Bay Area's booming tech economy even if AllDone were to fail.

Still, acceptance of AllDone San Francisco's organizationally sanctioned discourse and rituals was not complete, unchallenged, or universal among its staff. At the same time that organizational cultures prescribe the activities and sentiments of a firm's employees, they can simultaneously become objects that members reflexively consider and critique.[27] In meetings and conversations, employees raised pointed questions about the performance of the company or of particular projects, and some privately expressed skepticism about AllDone's leaders, their colleagues, or AllDone's long-term potential.[28]

After my departure from the field and his exit from the company, Sam, a software engineer who had worked at AllDone for almost five years, told me that he had maintained an "affirmation spreadsheet" during the latter part of his tenure at AllDone. Sam would copy exuberant e-mail messages penned by colleagues into the spreadsheet, eventually generating a long list of exclamations in order to poke fun at—and apparently to maintain some critical distance from—the office's culture of speculative optimism.

Attempting to assess the "authenticity" of the emotions expressed by individuals participating in an organizational culture can be a fruitless endeavor. The nature and depth of an individual's feelings are not static attributes, but are instead likely to vary depending upon the specific situation in which she finds herself.[29] Most AllDone San Francisco employees— including this researcher—appeared capable of holding both optimism and skepticism simultaneously, even as they largely suppressed public expressions of the latter.[30]

Additionally, although many AllDoners publicly professed their excitement about how the product they were creating could "change the world," some were also open about the fact that they were motivated by more prosaic considerations. During a break from work that Adam and I spent walking around the neighborhood near AllDone's office, he told me:

> 'Technically, building a marketplace for services doesn't matter to me. And I don't think Carter and Peter are passionate about it either. I think they just want to build a huge business. As a kid I always saw myself becoming a millionaire. And that's exactly what I'm doing.'

For some employees, the nature of the product they were creating and its impact on the world could be far less meaningful than how the company's success could change their own lives.

· · · · ·

AllDone's San Francisco–based employees performed engineering work while enmeshed in institutionalized rituals and practices of collective meaning-making. Both these material and cultural practices helped the company address valuation lag by bridging the gap between potential and profits. San Francisco staffers orchestrated continual change in AllDone's product in an effort to demonstrate growth to investors, while simultaneously enacting a relentless optimism about the company's capacity to make them rich and change the world.

In venture-backed startups like AllDone, the imaginary of a highly remunerative "exit" serves as a cultural resource that posits organizational goals and the means through which they should be pursued.[31] In raising expectations, the fantasy of success cultivates emotional displays and social and psychological investments in the firm among both internal and external audiences. Whether or not this vision was an accurate representation of reality is, from this perspective, immaterial. What matters is that this collective imagination of the future, shared by the company's investors, managers, and San Francisco–based employees, was *productive*. The firm's practices and rituals institutionalized its future orientation, enabling particular types of social interactions and interpretations of economic reality.[32]

Many corporate cultures emphasize how employees contribute to a mission related to the company's products or services—such as helping buyers and sellers of local services connect with one another. At AllDone, on the other hand, what the company actually *did* was incidental to the San Francisco team's workplace culture, which was oriented around achieving the goals promoted by venture capital investors. Workers were inserted into, and seduced by, a culture of speculative optimism that helped to build internal and external legitimacy in an organizational field rife with uncertainty. At the same time, AllDone San Francisco's workplace culture functioned as a tool for labor control, eliciting exuberant participation in work while orienting employees around the shared mission of achieving scale at all costs.

In Silicon Valley, as elsewhere, gendered labor makes resource acquisition and innovation possible. At AllDone San Francisco, employees' affective experiences were organized to generate expectations about the company's success. These experiences were enabled by the efforts of the women who cooked employees' meals, cleaned up after them, and organized the social events at which they sought out new recruits and promoted their brand. The stubborn persistence of gender inequality has long troubled observers of the tech industry, and scholars, practitioners, activists, and businesses have all mobilized in various ways to address the documented hostility, harassment, and stereotypes that women face in tech workplaces and at recruiting events.[33] My time at AllDone suggests yet another barrier to diversity in the tech industry: As new startups model themselves on more successful firms to boost their own perceived legitimacy to VC investors, they reproduce the field's norms, which, at this point, includes "bro culture."

The San Francisco office's culture of speculative optimism was also enabled by the company's geographic division of labor, which created physical distance between lower-status workers and the more privileged employees who held stock options. Lateral work relations and open expressions of excitement about striking it rich would likely have been far more difficult to sustain if the office were populated largely by low-wage support staff who were excluded from this version of the dream.[34] It is to the experiences of AllDone's remote workforce in the Philippines that we now turn.

PART II The Philippines

INNOVATION'S HUMAN INFRASTRUCTURE

3   Working Algorithms

When I began my research, AllDone had just secured its first round of venture capital funding, totaling \$4.5 million. The funding had preserved and enhanced AllDone's opportunity to generate value in its quest to build an "Amazon for local services." Although the influx of cash was cause for celebration, it also incited a sense of urgency among employees in the San Francisco office. As Carter, AllDone's president, intoned in an all-staff e-mail:

> We know what the future of local services is. But we're not the only people that know this is the future. And, more importantly, there's lots of people—smart, scrappy, and well-funded people—building our vision. Someone is going to do it. And it looks like it's going to happen soon. We just have to finish building faster than anyone else and we will win. We have to.

AllDone was bringing an important project to life—but it also faced an array of viable competitors. Carter's statement echoed an earlier all-office e-mail that Peter, AllDone's CEO, had sent to emphasize the same point: "The time is NOW!!! The limiting factor is our own creativity, hard work, and determination—we have to seize the opportunity!" Only by growing quickly could AllDone hope to secure the advantages that accrue to "first movers" in an industry that continued to welcome an ever-expanding array of competitors. The longer it took AllDone to advance its product and its standing in the market, the higher the likelihood that another firm would execute the cofounders' vision first and reap the rewards.

AllDone was facing a conundrum that all companies must ultimately address. For firms to survive, they must effectively balance the opposing yet complementary processes of "exploration" and "exploitation."[1] On the one hand, organizations need to explore by innovating, experimenting, and taking risks to develop new ideas, markets, or relationships that may yield benefits in the future. On the other hand, firms must also find ways to exploit their existing knowledge to realize the benefits of prior experiments by selecting, refining, implementing, and executing their most promising developments. Organizations that focus too much on exploration may discover that they are unable to fully take advantage of ideas that remain underdeveloped; those that focus too much on exploitation may find themselves surpassed by innovative competitors. Companies must demonstrate what management scholars Michael Tushman and Charles O'Reilly call "ambidexterity": ensuring the satisfaction of the current customer base, protecting the firm's reputation, and maintaining the organization's survival in the short term while simultaneously developing revolutionary innovations to position the firm for future expansion and success.[2]

AllDone faced extraordinary pressure to innovate and grow as quickly as possible. That would require developers to find new ways to attract users and increase their activity on the platform. At the same time, AllDone's leaders knew the firm would be worthless if it couldn't keep the product functioning properly and provide the services it had promised to an ever-expanding user base. For AllDone, developing this form of ambidexterity meant establishing separate organizational units to specialize in each function. The engineers in San Francisco took on the role of explorers, satisfying the expectations of venture capital investors by identifying new opportunities to grow the company and its valuation. A large team of contractors in the Philippines, meanwhile, exploited existing knowledge by supplementing or standing in for the computational processes that made AllDone's software work.

This chapter discusses a phenomenon I refer to as *technical drag*— organizational problems that arose when software developers' needs and imagination outstripped both the capacities of technology and their available engineering resources. Managers at AllDone hired Filipino workers to address technical drag by performing *computational work*, or routine, information-processing tasks that stood in for or supported the company's software systems.[3] Some computational work was applied to operations that software alone was unable to accomplish. Engineers also offloaded processes that software was *technically* capable of handling onto workers in the Philippines so employees in San Francisco could remain focused on their strategic goals. Additionally, Filipino workers directly supported engineers by taking on projects that accelerated their pace of innovation. Managers viewed AllDone's Filipino workforce as a crucial contributor to the company's rapid growth. They were, in the words of two executives, "the magic behind AllDone."

SOFTWARE WITHOUT ENGINEERS?

In the period immediately following the fundraise, AllDone's founders, in consultation with the board of directors, elected to prioritize two different kinds of expansion: growing the user base and hiring more employees for the San Francisco team. First, to have any hope of success, AllDone would have to bring a critical mass of users on board. Their previous efforts had been more successful in attracting sellers than buyers. As Peter explained in an e-mail update to AllDone's angel investors after the fundraise, "With 250,000 active sellers, we already have enough coverage to service almost all categories in all geographies."[4] The volume of buyers, in contrast, remained far lower: in the month when AllDone secured its VC investment, buyers had submitted just over seven thousand requests for services. During my first visit to the office, Martin told me that the team was targeting weekly growth in buyer requests of 2 to 3 percent over the next quarter, or up to 47 percent compounding growth during a three-month period. Continued expansion in the user base following its first VC investment would make AllDone an attractive target for future funding rounds.

AllDone's board of directors approved the executives' plan for improving the company's ability to attract and retain buyers. In a presentation to the board, the cofounders explained that buyers needed more information on what AllDone offered its customers. AllDone's software developers would thus be mobilized to "dramatically improve the public face of the website" by overhauling AllDone's homepage, as well as all the webpages buyers visited most frequently, to clarify the company's value proposition and to make their experience with the platform more intuitive and engaging.

AllDone therefore planned to use most of the new money to hire more engineers and designers. As Peter put it in a staff meeting, "we're spending lots now to get people onboard because we believe in what we're doing." But enlarging the four-person engineering staff would do more than increase the company's ability to expand its user base. It would also significantly increase AllDone's pace of innovation, enhancing the enterprise's ability to devise plans, run experiments, assess results, and implement changes to the product—activities that, over time, had the potential to generate substantial returns for those who held equity in the firm.

Recruiting engineers and designers to join the team became an all-consuming task that engaged AllDoners both inside and outside of the office, leaving little time for the staff to run the business. By the time an applicant had completed the interview process, he or she (though engineering candidates were virtually always men) had been assessed by an ad hoc hiring committee consisting of seven team members. The recruitment effort was led by Peter, AllDone's CEO. Peter hired a contractor named Hans to manage the details. Hans would review resumé submissions and schedule introductory phone calls between promising applicants and Peter. If Peter was able to convince the candidate to invest some time in completing a coding challenge devised by the company's four software engineers, the team would then review the applicant's submission and confer on whether to advance the candidate to the next stage in the process, in which an engineer would conduct a phone interview to further evaluate the individual's technical prowess.

Those who passed that test moved on to a daylong "onsite" interview in the office, which consisted of ninety-minute one-on-one sessions with each of the four current engineers. Candidates would also spend an hour with Josh, the product manager, and finally another hour with Peter before being sent off in the evening with a beer stein emblazoned with the AllDone logo. Each member of the hiring committee would then write an evaluation of the candidate that everyone involved would read, and then they would confer in person to discuss the candidate's fate. For weeks at a time, the hiring team interviewed one or two candidates per day.

Why was AllDone's hiring team so selective? In part, because the company lacked the managerial capacity to supervise its workers. One day at the lunch table, I asked Hans what kinds of applicants AllDone was looking for.

> 'At this point, we need people who are the best,' Hans replies. 'We have to be really picky, because nobody will be looking over them and their work—they can't make a mess of the code base. We need people who we know can work independently. Eventually, once we get bigger, we won't have to be so picky because they'll be managed.'

AllDone's developers had to be confident that a new hire could be trusted to make an immediate impact without putting their existing code at risk. For this reason, the hiring team believed that it was important for them to carefully assess an applicant's skills, rather than relying on evaluations based on his or her credentials. Managers also feared that diluting AllDone's standards in order to hire technical workers more quickly could compound the company's problems in the future. Hans told me that 'you have to find "A people" because "they bring in "A+ people." If you hire "B people," they pull in "C people." Managers believed that if AllDone compromised its standards in the name of expediency, the company could soon lose its way and find itself mired in mediocrity.

Given the engineering team's heavy involvement in recruiting, interviewing, and evaluating job candidates, they were invariably forced to sacrifice their short-term productivity as they built their team. AllDone's laborious and time-consuming hiring process thus threatened to slow the company's progress at a time when investors continued to expect immediate and precipitous growth in key metrics. Although I had come to AllDone because of my interest in studying work and life inside a startup, a month into my fieldwork, my fieldnotes reflected my surprise that "since I began at AllDone, there doesn't appear to be much *work* going on at all, at least as far as software production is concerned." My observations were later confirmed by Josh, AllDone San Francisco's product manager, when he reported that during the first quarter of the year, AllDone's four software engineers had "accomplished very little" in terms of their production goals because they had been "very, very focused on recruiting" activities that he said had consumed at least half of their work hours. By the time the San Francisco team wrapped up its hiring—over six months after the process had begun—they had received four hundred applications, which had resulted in one hundred completed coding challenges and four software engineers accepting offers to join the team. How, then, did AllDone simultaneously *run* and even *grow* its platform when its software developers were frequently too busy with recruiting to do their jobs?

TECHNICAL DRAG

As a tech startup that promised to use the power of algorithms to connect buyers and sellers of local services, AllDone's founders initially assumed that the company's software developers would be solely responsible for making the platform work. Soon enough, however, it became clear that AllDone had a *technical drag* problem: its software alone could not actually do all the things the company needed it to accomplish. To understand the challenges AllDone's developers faced, we must first understand how contemporary algorithmic systems work.

Artificial intelligence (AI) systems often appear to work "like magic": you ask your smart speaker to play a song and hear the first notes almost instantaneously; you enter your destination into Google Maps and it suggests a route that will help you avoid traffic; or you open up the Facebook app and the most interesting posts are waiting for you at the top of your screen. But even when AI can be taught to perform functions like these, programmers still need to hire humans to label the "big data" from which AI learns, to make sure the software continues to do what it's supposed to do as conditions change, and to step in to handle edge cases that can flummox automated systems. Anthropologist Mary Gray and computer scientist Siddharth Suri call these people the "ghost workers" who toil on digital assembly lines to make the internet run.[5]

Recent research has brought this work out from the shadows, revealing how a far-flung labor force keeps our social media feeds from being overrun by objectionable material, trains AI to recognize images and speech by labeling photographs and transcribing audio recordings, and fulfills a host of other functions behind the scenes of our global tech eco-system.[6] However, because such studies are largely based on interviews with workers and technologists, they offer a limited view of the invest-ment logics and organizational problems that call this work into being, and of the processes through which human labor and algorithmic systems evolve over time. How do software engineers conceive of the division of labor between humans and machines, and how do their views inform de-cisions regarding which processes to automate and which to delegate to far-flung workers? How are their judgments shaped by their perceptions of the digital laborers whose efforts support their products? And in what ways do their perspectives reflect the organizational contexts in which they operate, where goals and resources may shift over time?

At issue is what we mean when we refer to "artificial intelligence." Tech-nologists and journalists often portray algorithmic systems as "smart" and capable of solving an ever-expanding array of social and organizational problems. And programmers have long developed software that can sim-ulate human cognition by instructing it to follow precise instructions to sort data or complete mathematical calculations. However, there remain many tasks that cannot be simulated in this manner because humans can-not articulate the exact "rules" necessary for accomplishing them. Follow-ing philosopher Michael Polanyi's statement that "we know more than we can tell," economist David Autor observes that "the tasks that have proved most vexing to automate are those demanding flexibility, judgment and common sense—skills that we understand only tacitly."[7] For instance, most untrained human children could visually identify whether or not an ob-ject is a chair with a high degree of accuracy by reasoning about what the object is "for." It is far more difficult, however, to program a computer to consistently succeed at the same task because it is difficult to define a spe-cific set of attributes that a chair will possess: Some have four legs, while some have none; some have a back, arms, or wheels, while others do not.

Rather than telling software precisely how to perform certain opera-tions, a set of programming techniques known as "machine learning" al-lows computers to infer patterns approximating tacit rules from large sets of "training" data. Imagine again the task of visually identifying a chair.

Software engineers could "feed" their program a vast number of human-completed operations (i.e., thousands of images marked "chair" or "not chair"), and the software would use statistical modeling akin to inductive logic, rather than deductive reasoning, to "learn" how to perform the operation.[8]

Even when machine-learning systems do succeed, it would be short-sighted to conflate AI with autonomy from human intervention. As information scholar Tarleton Gillespie asserts, "Information systems are always swarming with people; we just can't always see them."[9] Human activity plays an essential role in the implementation of AI. Specifically, the software engineers who design algorithmic systems frequently rely on armies of workers performing what I call *computational work*. Here, I use the term "computation" to describe the process of transforming information according to a predefined set of rules. Humans perform computational work when they manually implement information-processing algorithms.[10]

Unlike software engineers, computational workers do not write computer code; however, their efforts constitute the behind-the-scenes human infrastructure that makes AI work. The tasks that people perform in and around algorithmic systems are as endless and dynamic as the demands of businesses and consumers. To keep pace with the scale of the data mobilized by AI systems and the near-instantaneous responses that software engineers and consumers demand, employers may recruit dozens, hundreds, or even thousands of far-flung workers to fulfill important functions. For example, in 2020 Facebook claimed to rely on fifteen thousand people located around the globe to filter out inappropriate user posts.[11] Wherever software developers have achieved breakthroughs in AI, that success has typically been predicated on combining the strengths of technology with access to cheap global labor markets to tap into the ingenuity, imagination, and dynamism of people.[12]

Management scholars Ted Baker and Reed E. Nelson have described how entrepreneurs with limited resources learn to "mak[e] do by applying combinations of the resources at hand to new problems and opportunities."[13] To accomplish their goal of achieving rapid expansion at a time when the company's technical team had little time to focus on maintaining and updating their software, AllDone's managers called upon the human resources that were readily available. At AllDone, addressing technical drag meant expanding the company's digital assembly line in the Philippines, where workers performed computational work that stood in for or supported software algorithms.

ALLDONE'S "HUMAN MACHINE"

AllDone had hired its first work-from-home Filipino contractor a few months after the company's launch. Within a year, the team had grown to 125 contractors, a number that held steady over the following six months. During the first phase of my research, the team began a new round of rapid expansion, growing by over 50 percent over the next six-month period, to 190 contractors. The vast majority of AllDone Philippines contractors were college educated and between the ages of twenty and forty, with a significant portion in their late twenties or early thirties. About 70 percent were women.

Contractors carried out long-term processes in support of AllDone's organizational goals. These workers performed their work by logging in to "portals," or administrative webpages created by San Francisco–based engineers to integrate Filipino team members into AllDone's computational infrastructure. Each portal allowed workers to complete a particular set of tasks. For example, a division of nearly one hundred staffers handled the company's primary function by manually matching buyer requests with sellers from AllDone's database of service providers. Another division "onboarded" new sellers by classifying the services they provided, running an array of checks to verify their trustworthiness, proofreading their profiles, and deleting inappropriate posts. A third division was responsible for generating tens of thousands of brief descriptions of All-Done sellers every month. These blurbs were then compiled on webpages designed to boost AllDone's position in search engine rankings. A fourth provided customer support by responding to user e-mail queries with text drawn from prewritten templates. Members of the fifth division carried out short-term "special projects" assigned by managers in San Francisco. In total, Filipino contractors executed over ten thousand routine tasks per day.

AllDone Philippines' labor processes were conceived by members of AllDone San Francisco through an activity they referred to as "establishing process." Employees would formulate a task, decompose it into its constituent parts, and write instructions for completing each part before offshoring the task to a distributed, online workforce.[14] AllDone San Francisco's technical workers wrote code in specialized programming languages to direct the hardware powering the company's technologies, and nontechnical workers wrote directives in plain English to guide the people who constituted what executives often called AllDone's "human machine." Like software engineers, nontechnical workers, too, crafted algorithms, or "sequence[s] of instructions that should be carried out to transform [any given] input to output."[15] And like computer code, the instructions they wrote were designed to leave nothing to the imagination. As AllDone's operations manager, I assumed responsibility for generating many such documents to guide the work of Filipino contractors.

I typically provided instructions in text, sometimes with supplemental images or video guides. Occasionally, for example, I included graphical decision trees to help workers understand how to handle all foreseeable contingencies. With every operation explicitly detailed, workers became, from the practical perspective of managers in San Francisco, nearly as interchangeable as computer processors in a network, with each person developing approximately the same interpretation of each task. Process engineers' algorithms were "debugged" by local leaders in the Philippines who reviewed each set of directions and posed questions to help managers clarify their instructions before they were distributed to team members for human computation.

Filipino contractors' wages and work hours were determined by workers' particular functions: some were paid by the hour, and others received a per-task piece rate; some were asked to log a set number of hours at particular times, while others maintained more control over their schedules. On average, contractors in nonmanagerial roles earned about $2.00 per hour and worked about thirty hours per week. While AllDone paid its Filipino workers only a tiny fraction of what San Francisco–based employees earned, their compensation substantially exceeded the Philippines' legal minimum wage, which varies by region, sector, and firm size.

At the time my research began, the smallest sum that employers could pay nonagricultural Filipino workers was between $5.36 per eight-hour workday in the outlying Ilocos region and $9.15 per day in metropolitan Manila.[16] During a typical month, the total cost of AllDone's Filipino workforce was about a quarter of the cost of the San Francisco team—even though the company paid ten times as many people in the Philippines as it had on payroll in San Francisco.

Building enduring relationships between members of AllDone Philippines and the organization allowed AllDone to exercise centralized control over its workforce. Given their reliance on AllDone Philippines (ADP), managers in San Francisco needed to have confidence that contractors would execute their tasks consistently and capably. Newly hired contractors read through documentation and watched video training modules to learn how to perform their assigned functions using AllDone's proprietary administrative software. Managers of ADP's divisions distributed weekly quizzes and offered coaching to ensure that workers understood AllDone's rules and procedures.

Companies seeking workers to complete routine, information-processing work often post tasks on on-demand "crowdwork" platforms like Amazon Mechanical Turk.[17] However, the importance of AllDone Philippines' tasks to the company's success meant that an "open call" fulfilled by anonymous workers distributed around the world simply wouldn't do. Although AllDone Philippines workers were contractors, rather than employees, they typically performed the same assigned task for a period of months or even years. Failure to log the expected number of hours was in fact the most frequent reason for dismissal from ADP.[18] If too many workers were insufficiently committed to their jobs, ADP's output could hamper the company's day-to-day operations and ability to meet its strategic goals.

All of this is to say: AllDone's managers weren't looking for just any person at any given time to perform information-processing tasks, but instead wished to coordinate the efforts of particular people, endowed with particular knowledge, at particular times. Workers were not instantly replaceable because each task required training, practice, and familiarity with AllDone's internal systems and procedures. They may not technically have been employees, but they were, nonetheless, essential workers.

AllDone moreover organized its computational workforce into teams to internalize and capture the value of human collaboration.[19] To ensure the quality and reliability of its computational work, AllDone built managerial systems designed to incorporate individuals into organizational processes as long-term "team members." Workers inhabited an organizational structure that more closely resembled a traditional firm than an agglomerated "crowd" of isolated individuals. Contractors were assigned to hierarchically organized divisions with varied, but stable memberships of twenty to ninety-five people. ADP was led by a general manager who oversaw four deputy managers, who themselves supervised a total of fifteen associate managers. Contractors communicated with each other and with managers via e-mail, text chat, and videoconference to ask questions, collectively identify and troubleshoot problems, and provide encouragement to one another. Workers got to know each other by name and participated in a digitally mediated work community. Some developed friendships through online activities and occasional offline meetings.

Perhaps most surprisingly, instead of contracting with an outsourcing firm, AllDone directly integrated these workers into its organizational processes. AllDone was able to run its digital labor platform for local service providers in the United States in part because it could use *another* online intermediary—a digital freelancing platform called oDesk—to recruit, supervise, and pay its Filipino workforce. There was no AllDone office in the Philippines; team members worked from their homes distributed across the country. Local managers in the Philippines posted job openings on oDesk to connect with applicants. After applicants were interviewed, evaluated, and hired, they logged in to oDesk before beginning each workday, allowing the platform to track their work hours and activities. The oDesk software recorded intermittent webcam photos and computer screenshots during work hours, ostensibly allowing managers to ensure that team members were only being paid for time spent working for AllDone. In exchange for its services as an intermediary, oDesk retained 10 percent of the wages that AllDone paid to workers. Managers and workers used Google's suite of free e-mail and office applications to create and share internal documentation, spreadsheets, and presentations with each other and with the team in San Francisco.

AllDone's staff in San Francisco considered AllDone Philippines an integral part of the organization. Like workers in San Francisco, members of AllDone Philippines were hired to fill what job postings called "full-time" positions. Working for AllDone was not framed as a short-term "gig," but instead as a "long-term" commitment of indefinite duration that would last for as long as both parties wished the relationship to continue. Contractors were referred to as "team members," and here the word *team* took on a different valence than it did in San Francisco. In a labor market where online employment relations were typically short-term and precarious, AllDone Philippines appeared to promise some degree of stability and community.[20]

Yet, if in some ways members of ADP appeared to share the characteristics of employees, in others they did not. Filipino workers' official employment status designated them as independent contractors. Workers did not receive any of the benefits associated with full-time employment, such as paid vacation or sick leave, health insurance, or retirement benefits, nor did they enjoy the perks (like free food) available to workers in the San Francisco office. Contractors were also responsible for providing their own computer equipment and internet connections. In short, Filipino workers were in many ways *related to* AllDone—and indeed constituted about 87 percent of its headcount—but they were not formally absorbed by the firm.

The top-down flow of power, information, and resources between managers in San Francisco and Filipino contractors highlighted the limitations of ADP's inclusion. Organizational hierarchies maintained distance between computational workers and the software developers whose projects they served. Supervisors in the Philippines helped to field questions from team members and provided immediate guidance whenever possible, reducing the number of queries that made it to managers in San Francisco. Unlike employees in the San Francisco office, Filipino contractors were not included in business decisions, nor were they privy to in-depth, up-to-date news about the company's strategies and progress toward its goals.

At times even high-ranking managers in the Philippines were not informed of product changes that would affect their teams, as I discovered one afternoon during a meeting with Carter, AllDone's president, and Josh, the product manager. Carter explained that AllDone's engineers had recently made a change that suddenly increased some contractors' workload by 60 percent. 'We should have told them ahead of time so they would know it's coming,' Carter said, wincing a little and shrugging sheepishly, 'but it just didn't occur to us.' As Carter's comments indicate, AllDone not only excluded Filipino contractors from the benefits of formal employment, but also from the organizational knowledge and decision-making capacities of their counterparts in San Francisco. In their daily work lives, most members of AllDone San Francisco (ADSF) experienced ADP as invisible, behind-the-scenes human "infrastructure" whose consistent functioning they could take for granted.[21] AllDone Philippines acted as organizational substrate that seemed to automatically pick up the slack generated by ADSF's innovations, such that employees could sometimes forget that they were there, running in the background as an ever-present computational resource.

Although Filipino contractors were expected to stay up to date on modifications to company policies or procedures, and though some were occasionally asked to switch teams as the startup's needs shifted, the fundamental nature of each division's labor process remained remarkably stable over time. ADSF software engineers rarely revisited the core operations that workers performed in AllDone's administrative portals after they had been established, nor did they typically pay attention to feedback from members of ADP about how their work processes could be improved. Software engineers believed that dedicating attention to improving the ease or efficiency of ADP's work would distract them from their more pressing strategic goals of innovation and expansion.

For their part, ADP managers had grown accustomed to having their requests for administrative features and bug fixes ignored by ADSF engineers who were busy orchestrating experiments with AllDone's product features and user interface. My fieldnotes document many ADP requests that went unfulfilled, and only one occasion when an ADSF engineer asked an ADP team leader for input on how a portal could be made to function more effectively. For example, I once found a seller who had listed his phone number on his profile page, which violated AllDone's guidelines. I notified Rebecca, the leader of the team responsible for proofreading seller profiles, assuming that one of her team members had reviewed this page and missed the violation. Rebecca replied:

> The text at the bottom of the service description has clearly been added by the seller after it was edited. ☺ I hope that every time sellers make changes in their posts, these posts will automatically go back to the [proofreader]

work queues. I've suggested this to Carter before, but he said that Engr. Adam is still swamped with work, so he couldn't make it happen for now. ☺

I heard a similar story late one night during a visit to the Philippines, when I joined three deputy managers around an outdoor table at a restaurant in the hills of Cebu City. We ate, drank, and looked out at the city lights below and the stars above, enjoying the feeling of the cool breeze cutting through the thick, humid air. Rebecca asked me what ADSF's engineers were like in person, because she had e-mailed them many times but had never met them.

> Rebecca says she used to notify Adam whenever members of her team found bugs in the administrative portal they use. She says Adam would always ask, "How many people is this affecting?" Ross and David both let out a knowing laugh as Rebecca goes on to say that no matter how she replied, Adam would inevitably respond, "We're not fixing it."

> 'No pleasantries, nothing,' Rebecca continues. David laughs again. 'He's just like, "Hi, no, no!"' she cries, breaking out into laughter herself. 'Actually, he doesn't even say hi!'

Because ADSF's software engineers were focused on innovating to create new sources of value, they were unlikely to view changing ADP work processes as a priority, given that improving the efficiency of these systems would not yield the explosive growth they sought.

Many startups hide their computational workforces from investors, believing that VCs prefer technologies that can "automatically" scale to accommodate more users over those that rely on human labor, which investors tend to view as costlier and more unreliable than software.[22] This was not the case at AllDone. In pitches to VCs, the company's leaders shared details of how many Filipino contractors they had hired and the functions they performed, highlighting the low cost that the company paid per task completed. AllDone executives believed that their extensive use of computational work made them look "smart" and "scrappy"—when technical and marketing resources were limited, they found innovative ways to organize human labor to accomplish their goals.

The efforts of AllDone's Filipino workforce allowed the company to meet venture capital's expectations for growth while relieving the burden on the overtaxed engineering team in San Francisco. During the first quarter of the year, AllDone met its user growth goal, receiving almost 50 percent more buyer requests than it had during the prior three-month period. During the second quarter, that mark would increase again by 75 percent.

AllDone's Filipino contractors made these substantial gains possible. Members of AllDone Philippines labored alongside computer code to adjust or complete the output of software algorithms. In some instances, computational labor complemented software systems because workers' tacit skills allowed them to perform tasks that were beyond the reach of computer code. In other cases, AllDone relied on workers to imitate software algorithms, taking on functions that computers were technically capable of performing but that developers believed would have been too costly or time-consuming to code up themselves. Although most of their work practices were invisible to users, their contributions were essential to supporting the company's expansion and upholding the reliable functioning of AllDone's technological systems.[23]

RELENTLESS GROWTH

Demonstrating a venture-backed startup's potential for explosive growth is its founders' highest priority. The imperative for rapid expansion shapes both corporate strategy and organizational structure. AllDone's team in the Philippines advanced this goal by helping to attract new buyers to the platform, facilitating users' day-to-day activities, and supporting software engineers' experiments with new product features.

As a startup, AllDone lacked a marketing budget that would allow it to blanket national airwaves with advertising to attract potential buyers. The company thus focused its buyer acquisition efforts on "search engine optimization," a phrase that describes techniques designed to bump a website's pages to the top of the results on search engines like Google.

One way that websites can enhance their standing in search engine results is by obtaining incoming links from other websites—particularly from those that search engine companies believe are widely respected by web users, such as newspapers and government webpages. As the first phase of my research was getting underway, two members of the San

Francisco team's marketing department, Martin and Paul, conducted a nationwide online survey of AllDone sellers about the local business environments in which they operated. They then packaged the survey results on AllDone's website and tried to get other websites to link to those new pages. AllDone paid a public relations firm $30,000 to assist with outreach to news organizations that might be interested in publishing articles about the survey results—stories that would invariably include valuable links to AllDone's website.

Simultaneously, Martin and Paul orchestrated a "data mining" experiment to find out whether a combination of technology and low-wage workers could outperform the professional PR firm. Martin asked Christine, a team leader in the Philippines, to recruit two dozen contractors. These workers were invited to join a temporary "survey team." Martin and Paul created detailed documents instructing members of this new team how to systematically scour the web for the first and last name, e-mail address, Twitter handle, and organizational affiliation of every person and platform in the United States that might publish a story about local business issues. It would have been exceedingly difficult to teach software to accurately gather unstructured data from such a vast array of sources, each of which was formatted in a unique manner. AllDone Philippines' human workers, however, possessed a tacit understanding of how to identify the desired information, and they could perform these operations with relative ease.

Over a span of three months, survey team members accumulated and classified data about fifty thousand journalists, bloggers, nonprofits, politicians, and think tanks, and recorded their findings into a complex series of spreadsheets. Martin then asked me to write detailed instructions for ADP survey team members to "clean" and standardize each entry. This would ensure that Paul could use an automated system to send each target a "personalized" e-mail pitch. For example, a newspaper reporter would receive a message that included her first name, the name of her publication, and the city or region it covered. ADP's survey team then recorded recipients' responses to the automated e-mails in the spreadsheets (e.g., "This seems to raise some interesting questions" or "I'd have to question the methodology") so that Martin or Paul could reply to them individually. Finally, I wrote instructions specifying under what conditions survey team members should follow up via e-mail or Twitter with contacts who

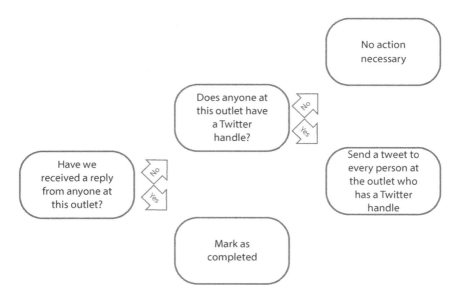

Figure 3. Example of algorithmic decision tree

had not yet responded to make sure they hadn't missed AllDone's message (figure 3).

The experimental survey team logged thousands of human-hours of work. Their efforts were wildly successful, yielding hundreds of online news articles and blog posts, each of which generated a valuable "incoming link" to AllDone's website. In fact, the survey team's efforts resulted in fifty times as many stories as had the PR firm that AllDone had retained for the same purpose, at one-third of the cost.

Another technique for optimizing websites' search engine results involves creating web pages rich in the "keywords" that potential users are most likely to enter (e.g., "best locksmith," "affordable tutor"). Ideally, AllDone's engineers would develop software algorithms to automatically add vast amounts of keyword-rich text to their webpages. However, this strategy was deemed too risky because search engine companies deploy their own algorithms to detect and penalize websites that attempt to "game" their systems by posting auto-generated content. AllDone therefore turned once again to computational workers in the Philippines.

Are you looking for painting, flooring, fence, patio, or remodeling work? Mike O Repairing is a local handyman and painter who offers home repair services.

 155 characters, Target range: 150-175. Good!

ServiceTitle

Handyman Services

Business Name

Mike O Repairing

Service Description

General home repairs outside and inside, painting, flooring, fence, patio, patio covers (some wood carving, decorative), closets, remodeling and many more.

- handyman services
- handyman service
- handyman business
- home repair services
- home repair contractors
- local handyman
- handyman home repair
- master handyman
- professional handyman
- handyman companies
- handyman special
- handyman company
- handyman help
- handyman home improvement
- licensed handyman
- handyman repairs

Figure 4. A demonstration of AllDone's blurb-writing portal

One of AllDone's software engineers set up an administrative portal that would show members of the writing team in the Philippines two key pieces of information. At the bottom of the portal was the description of services that an AllDone seller had already written for display on her profile page. On the right side of the portal was a list of the most popular keywords that buyers use to search for the services the seller offered. ADP team members rewrote the seller's description, creating an eye-catching blurb that would include one or more of the popular search terms.

In figure 4, the blurb that appears at the top of the portal contains two keywords that are missing from the seller's description: "handyman" and "home repair services." Software engineers in the San Francisco office then added the blurbs written by members of ADP's writing team to thousands of AllDone webpages designed to be found by potential buyers via web searches. Engineers believed that this system introduced enough human variability into the process that search engines' algorithms would not punish AllDone for publishing auto-generated content. During the first phase of my research, the writing team more than doubled its output from thirty-seven thousand to nearly seventy-nine thousand blurbs per month, as managers in the Philippines increased the size of the team by 50 percent, growing it from thirty-seven to fifty-five contractors. Managers moreover implemented a change in the team's pay scale (from an hourly wage to a piece-rate) to boost productivity.

BEHIND THE "MAGIC"

Because AllDone's search engine optimization strategy was yielding an ever-increasing volume of buyer requests, the company had to connect far more buyers with sellers than ever before. Indeed, AllDone's core function was to link potential buyers with sellers of local services. However, developers chose not to create software algorithms to perfect this process. Instead of devoting its scarce engineering resources to matching buyers with sellers, AllDone relied on staff in the Philippines to manually construct every introduction. This allowed software engineers to devote their energies to new projects that could "move the needle," or significantly increase the key metrics that VC investors watched to assess a startup's success.

Members of ADP's matching team used a web portal that displayed the details of each new buyer request. They began their work by vetting requests and deleting those that appeared to be fraudulent (e.g., a request placed by "Mickey Mouse"). The portal then provided team members with a rough, algorithmically generated list of local AllDone sellers who might be eligible to receive the request because they worked in related service categories. Workers would select all the sellers whom they judged to be an appropriate match, and the sellers would then be automatically notified via e-mail and/or text message of the incoming request. ADP contractors effectively functioned as "artificial artificial intelligence," simulating the output of software algorithms that had yet to be completed.[24]

Figure 5 provides a screenshot of the matching process as it would appear to a worker processing a buyer request for hairstyling services. In this case, the contractor would click on the boxes next to the hair care providers, while leaving the boxes next to the commercial cleaner, the photographer, and the skincare specialist un-checked.

AllDone's users would never know that human workers, rather than a computer algorithm, had handcrafted each introduction. To keep up with

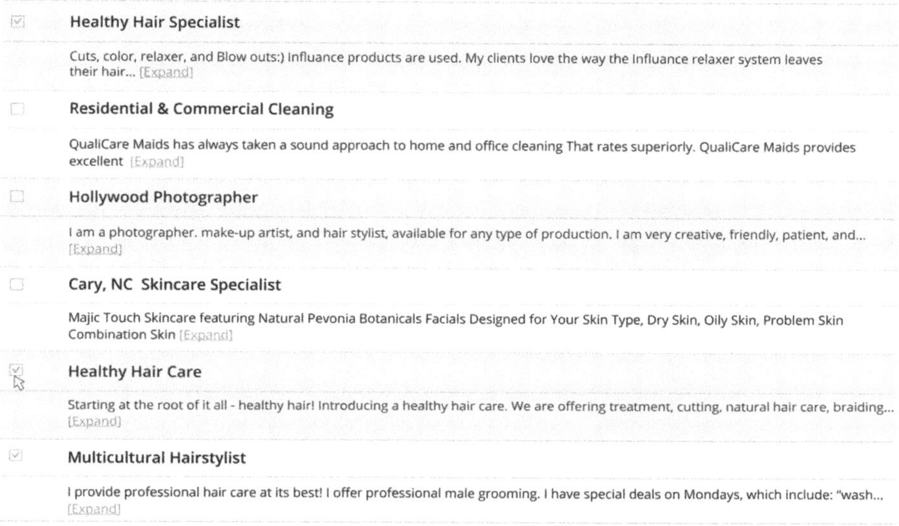

☑ **Healthy Hair Specialist**

Cuts, color, relaxer, and Blow outs:) Influance products are used. My clients love the way the Influance relaxer system leaves their hair... [Expand]

☐ **Residential & Commercial Cleaning**

QualiCare Maids has always taken a sound approach to home and office cleaning That rates superiorly. QualiCare Maids provides excellent [Expand]

☐ **Hollywood Photographer**

I am a photographer. make-up artist, and hair stylist, available for any type of production. I am very creative, friendly, patient, and... [Expand]

☐ **Cary, NC Skincare Specialist**

Majic Touch Skincare featuring Natural Pevonia Botanicals Facials Designed for Your Skin Type, Dry Skin, Oily Skin, Problem Skin Combination Skin [Expand]

☑ **Healthy Hair Care**

Starting at the root of it all - healthy hair! Introducing a healthy hair care. We are offering treatment, cutting, natural hair care, braiding... [Expand]

☑ **Multicultural Hairstylist**

I provide professional hair care at its best! I offer professional male grooming. I have special deals on Mondays, which include: "wash... [Expand]

Figure 5. A demonstration of the matching process

the rapid rise in request volume during the first phase of my research, the matching team's managers more than doubled the team's size, increasing it from thirty to sixty-eight. Additionally, local managers cross-trained members of another division of ADP on the matching function so that when user activity peaked to unanticipated heights, more workers could be mobilized to immediately log into the matching portal and assist with clearing the backlog. AllDone Philippines thus provided important "organizational slack" that helped the company adapt to rapidly changing conditions.[25]

There were many other long-term organizational processes that AllDone's engineers agreed could technically have been automated, yet were instead handled by members of ADP. These included screening out sellers whose names appeared on the Department of Justice's national sex offender registry; adding badges to seller profiles that passed a series of verifications; checking sellers' professional license numbers against relevant state databases; running voluntary criminal background checks on sellers; and sending semi-personalized e-mails apologizing to buyers whose requests received zero quotes from sellers.

The survey project demonstrated the ease with which managers in San Francisco could take advantage of AllDone Philippines' functional and numerical flexibility. The experiment proved so powerful that soon members of AllDone San Francisco began to envision new information-processing tasks that could only be completed by human workers, and colleagues asked me to devise algorithmic instructions for their own "special projects." For example, to support ADSF's recruiting goals, I established a process through which members of ADP would promote job openings at AllDone by gathering contact information for and reaching out to college computer science departments.

I initially offered such projects on an ad hoc basis to ADP team members who wanted more work, but later Christine, who had led the temporary survey team, was asked to reconstitute her group as a permanent special projects team. ADSF staffers could call upon this group whenever they wanted to quickly and cheaply execute a "random" data-gathering or -processing task without requesting and waiting for help from AllDone's small team of software engineers. Just as software developers often rely on "software-as-a-service"—integrating other companies' ready-made software products into their own code—members of ADSF could access ADP's "humans-as-a-service," using a flexible, on-demand workforce to pick up or drop projects at a moment's notice.[26] Managers encouraged all ADSF employees—from software engineers to the office manager—to "outsource" as many tasks as possible. As Martin wrote in my first performance review:

> If you spend all your time on grinder projects that take many hours, we lose you for other projects that could be equally valuable for you to work on. You should always think about how you can set up a process, delegate to someone else (an outside contractor or someone on ADP/[AllDone Las Vegas]), and move on.

Delegation freed more costly workers from routine tasks, allowing them to spend more time on the ostensibly more "valuable" work of innovation.[27] In this way, ADP altered ADSF employees' vision of technology's horizons, expanding the company's scope of action by unlocking innovative schemes like the survey project that could be completed quickly, cheaply, and effectively only by combining software with human workers.[28]

ADSF also deployed computational work to reduce the engineering burden that came with developing new and experimental product features. ADP contractors often supported what software engineers referred to as "quick and dirty" tests. By manually executing algorithmic tasks, they provided a rough approximation of a project's potential before developers invested time and resources in devising software solutions.

In one such case, ADSF deployed ADP members to test whether it would be worth an engineer's time to "code up" a new product feature. ADSF's product team wanted to determine whether including information from an AllDone seller's profile on Yelp (a consumer review website) on her AllDone profile page would increase buyers' likelihood of submitting a request, presumably because this additional information would enhance the perceived trustworthiness of AllDone sellers. Yelp offers free tools that allow software developers to embed Yelp users' business information directly into their own websites. However, Bill, the engineer in charge of the project, preferred not to spend his time learning how to use Yelp's tools without first knowing whether the new feature was likely to succeed. He devised a test whereby members of ADP substituted for software algorithms by manually searching for nine thousand AllDone sellers on Yelp and gathering information about the contents of their Yelp user profiles. Bill experimented with putting some of this information on relevant AllDone pages, and, upon finding that that it did not have a statistically significant effect on buyer behavior, abandoned the test. By using workers to stand in for software infrastructure, Bill was able to save valuable engineering time that would have been wasted learning how to use development tools to conduct a test that was destined to fail.

Maintaining a computational workforce in the Philippines allowed the company to undertake projects that would have otherwise been infeasible. During one dinnertime conversation, Carter explained how, without access to inexpensive labor in the Philippines, the jobs contractors performed would not be moved to San Francisco—they simply wouldn't exist at all:

'[Blurb] writing, we wouldn't do. Categorization [of sellers] would be automated. So would matching. We just wouldn't do proofreading. Background checks—' Adam interrupts, 'We can already automate them. We'd just need to run a script to parse an e-mail. It's just not worth it because Team Philippines is so cheap.' Carter concludes that if AllDone hadn't been able to offshore so many tasks, virtually all of ADP's job functions would disappear, aside from 'two people making minimum wage in San Francisco answering [customer support] e-mails.'

Throughout the duration of my research, AllDone had between four and eight software engineers on staff. Without ADP, the startup would have been forced to abandon some functions of its software, and to re-allocate some of its engineering resources toward building software infrastructure. ADP's reliable performance of important tasks thus supported the company's mandate to experiment and expand as quickly as possible.

Even as AllDone's software engineers were consumed with recruiting new colleagues, the company exceeded its user acquisition goals by tripling the volume of buyer requests during the first six months of my research. Amid substantial constraints on the product team, AllDone turned to a resource that was more readily at hand—an online computational workforce in the Philippines. ADP's relatively low cost, adaptability, and scalability allowed AllDone to quickly achieve the precipitous growth demanded by venture capital investors to rapidly increase the company's valuation.

· · · · ·

During the first phase of my research, AllDone's executives hoped to take advantage of the company's first round of venture capital funding by increasing demand for the product. At the same time, they sought to double the size of the software engineering team in San Francisco. These dual expansionary pressures created technical drag, or a gulf between AllDone's aims and the realities of technology's limitations and the firm's scarce resources. Managers addressed technical drag by deploying computational labor in the form of Filipino workers who supported or stood in for software algorithms.

Members of AllDone Philippines performed repetitive operations that would have been costly, time-consuming, or impossible to complete using computer code alone. These tasks helped AllDone attract new buyers to the platform, facilitated their activities once they were on the website, and helped software developers accelerate their pace of experimentation and growth. Combining software with human workers allowed ADSF's software developers to offshore processes aimed at adapting the firm to present needs, freeing them to pursue new opportunities to please investors by generating new sources of value. The innovations emerging from All-Done's San Francisco office were thus predicated on the consistency and stability of the company's workforce in the Philippines.

The case of AllDone highlights how, rather than consisting of software alone, algorithms are comprised of decentralized and dynamic configurations of people and code. While the team in San Francisco threw parties for new recruits, enjoyed catered meals, and created the impression of technological wizardry, Filipino contractors were toiling behind the scenes to support both systematized and ad hoc organizational processes. Members of AllDone Philippines handled vital, long-term functions such as matching buyers with sellers and writing blurbs to support search engine optimization. But they also performed temporary, experimental tasks. Some tests were short-lived, as when a software developer enlisted computational workers to support an experiment that placed Yelp review information on AllDone sellers' profile pages. Others succeeded and were institutionalized, as in the case of the survey project, which would go on to be repeated annually.

Many theorists of the future of work expect computers to replace humans in "codified, repetitive information-processing tasks."[29] At AllDone, however, resource constraints or the experimental nature of new product features could lead to the reverse outcome, with low-wage human workers performing programmable digital processes by hand. The existence of software solutions did not dictate that AllDone would use them; rather, the choice to automate a process or offshore it to the Philippines depended on the organizational context as well as the availability of low-cost, online labor. When researchers have written about the behind-the-scenes workers who perform this sort of labor, they often imply that software developers turn to human workers to "fill the gap" between the promise of artificial intelligence and the realities of its limitations."[30] The evidence presented in this chapter points to another source of demand for computational work: the gaps that emerge between software developers' vision and organizational limitations. Because AllDone faced venture capital's demand to achieve rapid growth under conditions of resource scarcity, developers learned to solve problems by turning to the relatively inexpensive computational labor that was readily available to them.

AllDone's use of computational labor highlights the role of human workers on the frontiers of automation, demonstrating why it is shortsighted to forecast a future of full automation or a world without work. The division of labor—and interdependence—between generously compensated software engineers in San Francisco and low-cost computational workers in the Philippines suggests that advances in software automation rely not only on the application of human labor, but also on a broader context of global inequality.

Venture capital investors use tech companies as vehicles to produce windfall returns. To get big enough fast enough to create the kinds of enormous profits investors seek, tech companies frequently rely on people living far from corporate headquarters who receive in compensation only the tiniest fraction of the massive value they help to create. Sometimes investors are aware of how startups employ computational workers as a "shortcut" to innovation, while at other times founders may conceal the depth of their use. At AllDone, an uncommon arrangement prevailed: not only were computational workers integrated into the company's org chart, but managers also sought to win their hearts and minds by promoting an organizational culture of familial love.

4 All in the Family?

Before my first day of work as an intern at AllDone's San Francisco headquarters, I received an introductory e-mail that the company's cofounders sent to new hires to welcome them to the team. The message began with an explanation of "our first guiding principle at AllDone: "**Play to win**: We're a professional sports team, not a family. We're not here to have a good season. We're here to win the Super Bowl." The e-mail contained a link to an online reference guide for new employees. Amid descriptions of company policies and procedures was a link to another website maintained for prospective and current members of AllDone Philippines. I clicked on the link and was surprised to find text that contrasted starkly with the message I had just read. The homepage stated: "AllDone is more than just a job—*we're a community and a family*. We love our jobs and we love working with each other. And we hope you will feel the same way soon." I then clicked on a video embedded in the page below the introductory text. My fieldnotes captured what I saw:

> As U2's "Beautiful Day" plays in the background, workers are shown laughing with each other, high-fiving and snapping pictures in the conference room and on the streets of a Philippine city. These images are interspersed with clips of individuals speaking directly to the camera in various indoor

and outdoor locales, offering testimonials about their experiences with the company: "Whenever I get online, it's like saying 'hi' to my own family"; "We are brothers and sisters in AllDone"; "Now that I've found a family in All-Done I don't want to leave."

Later, stills of parents and children appear onscreen, and female contractors provide commentary: "Working as a mom at home and with AllDone makes really my life as a mom easier. I can see my daughter anytime, kiss her, hug her."

Carter [AllDone's president] appears onscreen: "We want people who are looking for a community, who are looking to work someplace for years." Then contractors offer more testimonials: "I really like and love AllDone so much, and I'm very willing to work for AllDone for the rest of my life."

My mind was flooded with questions. How did accounts emphasizing community and longevity square with the fast-moving world of venture-backed startups? How could workers and managers conceive of this far-flung group of independent contractors as a "family"? Did these people, who performed routine and seemingly monotonous tasks on a digital assembly line, really "love" their jobs? Perhaps the video represented a slice of corporate propaganda designed to gloss over the harsh realities of toiling in an electronic sweatshop—or perhaps AllDone was in fact a uniquely benevolent employer of Filipino labor. What aspects of workers' reality did the imagery and rhetoric in this video reveal, and what did it hide?

In this chapter, I unravel this puzzle by examining the social and organizational conditions in which AllDone Philippines' shop-floor culture could make sense to the people involved with the team. Like any organizational culture, it called upon workers to engage in speech and behavioral performances that matched the prevailing "feeling rules" of the workplace.[1] But team members' expressions of love, gratitude, and familial belonging also reflected the complementary configuration of AllDone's organizational needs and Filipino workers' labor-market conditions.

At AllDone Philippines, corporate feeling rules delineated an organizational culture of *familial love*. The rituals and practices associated with what managers and workers came to call "AllDone Love" evolved through the interplay of leaders' management philosophies and interactions between members of ADP and ADSF. ADSF managers viewed ADP's distinctive style of communication as having originated on the "virtual" shop floor as a creative response to computational work. Veronica, ADP's general manager and its first contractor in the Philippines, recounted how, early in ADP's history, she was mortified to discover that a new hire was including rafts of emoticons and exclamation points in her e-mails to colleagues. Veronica worried that Carter (her supervisor in San Francisco) would find such messages "unprofessional," and that this judgment would reflect poorly on her leadership of the team. Instead, to her surprise, Carter informed Veronica that he "loved" the new hire's e-mails. Effusive expressions of sentimentality soon became a central feature of ADP's online and offline communications.

In analyzing ADP's organizational culture, I put aside questions pertaining to the "authenticity" of Filipino team members' emotional displays.[2] My argument is neither that contractors' emotional expression on the job corresponded to their "genuine" feelings about their work or colleagues, nor that their displays were calculated responses designed solely to further their careers.[3] Emotional expression can be particularly complex when traversing power differentials, as material support and affective attachments are often intermingled. Instead of trying to understand what these displays *mean*, then, I try to understand what they *do*. I follow the multifaceted linkages between political economy and affect, examining how the emotional displays exchanged between ADP workers and ADSF managers were coproduced to achieve stable employment relations within the context of longstanding inequalities between the U.S. and the Philippines.[4] Examining ADP's organizational culture as a performance allows us to consider how managers and contractors constructed emotional displays and how these displays supported the smooth functioning of AllDone's product amid the company's push for relentless experimentation and growth.

As we have seen in chapter 3, AllDone's leaders in San Francisco depended on the computational work provided by AllDone Philippines, which allowed ADSF employees to focus on projects that could immediately increase the company's value to venture capital investors. AllDone's Filipino workforce was accordingly organized to bolster the team's stability and reliability, offering workers jobs rather than "gigs," competitive wages, and opportunities for advancement in a fast-growing organization. For many Filipino contractors, working for AllDone was simply a more attractive option than the alternatives available to them in both local and global labor markets. Expressions of familial love were thus rooted in the mutual—though fundamentally unequal—dependence between Filipino workers and San Francisco–based managers.

THE TWO MEANINGS OF *TEAM*

At first glance, the variation in AllDone's characterizations of its San Francisco and Filipino workforces seem overdetermined. The young, male, individualistic entrepreneurs manning the office in San Francisco rejected a cultural trope evoking femininity in favor of the more traditionally masculine metaphor of competition on the gridiron. After all, they were participating in a notoriously male-dominated industry, and for most of my time in the field, the San Francisco workforce was 90 percent male. By the turn of the twenty-first century, many US-based corporations had long ago abandoned the language of a "corporate family" so popular with mid-twentieth-century industrial employers, instead offering employees the promise of "flexibility."[5] The workplace as family metaphor may seem particularly anachronistic at a startup like AllDone given the uncertainty surrounding the company's long-term solvency.[6]

The cofounders' equation of the San Francisco workforce with a professional football team implies that AllDone is a *temporary* community—a talented group of free agents who have come together to coordinate their efforts and beat out the competition on the world's biggest stage. As football fans know, winning the Super Bowl requires togetherness, but also ruthlessness. Unlike a family member, an NFL player cannot take his membership on his team for granted. In the world of professional sports, one's participation is linked directly to one's performance on the field. Teammates are not bonded by kinship, but by their shared goal and commitment to high performance. Those who fail to meet management's expectations will be cut from the team.

The emergence of a so-called "family" of work-from-home contractors in the Philippines, however, is more puzzling. Many US-based business consultants and executives believe that Filipino workers' commitment to collectivist principles makes them "naturally" family-oriented and compliant, but this is a myth: scholars have documented numerous examples of hostile relations between Filipino workers and employers, undermining the notion that Filipino culture inevitably generates harmonious workplace cultures.[7] As independent contractors, AllDone's Filipino workers were more tenuously connected to the organization than their counterparts in San Francisco, and they received none of the employment benefits typically thought to signal a tech company's commitment to its workers, including health insurance, paid time off, and stock options.[8] While members of AllDone San Francisco worked in close physical proximity to each other in the office five days a week, members of AllDone Philippines were geographically dispersed; most workers rarely, if ever, found themselves in the physical presence of colleagues. Yet it was the team in the Philippines that AllDoners described using language that emphasized their enduring attachment to the firm and their ties to each other.

The notion that AllDone Philippines could be thought of as a "family" gets still more perplexing when we consider prior accounts of the working conditions faced by the those who labor in the shadows of today's high-tech innovations. Researchers and journalists have long warned of the potential for exploitation when companies headquartered in the Global North locate production processes in the Global South in search of cheap labor and fewer regulatory constraints. For example, in 2010, a spate of worker suicides in China drew public attention to working conditions on modern assembly lines. Foxconn, the manufacturer that produces iPhones for Apple, became notorious for its harsh working conditions, demanding production quotas, and strict codes of conduct for workers in both factories and dormitories.[9] Although workers performing routinized information-processing tasks on home computers are unlikely to incur some of the bodily risks and injuries that can accompany manufacturing work, they too are often subjected to various forms of exploitation. On platforms like Amazon's Mechanical Turk, workers label images, screen violence and pornography out of social media posts, add text captions to video files, and complete myriad other operations for as little as one cent per task.[10] Existing scholarship provides numerous additional examples of nakedly exploitative digital labor arrangements that push wages and working conditions into a global race to the bottom. How, then, can we explain the emergence of a self-proclaimed work "family" at AllDone—including professions of love and loyalty—surrounding precisely the types of workers among whom we might least expect to find it?

Understanding why AllDoners would refer to Filipino contractors as "family members" requires that we return to the organizational context in which workers uttered their professions of love. Without its Filipino workforce, AllDone had no hope of meeting investors' expectations for rapid growth. The imperative of constant innovation meant that the company's computational workforce had to be not only inexpensive, but also steady and trustworthy. For their part, the company's Filipino workers interpreted their positions in relation to alternative employment options. Understanding each party's needs and constraints can help us make sense of AllDone Philippines' employment relations and organizational culture.[11]

MUTUAL ATTRACTION, MUTUAL ATTACHMENT

AllDone established its team in the Philippines just months after the startup launched its website. The company's cofounders had encountered an unanticipated problem: They found that many of the sellers who signed up to use AllDone were (presumably) far better at painting houses, fixing plumbing, and the like, than they were at using proper spelling, grammar, and punctuation in describing the services they offered on their AllDone profile pages. This discovery raised concerns that potential buyers would find AllDone's sellers—and, by extension, AllDone—unprofessional and untrustworthy.[12]

At first, the cofounders copyedited seller profiles themselves. As AllDone grew, however, they found it difficult to keep up with the volume of new users. They decided to seek outside assistance by posting a proofreading gig on oDesk, the digital labor platform. Freelancers bidding on the job hailed from the United States, Jamaica, India, and the Philippines. Carter, AllDone's president, asked each of the applicants to complete a sample set of tasks so he could assess the quality of each person's work in light of his or her speed and asking price.

Carter would later claim that the applicant who possessed the best English-language skills, performed the task most quickly, and presented herself in the most professional manner happened to be a young woman in her mid-twenties named Veronica, who lived in the Manila metro area. What's more, Veronica had asked for 90 percent less pay than had the American applicants. Carter later called this discovery a "mind-blowing, jaw-dropping moment" that led him to realize that "there is so much opportunity here [in the Philippines]." When they were launching AllDone, the cofounders had never imagined that they would be building a team overseas. But soon, Carter recalled telling Veronica, half-joking, "I want to hire you, your friends, your family, everyone you know."[13] Over time, AllDone expanded an English-speaking Filipino labor force that managers in San Francisco perceived as hardworking, loyal, and inexpensive.

At the time, Carter didn't realize that his experience was being replicated at hiring desks across the United States. Due to the legacy of American colonial rule, English-language education is widespread in the Philippines. This fact, combined with the country's position in the global economy as a developing nation with relatively low prevailing wages, make it a particularly attractive site for US-based companies wishing to offshore knowledge work.[14] Over the past two decades, the Philippines has emerged as a popular destination for both call centers that cater to American corporations, and much of the high-tech "hand work" that supports American software products.[15] Hiring Filipino workers via a digital labor platform allowed AllDone to practice *labor arbitrage*: purchasing English-speaking labor power located in a nation where it was relatively inexpensive. Sourcing online, work-from-home contractors from developing nations also allows American firms to evade employment taxes; to shift overhead costs like office space, computer equipment, and internet connections onto workers; and to pay workers only when there is demand for their services.[16]

Although American tech companies like AllDone may often prefer to hire Filipino workers to perform offshored knowledge work, managers' desires alone do not guarantee that Filipino workers will be willing to accept these jobs. Why would people in the Philippines want to work for AllDone? If AllDone executives understood hiring Filipinos as labor arbitrage, Filipino workers often viewed engaging in online work as *skill arbitrage*: Seeking employment via the internet afforded them access to opportunities beyond those available in local labor markets.[17] This may explain why members of AllDone Philippines frequently attested that they loved their *jobs*, even as they rarely spoke of loving their *work*. They did not necessarily enjoy performing repetitive information-processing tasks, but they appreciated the lifestyles that working for AllDone enabled them to experience.

The Philippines' colonial history has played a crucial role in shaping both the economic landscape confronted by its contemporary workforce and its appeal to foreign capital. Political corruption, widespread poverty, and minimal social welfare programs are among the systemic problems that limit economic opportunity for the vast majority of the Philippines' 109 million residents.[18] Although sending a child to college remains a crucial component of Filipino families' economic mobility projects, in this context a college degree is no guarantee of a decent life for oneself and one's family. The year my research began, government statistics counted 27 percent of Filipinos as unemployed or underemployed. College graduates represented about 20 percent of jobless Filipinos.[19]

The Philippines' demographic composition, coupled with limited economic opportunity, drives college graduates to look for jobs wherever they can find them. Many young graduates migrate to work abroad. In 1974, the Philippine state established government agencies designed to manage the flow of contract workers out of the Philippines to destinations around the globe.[20] At any given time, nearly 10 percent of the Philippine population—between 10 and 12 million people—are working outside of their homeland. The pay is relatively good—typically around $1,000 per month—but the expenses and bureaucratic hurdles associated with migration, not to mention workers' vulnerability to exploitation in a foreign land and the heartbreak that comes with prolonged separation from friends and family, can greatly reduce the appeal of working abroad.[21]

Those who choose to stay at home may seek to move into the professions for which they trained in college, but they face a daunting job market. In Manila alone, three hundred institutions of higher education enroll about seven hundred thousand students and award two hundred fifty thousand bachelor's degrees each year. Companies take advantage of the surplus of qualified workers by requiring applicants for nearly all formal-sector jobs to endure months or even years of "On the Job Trainings," or unpaid internships that prolong young graduates' dependence on family members or loans for financial assistance. Once they begin earning money, workers can expect to take home Manila's minimum wage of about $150 per month, enough to support only a spartan existence in a shared living arrangement with little money left over for nutritious meals and only the rarest of leisure expenditures.[22]

The recent emergence of outsourced call centers has provided Filipino college graduates with a "middle path" between relatively well-compensated migrant labor and minimum-wage "professional" work. Unlike workers pursuing the aforementioned options, successful job applicants needn't wait to begin paid employment—many are able to begin work the day after passing an English-language exam and interviewing for a position. On average, call center agents take home just over $3 per hour, or $500 per month, with some earning up to $750. Although call center work does not advance the professional goals of graduates dreaming of breaking into the fields they prepared for in college, and although many positions require overnight shifts (during American business hours), offshored workers are able to provide themselves and their families with a relatively comfortable life without leaving their communities. Given the opportunities and resources available to them, many young Filipino college graduates view this path as a strategic and sensible option.[23]

Positions with AllDone Philippines shared many of the advantages of call center jobs while also offering unique benefits, along with some tradeoffs. Call center work, after all, is hard work. During my first trip to Manila, Carter, Veronica, and I met with Alex, an assistant vice president at a major outsourcing firm who oversaw five hundred call center employees for an American telecommunications company. Alex told us about the attractive compensation available to young Filipinos with the right skills: wages for new employees were similar to those offered by AllDone (about $2 per hour), and could double through incentive pay for top performers. But because their call centers served American clients, workers' shifts typically lasted from 11 p.m. to 7 a.m., with commutes on crowded jeepneys (small buses) through chaotic and traffic-choked streets commonly stretching up to two hours each way. Call center work, Alex admitted, was taxing: workers absorbed abuse from customers, experienced constant surveillance from managers, and were evaluated on a bell curve.[24] These conditions resulted in high turnover, as workers displayed what Alex called a "mercenary attitude" by seeking better compensation at rival call centers.

AllDone could eliminate some, but not all, of these headaches. Even if some contractors were expected to clock in around 11 p.m., getting to work with AllDone was as simple as opening a laptop. And in fact many positions with AllDone offered workers more favorable or flexible hours than call centers' unrelenting night shifts. Whereas the subcontracting firms that run Filipino call centers push workers to meet strict performance standards dictated by their agreements with clients, AllDone directly oversaw its own workforce in the Philippines, and managers were reluctant to implement practices that might damage the team's morale (more on this below). Additionally, working for AllDone was far less stressful than working in a call center because virtually none of the jobs required live interaction with customers. Indeed, many ADP staffers had previously worked in outsourced call centers, suggesting that they viewed AllDone as a favorable alternative.

Work for members of AllDone Philippines was repetitive, but not overly stressful. ADP managers had access to a suite of electronic surveillance software to monitor workers' performance, but in practice, supervision was relatively lax. Managers could view intermittent images of workers and their computer screens, but they did not act as "time-study men" hovering over employees' shoulders to identify and correct inefficiencies.[25] For example, Veronica, ADP's general manager, once told me that occasionally customer support representatives would sleep through half of their eight-hour overnight shifts, and that this was OK with ADP leadership "as long as you get your e-mails done."

Supervisors issued upbeat weekly or monthly reports comparing team members' output, praising top performers, and sometimes setting goals. For example, one such report intoned,

> I want to remind you of our team goals for the month of May (yes, THIS May 😄).... With Jocelyn in the lead, we will try our best to process at least 80% of [tasks] daily. . . . This requires hard work, commitment and, yes, AWE-SOME teamwork. . . . We have done 100% of [tasks] in May 7 (although it was one of the "quietest" days with only 900+ [tasks] 😄) but we will do it!

Some contractors whose performance consistently lagged behind those of their colleagues (in terms of the quality or quantity of tasks performed) received warnings that could eventually result in their dismissal. However, local managers typically focused more on aggregate team output than individual performance, as in the above example.

Well-compensated managers in AllDone's San Francisco office saw little incentive in maximizing individual contractors' productivity at the expense of the team's morale. For example, when Rebecca, an ADP deputy manager, proposed restricting her team members to one hour of paid time checking e-mail per week as a "way of helping out in minimizing costs," Carter, AllDone's president, replied that "it's totally fine for team members to spend some time each week chatting via e-mail—there's no need for us to be stingy with that. It's not much money." Additionally, a fast-growing workforce reduced the visibility of, and pressure on, any individual team member.[26]

Working from home also allowed AllDone's contractors to exert an unusual degree of control over their time. In the Philippines, women often assume the roles of both caretaker and breadwinner in supporting their extended families.[27] On a team that was largely composed of women—a majority of them mothers—many found working from home particularly appealing. Malinda was typical in this respect. After graduating from college with a degree in nursing, Malinda had, like so many young Filipinos, been unable to find employment in her chosen field. She instead put her fluency in English to work at a Baguio call center for three years, where she booked appointments for American doctors. When I met Malinda at 50's Diner (an American-themed eatery with retro décor), she had been working for AllDone for nearly two years. Malinda now began her workday at home at 3 a.m. Some hours later, she would log off to get her two children ready for school; once they were gone, she would log back on until they came home for lunch. Malinda got some more work in here and there between napping and preparing the family dinner, before catching a few more precious hours of sleep at 10 p.m.[28] Working from home allowed women like Malinda to fit their work around their lives, rather than fitting their lives around night shifts in call centers.[29]

Jobs with AllDone also gave Filipino workers the chance to choose where they lived, an enormous benefit in a country where so many seek work overseas. Many of the ADP workers I met had previously lived abroad. John, whose most recent travels included stints doing janitorial work in London and Aberdeen, told me he considered his job with

AllDone "a blessing" because it let him earn money while living close to his family. George, in his early thirties, told me a similar story when I sat next to him on a bus ride following an AllDone party in Manila. He explained that he was thrilled to be able to work from home in the Philippines—as a gay man, he found the extreme heat and social strictures of Bahrain, where he had lived for six years, to be stifling. Within the country, call center work is heavily concentrated in Manila, a relatively expensive and crowded city.[30] Only about a quarter of ADP team members resided in metropolitan Manila, and nearly half lived outside of Luzon, the Philippines' largest and most populous island. Some logged on from villages that had only recently acquired high-speed internet connections.

Last but hardly least, working for AllDone offered contractors the possibility of advancement in a rapidly growing operation. When I left the field, some of the team's most senior contractors had been with the company for up to four years, receiving periodic raises (typically an additional $0.25 per hour), bonuses for reaching performance milestones or for their long-term loyalty to the company (ranging from $5 to $150), and promotions into supervisory positions. During the course of my research, the number of ADP contractors grew by about 50 percent, while the ranks of middle management nearly doubled, rising from eight to fifteen associate managers, with some making up to $4 an hour, or double the average rate for team members. Youth was not a barrier to ascending the organizational ladder: three of ADP's five top leaders had originally been promoted into their positions while in their mid-twenties. Such internal labor markets engender commitment by allowing workers to envision enduring careers within a company.[31]

Yet not all was well at ADP. When management conducted an anonymous survey, multiple respondents objected to their status as independent contractors working for oDesk, rather than as employees of AllDone. As an "online" employer that was not formally established in the Philippines, paying Philippine taxes, or subject to Philippine law, AllDone did not offer health insurance or paid sick leave, nor did it contribute to workers' social security accounts or provide proof of employment that would ease workers' access to credit.

Additionally, some contractors spoke of the emotional challenges that can come with inhabiting a "virtual" workplace. During a team meetup in

Cebu City, a recent college graduate named Cynthia explained to ADSF managers that 'working online means working at home—it gets lonely.' Survey responses reflected this sentiment, with some contractors requesting that AllDone offer more in-person work activities and "get-togethers." The repetitive nature of ADP team members' tasks could also affect their emotional states. Managers reported that some staffers felt "bored" with their work, and some surveyed workers asked for "more challenging position[s]/task[s]" and job rotation to stave off monotony. Others requested wage increases, an employee equity program, and more opportunities for career growth. For many, working conditions were far from ideal, with some contractors spending hours each day hunched over their laptops in bed, facing frequent interruptions in crowded homes. Some reported experiencing intermittent disruptions in internet service and electricity. And although many enjoyed having some control over their work hours, some were frustrated when there was less work available than usual, temporarily impacting their ability to provide for their families.

In spite of these complaints, however, AllDone's Filipino contractors generally reported satisfaction with jobs that they considered favorable compared to other options available to them.[32] Team members' general preference for working for AllDone over (or in addition to) other jobs was reflected in the team's relatively low rate of voluntary attrition: the percentage of contractors who chose to leave the company each month was typically between zero and two.[33] One question on the company's internal, anonymous survey asked how likely ADP contractors would be to recommend working at AllDone to a friend. The average score was 9.5 out of 10, which Carter proudly declared was "even higher than Apple's."

CULTURE IN THE CLOUD

The mutual attachment between members of AllDone Philippines and the firm was reinforced by an organizational culture that emphasized love, gratitude, and loyalty. As noted in chapter 2, organizational cultures consist of "rules for behavior, thought, and feeling" that in the aggregate constitute a "well-defined and widely shared 'member role.'"[34] Managers may cultivate organizational cultures in an attempt to build collective identities, coordinate decision-making, and align members' goals with those of the company. The organizational culture that emerged among AllDone's Filipino workforce supported an aim shared by both the firm's management and its employees: knitting distributed workers into a stable and reliable team.

As the team grew, Carter collaborated with ADP managers to self-consciously codify the group's "family values." He encouraged them to model aspects of their organizational culture on Zappos, an online retailer in the United States known throughout the tech industry for, as Carter explained in an e-mail, its uniquely "silly, upbeat, warm, family-oriented" work culture.[35] ADP contractors increasingly adopted the trappings of AllDone Love in their communications with each other and with managers in San Francisco. Because they worked from home, the vast majority of ADP contractors' interactions with colleagues occurred online. Many ADP staffers emphasized how online communications had contributed to their enculturation: In a survey of contractors conducted by management, one recalled that "when I was a newbie at AD, I remember that the first inkling I had of how AD's culture was, was by reading the e-mails and seeing how other AD members responded to e-mails."

Everyday communications among members of AllDone Philippines were often laden with ritualized professions of love, loyalty, and gratitude. Team members bombarded new hires with cheery and colorful messages welcoming them to the AllDone "family" and proclaiming that they were sure to love their jobs. Workers responded to e-mailed descriptions of ADP's performance with expressions of breathless enthusiasm, as in the following three examples following the distribution of an annual report:

> I am very inspired! ☺ Thank you so much Ma'am Veronica! WE WUV YOU so much! 🤗 Cheers to more AllDone years! 🍻

> Thank you for this inspiring e-mail, Veronica!!! 🤗 So happy to be a part of this wonderful family!!! Praying for more better years to come!!!! 🎉 🎉 🎉

> AllDone is such a blessing
> I always thank God for it every morning 🙏
> AllDone is 🖤.

Thanks so much for this amazing, wonderful job!
More AllDone ♥ and happiness this [year], rockstars! 🍺

Similarly, when contractors received promotions, bonuses, or recognition, they would typically e-mail their supervisors in the Philippines, as well as managers in San Francisco, to express gratitude and share proclamations of their loyalty to the company. "I'm so blessed to be a part of this wonderful family," one contractor wrote to Veronica on such an occasion. "I'm really looking forward to sticking with AllDone, as long as you want me to be here. Of course, that goes without saying that you can rely on my commitment, hard work, honesty, and loyalty.☺" AllDone Philippines' leaders, too, often wrapped their messages to managers in San Francisco in extravagant expressions of love and gratitude. In a weekly e-mail update, Ross, a deputy manager, wrote:

> I treasure my AllDone life. . . . My dear bosses, wait for more weeks to come and we have more surprises for you—more amazing systems, more amazing TOOLS to make our team happier, and more amazing ideas. :) We do this because we OWE you and ALLDONE a lot and we want to pay you back by showing to you our commitment and love. . . . *I want to recommit to you now my 200% commitment, love, and loyalty to ALLDONE.*

Ross used schemas of debt and reciprocity to frame contractors' hard work as stemming from their obligation to give back to the company that had placed its faith in them.

ADP's organizational culture of familial love is inseparable from the United States' and the Philippines' intertwined historical and geopolitical legacies. Spanish and US colonialism were legitimated through the notion of an idealized, "benign" hierarchy that ensures that benefits are transmitted from the upper reaches of society to the bottom.[36] This political history, marked by clientelism and colonialism, has contributed to an expectation among workers that supervisors desire performances of workplace familism. *Clientelism* refers to a relationship "in which an individual of higher socio-economic status (patron) uses his own influence and resources to provide protection or benefits, or both, for a person of lower status (client) who, for his part, reciprocates by offering generous support and assistance, including personal service, to the patron." Such "instrumental friendship[s]" are structured by enduring power asymmetries.[37]

Managers in San Francisco generally appreciated the work these norms of familism did for them in the Philippines. In organizations that abide by principles of familism, interpersonal relations and communications emphasize mutuality between supervisors and workers. Subordinates offer loyalty, respect, and obedience to leaders, who in turn may take on a paternalistic role akin to a "benevolent autocrat" who supports, protects, and cares for workers.[38] In such settings, workers may be less prone to discuss conflicts openly, acting instead to preserve amicable interpersonal relations. Deference can make subordinates less likely to share information that they believe leaders might find unwelcome.[39] ADSF leaders remained distant from the everyday lived experiences of ADP workers and expressed gratitude for how ADP managers built processes that took work out of their hands and shielded them from having to deal with—and in many cases even know about—personnel issues involving individual contractors.

Both ADSF managers and ADP workers came to express the view that AllDone Love was concordant with preexisting local norms. In a message to San Francisco staffers, Carter posited that Filipino team members were predisposed to conform to an organizational culture of familial love: "We can in no way take all the credit for the amazing culture on Team Philippines. Much of the warmth and generosity is deeply engrained in their culture. We've just promoted and amplified and institutionalized it."

Workers themselves often identified with these supposedly national attributes, arguably both because they served as sources of dignity and meaning and because they allowed contractors to assume the role of the "authentic" Filipino whom their visitors could embrace.[40] In their responses to surveys conducted by management, some contractors explicitly cited ADP's resonance with what they viewed as characteristics of their national culture: One noted approvingly that AllDone adhered to "true Filipino values that are essential in a workplace." During my visits, some workers proudly quoted the Philippine Department of Tourism's new slogan, "It's more fun in the Philippines," when explaining that "Filipinos are known for" being friendly, happy, and welcoming. These statements accorded with an image of Filipino workers that has achieved global currency, particularly among American managers. The Philippine state's labor migration bureaucracy—an important pillar of the national economy—has long marketed its workers' purported strong work ethic and patience as positive attributes that make them particularly docile and employable.[41]

I overheard Veronica reflecting these stereotypes back to an American reporter when she was being interviewed for a story about AllDone. "Filipinos love guidelines," she told the reporter. "Filipino workers do what they're told. They're pretty submissive. I'm not saying it in a—*submissive* is not a good term generally, but I hope you get my point, they will do what they are asked." This essentialized image of the compliant Filipino worker is belied by numerous real-world examples of Filipino workers resisting employer dictates, but the cultural expectation that subordinates will accede to those with higher levels of authority and foreign status remains strong.[42] Such performances were on vivid display during cross-cultural encounters between members of ADSF and ADP.

WAGE-LABOR MEETS CLIENTELISM

The messianic language associated with Silicon Valley startups slips easily into the practices and discourses of clientelism in the Philippines. Founders frequently claim that the companies they build are more than mere profit-seeking enterprises: they are also vehicles for, in the words of Google cofounder Larry Page, "making the world a better place."[43] The sociotechnical imaginaries fueled by tech industry leaders are imbued with a moral valence: corporate leaders claim they are "doing well while doing good," implying a harmony between piling up billions of dollars for investors and social progress. AllDone executives, too, asserted that their company was making the world, and particularly the Philippines, a better place. Carter would occasionally send e-mails to the staff in San Francisco to remind them of how AllDone's success could transform the lives of people far beyond the office walls. After his first visit to the Philippines, he wrote a message that included this story:

> While I was doing e-mails with Veronica one day, she showed me an e-mail she gets *every day* from someone who applied to be a proofreader. He didn't pass the test and has been e-mailing Veronica daily for weeks telling her that he can't feed his family and he needs this job so his children can eat. . . .

> If this is making you feel guilty about not helping the poor enough . . . just work harder at making AllDone successful. If we make AllDone a billion dollar company we will do more good in the Philippines and elsewhere than most non-profits could ever dream of. I actually developed a somewhat righteous anger for people who don't appreciate the good that for-profit companies can do in develop[ing] countries. It's so blindingly obvious it hurts.

Carter's conviction that AllDone was changing the world for the better did not emerge solely from the firmament of a narcissistic and self-serving Silicon Valley culture. Instead, it was reinforced by—and, indeed, coproduced through—interactions with members of AllDone Philippines that positioned managers in San Francisco as heroic altruists and Filipino workers as deserving beneficiaries.

Because AllDone was relying on an ever-expanding team in the Philippines to support its growth, and because its founders saw themselves as holding the unique power to transform workers' lives, San Francisco-based managers believed that it was important for the company to ensure the happiness and loyalty of Filipino contractors. Executives envisioned ADP's organizational culture as a sort of compensation for work that, while an improvement over the alternatives, might nevertheless feel isolating, alienating, or meaningless. They endeavored to create positive emotional experiences for Filipino team members to sustain contractors' motivation and commitment.

ADSF managers planned occasional visits to the Philippines to advance this goal. Less than four months into my tenure at AllDone, I joined two of the company's cofounders, Carter and Martin, on my first of three trips to the Philippines to visit team members. As we prepared for our journey, Carter explained to Martin and me that the purpose of the trip was not to conduct business meetings. Instead, the three of us, along with ADP's general manager and at times other ADP leaders, would travel from city to city hosting parties for the workers who lived in each region.[44]

As Carter detailed in e-mails to the ADSF staff before the trip, one of the primary goals of the visit was to build camaraderie among Filipino team members who rarely, if ever, saw each other in person. "Getting team members to meet each other" would encourage them to "treat AllDone more like an offline job than an online one," helping "to foster community and relationships so they see AllDone not just as a job but a place where their friends and family work." The meetings were thus designed to build workers' emotional attachments to the startup and to each other. An additional aim of the trip was to "build love team wide: Make everyone feel appreciated and loved from Team SF and from ADP [leaders]." Carter hoped the parties would make contractors feel good about their jobs in spite of the fact that they did what he called "unglamorous work," and that the celebrations would encourage team members to preserve the team's joyful culture as it grew.

During their visits to the Philippines, managers from San Francisco attempted to cultivate emotional bonds with Filipino workers. Informality, friendliness, and the elision of hierarchy were central to ADSF managers' interpersonal interactions with ADP contractors. As in sociologist Pierre Bourdieu's observations of social life in northern Algeria, at times members of the dominant group "mask[ed] the dyssymmetry of the relationship by symbolically denying it in [their] behavior."[45] When I traveled around the Philippines with a small contingent from ADSF, we would typically arrive at each stop early in the day to spend time with team members who lived in the area. This included, for example, visiting Manila's massive Mall of Asia, picking strawberries in foggy Baguio, or packing into a van to take in views of Cebu City from a nearby peak. ADSF managers typically avoided asking contractors questions about their jobs, and instead tried to learn about their lives outside of work, inquiring about their education and employment backgrounds, their families, and their hobbies.

I was initially relieved that I would not be expected to discuss work activities with ADP staffers because I felt guilty that most were responsible for what I perceived at the time to be tedious, mind-numbing operations.[46] During a day trip that featured a hike near Taal volcano, for instance, I was instead delighted to have a long conversation with a contractor named Mac about topics including religion, philosophy, and literature. As one travel companion from San Francisco put it during my second trip to the Philippines: 'We just go to hang out. It's easier this way. People like to feel like they're part of the team.' ADP contractors reciprocated, and were far more likely to inquire about ADSF managers' love lives than about their job functions or employment benefits and perks. As anthropologist Mary Leighton argues, work cultures that blur hierarchy through practiced informality can mask inequalities.[47] By orienting activities around "friend-ship," hanging out, and having fun—rather than work—ADSF managers avoided drawing attention to status differentials that were associated with vast disparities in authority and compensation between the two teams.

At evening parties, managers took on more formal roles as appreciative patrons. Following a round of icebreaking games, Carter, Martin, Veron-ica, and I would deliver short speeches to the assembled team members touching on AllDone's growth and ADP's role in the company's success. Carter would explain that we hadn't visited the Philippines "just to eat, talk, dance, and have a fun time with you all."

> "Martin, Ben, and I traveled seven thousand miles—halfway around the world—so we could each say '*mahal ko kayo*' [I love you all] and '*salamat*' [thanks]. Team Philippines does incredibly important work for AllDone, and Team Philippines is filled with incredible people and we wanted each of you to know how much we appreciate and love and care for you all."

Carter underscored the lengths to which ADSF managers had gone not simply to thank workers for their efforts, but also to demonstrate man-agers' love and care for them. He would then marvel at the sheer volume of tasks that ADP staffers had performed and praise workers for being "smart," "talented," "hardworking," and "fun."

Most important, managers emphasized, was how team members must be "guardians" of ADP's unique culture as the team rapidly expanded. "Each of us needs to keep living the AllDone values, like treating each other as family and sharing AllDone love, joy, and optimism every day," Carter pronounced to applause from the gathered contractors. "And, even more important, we need to make our family values contagious, so all the newbies are infected with our spirit as well." Visitors from San Francisco would then circulate around the room and strike up informal conversa-tions with team members. This required "code switching" on the part of Carter, Martin, and me, as we took on manners of speaking and behav-ing that would have been out of place in the San Francisco office, liber-ally doling out hugs and in some cases putting our arms around "family members'" shoulders.[48] Members of ADP and ADSF ate, drank, sang, and danced together (and even shed an occasional tear), ending every evening with warm embraces and mutual expressions of love and gratitude.

Just as ADSF managers mobilized ADP's culture of love to build worker commitment, so too did ADP contractors draw on the symbolic resources afforded by the company culture to reinforce the loyalty of the bosses from San Francisco to the team in the Philippines. San Francisco managers' attempts to reduce the apparent social distance between the groups and obscure differences often prompted responses from Filipino workers that reaffirmed distinctions between the two teams. Contractors' performances tended to highlight ADSF's benevolence and ADP's dependence on management, construing the Americans as benefactors who were transforming Filipinos' lives for the better.

After San Francisco managers' visits to the Philippines, ADP workers flooded their inboxes with messages thanking them for being "cool" bosses who would fly halfway around the world just to hang out with members of their workforce as "friends" and get to know them as people; who were brimming with expressions of joy and enthusiasm when visiting their Filipino colleagues; who took the time to reply to ADP team members' e-mails and "like" their Facebook posts; and who recognized their contributions and reciprocated their expressions of "love." As two members of ADP, Terry and Zach, expressed via e-mail after a visit from management:

> Carter, Martin, and Veronica, no words can explain how huge a blessing you are to many lowly people like me. You have inspired so many lives. You're everything anyone could ask for in a boss. I know I can't say it enough, but each day I wake up, I keep thanking God for sending over what is now widely known as **AllDone love**. You three never fail to expound what that phrase means, and you've personally shown that to us during your visit. (Terry)

> A million thanks to [AllDone's cofounders] for continuing to provide Filipinos like me, opportunities to grow and prosper. The quality time that I spend with my wife and kids right now, it's priceless, and as I've said, I owe it all to you guys and AllDone. I hope that I can still contribute to AllDone's success in my own little way. (Zach)

Terry explicitly framed his position vis-à-vis management as "lowly" and heaped praise upon his bosses for their beneficence. Zack lauded AllDone's founders for bringing good fortune to Filipinos' financial and family lives while also expressing his obligation to dutifully serve the company "in my own little way" in exchange for the opportunities it had provided. In a survey that solicited ADP staffers' opinions about working for AllDone, some expressed dismay with colleagues who "forget to reciprocate" the company's generosity, or "forget to show how thankful they are" for their jobs. Veronica echoed these sentiments, as well as contractors' appreciation of the relative stability AllDone provided, in her concluding speeches at each of the parties. She began by stating that 'the theme of the night is how grateful we feel,' and ended with a smile and a glance toward Carter that "I'm sure we will be with AllDone for the long haul."

Veronica's comments highlight an unspoken truth. In the promotional video described above, Carter claimed that AllDone was seeking Filipino workers "who are looking for a community, who are looking to work someplace for years." And, indeed, by the time my fieldwork ended, some had already worked for AllDone for up to four years. At the same time, contractors were doubtless aware that there were no guarantees that a startup like AllDone—which hired them as independent contractors and which was itself inherently dynamic—would be willing or able to provide them with long-term employment. Martin hinted at this during my first visit to the Philippines, when he told Carter, Veronica, and me that his speech at each team gathering would emphasize the recent growth in AllDone's search traffic, because 'what they want to hear about is the stability of the company.' In an uncertain environment, contractors sought to cultivate ties with American managers by deploying schemas of debt and reciprocity that highlighted team members' reliance on and loyalty to American managers. These expressions carried an implicit expectation that managers should reciprocate their commitment.

Although ADSF managers' habit of eliding inequalities in interpersonal interactions with members of ADP enhanced my own comfort during my visits to the Philippines, I was also surprised and unsettled by ADP team members' outward displays of adoration for the visitors from San Francisco. I felt as if Filipino team members sometimes treated Carter, Martin, and me as if we were celebrities. Every year, ADP staffers crafted elaborate video messages to mark the cofounders' birthdays. During our visits, contractors often welcomed us at airports holding large, full-color banners printed with our names and photographs of our faces. After one party, local team members arranged for a surprise performance by a drum troupe and fire dancers in our honor. When we departed, ADP staffers gave us ornate, handmade scrapbooks filled with adoring messages to take home to San Francisco. Carter wrote to the team back in San Francisco that "they treated us like total rock stars."

These activities represented an undoing of the work of leveling that had provided me, and presumably the other managers, with some measure of comfort during interpersonal interactions that were shaped by vast socioeconomic disparities. One member of ADSF who saw pictures of management's visits to the Philippines on Facebook suggested that his Filipino colleagues "worshipped" the managers from San Francisco. I couldn't deny that, from the remove of the ADSF office, appearances could suggest as much. After a party, an ADP team member named Joy texted Carter:

> Wat u did for us is more than we cud ever ask. For many of us, just getting to see u visit us in person is a dream come true. Im not joking, I really heard team members express this behind ur back, hehe. Thank u so much for everything. . . . Just promise us that u will visit us again. :)

Joy's message frames Carter's visit as a gift to workers in and of itself. I was disturbed by the notion that contractors would cite simply seeing their American boss in person as "a dream come true" because this statement seemed to diminish the value of Filipino workers in comparison to the Americans, none of whom had made such a statement about their Filipino counterparts. In another postcolonial setting, sociologists Ann Swidler and Susan Cotts Watkins observe that "Westerners view patron-client ties as demeaning to the subordinate," whereas clients may view such ties "as empowering the subordinate because patrons have obligations to their clients."[49] I have since come to understand Joy's message as at least in part an attempt to build emotional attachments to cultivate the commitment of powerful actors and stake a claim to their resources.[50]

ADP team members' performance of the role of the deferential and grateful client contributed to how ADSF managers understood their relations with and obligations to Filipino workers. The members of ADSF who had the most direct contact with ADP became emotionally invested in their Filipino colleagues. Each independently told me that one of the most painful aspects of the company's earlier financial difficulties, before the infusion of venture capital funds, had been drawing up contingency plans to lay off much of ADP. One night during a visit with team members

in Las Vegas, Carter and I had dinner at a restaurant in a flashy new ca-
sino on the Strip. Over roasted salmon and cocktails, he described his affection for members of ADP's management team.

> We're talking about if either of us ever wants to have kids, and how much
> parents have to sacrifice for their children. 'I kind of feel that way about
> Ross,' he says. 'I'm just so proud of him and so excited to see him live up to
> his potential. When I think about AllDone getting huge, half the time I'm
> not even thinking about myself—I'm thinking about Ross, and Veronica,
> and partying with them, and seeing them just have "*unfathomable*" amounts
> of money.'[51]

> I say sometimes I can't believe how young ADP's managers are, given all the
> responsibilities they handle. Veronica, I note, is only twenty-nine, and she's in
> charge of a two-hundred-person team. 'I think of Veronica as my little sister,'
> Carter says. 'If she had a boyfriend, he would never be good enough. I have an
> amazingly strong love for Veronica. It's like "platonic-romantic" love.'

Carter expressed feelings of paternal pride for Ross and what he imagined to be a big brother's (paternalistic) protectiveness toward Veronica,
whom he first described as akin to 'my little sister,' even though they were
approximately the same age. At the same time, he struggled to articulate the depth of his feelings for Veronica. Although their relationship was
platonic, he equated the strength of his feelings for her with feelings of
romantic love.[52] In both cases, Carter expressed his deep care for members
of AllDone's Filipino workforce.

Contractors' testimonials reinforced ADSF staff members' predisposi-
tion to believe that AllDone was transforming Filipino lives for the better.
When Carter reported back to the San Francisco office about his first trip
to the Philippines in a series of missives, he documented the stories he'd
heard of the trials and tribulations faced by team members before they
joined AllDone, and how, in the words of one team member, "AllDone has
changed my life."[53] Carter detailed narratives shared by a college graduate
who had long struggled to find work, and a nurse whose salary quadru-
pled after joining AllDone, allowing her to achieve financial independence
and purchase health insurance for the first time.[54]

"At this point in the night, I was almost overcome [with emotion]," Carter writes before describing three team members who

had taken some crappy, packed, un-air-conditioned bus 7 hours through winding, dirty roads across their island. They had spent a few days' earnings to pay for their tickets.[55] And there they were—not listening to me thanking them for writing thousands of blurbs for $2.50/hr—but I was listening to them thank *me* and thank *AllDone* for the wonderful opportunity we were providing them. "Every Sunday I go to church and I thank God for AllDone. AllDone has blessed our lives." They said it again and again.

"These guys live such hard lives" in comparison to Americans, Carter continued. "It's hot, humid, congested, and dirty everywhere. They have no AC or privacy." After describing various indignities and iniquities suffered by team members, he concludes:

> And in the face of all this ugliness, they smile and are thankful for everything they do have. And, oh how thankful they are for AllDone. An employer who pays well and cares about me and invests in me and provides a community and an opportunity and rewards me when I work hard. If you've never had those things it truly must be a God send.

> If AllDone is as successful as we all hope, we'll create an amazing organization and we'll all make some money and have more freedom and luxury in our lives than we would otherwise. And that'll be awesome. But nothing—nothing—will give me more pleasure or satisfaction or *meaning* than to create an enormous, profitable company that employs thousands and thousands of wonderful, deserving people like this around the globe.

Carter appeared to feel some discomfort with employment relations at AllDone—when he praised members of ADSF for doing a good job, their wages did not enter the picture, but he was traveling around the Philippines thanking workers "for writing thousands of blurbs for $2.50/hr." However, Carter described feeling overwhelmed by their gratitude for their jobs and their appreciation for his care, which seem to have dissolved his discomfort and redoubled his commitment to providing jobs for "wonderful, deserving people like this around the globe." Filipino workers' emotional displays relieved Carter's guilt, reframed entrepreneurship as an act of altruism, and repositioned him as a hero in a "rescue narrative" that enfolded assumptions about and realities of gender, race, class, and nationality.[56]

Martin's first visit to the Philippines appeared to have a similar effect on him. Upon his return, he sent a message to ADSF staffers that reflected on "just how much the work we do in SF has improved—sometimes dramatically—the lives of hundreds of people in a place most of us will never visit." I, too, found myself feeling an outpouring of warmth—and even a sentiment that I recognized as "love"—for my colleagues. During my second of three trips to the Philippines, a group of team members from the Manila area gathered for a sightseeing trip to the countryside. On the van ride back to Manila, I sat next to Mac, a colleague who was about my age. As he fell asleep and his head drooped onto my shoulder, I reflected on the powerful bonds that our trip was creating: "It feels like summer camp," I wrote in my fieldnotes, "creating closeness by taking people out of their everyday lives and putting them in close proximity to each other so they can experience new things together."[57]

The notion that AllDone treated its remote workforce humanely was also important to members of ADSF who had never met their Filipino colleagues. At one ADSF party, Paul, who managed marketing projects, asked me about my upcoming trip to the Philippines.

> I start to tell Paul about our plans to attend gatherings for workers in each of the cities we'll visit. Paul says he sometimes struggles with feeling that members of ADP are "exploited," but then he remembers that these are good jobs in the Philippines. 'Who am I to judge? They seem happy!' He continues: AllDone pays fair market wages in the Philippines. But, he claims, AllDone could pay twice as much and the workers *still* wouldn't be as happy as they are now if the company didn't treat them well.

Most ADSF employees were only vaguely aware of ADP team members' daily activities, but some did express ambivalence about the disparity in compensation between the teams. Still, members of ADSF could take pride in management's reports about the "happy family" that AllDone was supporting in the Philippines, which drew attention to workers' emotional displays while downplaying global inequalities.[58]

Others seemed less troubled by the relationship between the two teams. During a toast at another ADSF party, James, a software engineer, unwittingly echoed American political and military leaders' rhetoric from the colonial era when he proclaimed he was glad that AllDone was "bringing the advantages of the modern world to people who haven't felt it."[59] Highlighting the difference that Filipino workers' income could make in their lives made it easy to justify the stark pay gap that separated workers from each team.

Emotional bonds between ADSF and ADP team members could also have material consequences. Through word and deed, AllDone's cofounders gave every indication both that they had come to feel a burden of responsibility for Filipino contractors' well-being, and that they hoped to provide jobs to Filipinos for years to come. Yet AllDone remained a startup that was obligated to prioritize investors' interests as it adapted to rapidly changing conditions. Managers eventually found that as the number of buyer requests submitted each day multiplied, it became impractical for human workers to continue to handle the matching function. ADP's matching team was unable to keep up with request volume during particularly busy periods, at times falling more than two hours behind. The longer buyers had to wait to hear from sellers, the more likely they would lose interest or find other means of completing their job, leading to fewer paying jobs for AllDone sellers. AllDone's engineers started to prepare for the automation of ADP's most labor-intensive function.

The cofounders began planning for the human consequences of the change nine months before the automated system was scheduled for implementation. First, they tried to, as Carter put it in an e-mail to leaders in the Philippines, "find another company to hand off [the] team to (e.g. find a soft landing) so they won't lose their jobs." AllDone's cofounders worked their professional networks for months in an effort to find another startup that would be willing to absorb the contractors whose livelihoods were at risk. None, however, ended up expressing interest in hiring the entire team.[60] Carter then consulted with Josh, the product manager, and the rest of the San Francisco staff to brainstorm new projects that they might be able to find for the affected contractors. Leaders of other divisions in AllDone Philippines were also asked to assess whether their teams had needs that the workers affected by automation could help them address. Eventually, the planned cuts were reduced to thirty-five, and most of those who were let go were recent hires who had been informed that their positions may soon be eliminated. AllDone also provided severance pay to those whose contracts were terminated commensurate with their employment tenure—up to six weeks for those who had been with AllDone for at least two years.

It is likely that San Francisco–based managers were motivated to save as many Filipino contractors' jobs as possible both because they worried that mass layoffs could jeopardize the team's morale—and thus potentially the reliability of the team as a whole—and because of their personal feelings of obligation to protect contractors' well-being. Regardless of their motivations, their actions reveal their desire to keep AllDone Philippines' culture of familial love intact, standing in sharp contrast to dominant accounts of employers of computational work, who tend to treat the people behind AI systems as interchangeable and expendable.[61]

At AllDone, expressions of familial love inflected wage-labor relations with patterns of clientelism. For managers in San Francisco, AllDone Love supported the notion that, by practicing labor arbitrage to generate jobs that wouldn't otherwise exist, the company was simultaneously supporting its own growth and changing the world for the better. Leaders believed that sourcing contractors via a global digital labor platform allowed AllDone to transcend geographic boundaries and to provide meaningful work to talented and hard-working people in the Philippines who had difficulty securing decent employment. Viewing themselves not just as employers, but also as benevolent patrons, was gratifying, helping ADSF managers assuage the guilt that might otherwise be associated with asking Filipinos to perform what Carter called "unglamorous work" at a wage that was orders of magnitude lower than the compensation reaped by workers in San Francisco. In this way, the culture of AllDone Love legitimated the vast inequalities between the teams.

.   .   .   .   .

Paradoxically, it was the imperatives of venture capital investors—which motivated endless change in the activities of workers in the San Francisco office—that generated the conditions of possibility for AllDone's culture of familial love in the Philippines. In order to maximize the resources dedicated to experimentation, AllDone's software engineers relied upon the consistency and relative stability of what managers called AllDone's "human machine" in the Philippines, which constituted the hidden underside of innovation. And for reasons having as much to do with the political history of the relationship between the United States and the Philippines as with investors' expectations, workers in both ADSF and ADP came to describe their organizational arrangements using the language of love, loyalty, and gratitude.

Members of both teams played scripted roles in a game of emotional display intended to instill feelings of obligation in the other. Managers came to be enamored of—and arguably even fetishized—AllDone's Filipino contractors, who presented themselves as ideal workers. Managers in San Francisco believed that ADP's culture of familial love helped to secure contractors' effort and ensure their commitment to the firm, suggesting how strategies of normative control aimed at winning workers' "hearts and minds" can be layered atop what may at first glance appear to be cold and rationalized algorithmic systems.[62] In this way, "AllDone Love" served the interests of the powerful venture capital investors driving AllDone's development. Filipino workers, too, used the symbolic terrain of familial love to endow computational labor with meaning. At the same time, they promoted affective ties and long-term bonds with managers in San Francisco by strategically infusing formal, contractual wage-labor relations with symbolic elements of clientelism. Contractors mobilized schemas of debt and reciprocity to instill in managers a feeling of obligation to expand opportunities for a deserving and underserved population.

Figuring employers as patrons and workers as clients created the appearance of a win-win relationship: what was good for the business seemed to be good for workers, and what seemed to make workers happy also pleased managers. Receiving team members' expressions of love and gratitude affirmed the Americans' identities as altruistic entrepreneurs whose technologies were transforming lives for the better. Both sides thus had a common interest in euphemizing wage-labor relations—which can be laden with unsettling inequalities and destabilizing conflict—as patron-client ties.

And yet: the relationship between managers in San Francisco and contractors in the Philippines was also fundamentally unequal. AllDone Philippines' culture of familial love served the immediate interests of both American and Filipino team members, but it also legitimized the immense disparity in the firm's distribution of rewards. Members of the team in San Francisco received compensation that was orders of magnitude greater than the wages on offer in the Philippines, and their stock options also allowed them to directly benefit from the increasing value of the firm in a way that their Filipino counterparts could not. The language of "friendship" masked the inequitable distribution of economic rewards. "AllDone Love" afforded managers the opportunity to transform their ambivalence and guilt about this inequality into unambiguous altruism.

For all the talk of loyalty and family, there was much that members of both teams were *not* speaking of. There was no guarantee that AllDone would still exist a couple of years down the line. Even if the company was successful, it could eventually face pressures to automate AllDone Philippines out of existence. The meanings associated with AllDone Love may have helped both managers in San Francisco and workers in the Philippines cope with this uncertainty, keeping both teams focused on their missions in the present in part by directing their attention away from how unstable the company and its employment arrangements might actually be in the long run. Strongly identifying with the organization may have also helped contractors soothe the anxiety associated with the potentially transient nature of their employment.[63]

AllDone Philippines was not the only remote team whose efforts were integral to the company's business. Whereas team members in the Philippines largely operated behind the scenes of AllDone's software systems, another set of contractors working from their homes in the Las Vegas area were situated on the front lines, serving as the primary point of contact between the company and its most confused, angry, and dissatisfied users.

PART III   Las Vegas

THE CALL DE-CENTER

5 Working the Phones

One night in downtown Las Vegas, I found myself staring down a full glass of red wine at a dimly lit cocktail bar. Carter and I were in town to honor AllDone's small phone support team and its extraordinary contribution toward helping the company transition its users to a new payment system. After doling out hugs and goodbyes to team members, only the two of us were left to finish off the last bottle. Carter grinned and told me he had just sent a text message to a fellow cofounder back in San Francisco: 'When we started AllDone, did you ever think we'd spend so much time drinking with middle-aged women?' He raised his voice to cut through the din of club music, adding, 'Because that's what we do—here, and in the Philippines. Middle-aged women are what make AllDone work.'[1]

Investors dream of platforms that are entirely automated, powered by technological systems that seamlessly and inexpensively "scale" to accommodate an ever-expanding user population.[2] The more people who use a platform, the more the utility of joining its network increases, fueling a cycle of further expansion and heightened utility that can swiftly lead to market dominance and exponential increases in a company's valuation.[3] As we have seen from the work of AllDone Philippines, the kinds of platforms coveted by investors are often powered in part by low-wage workers who conduct digital labor in and around algorithmic systems. As platforms grow, they encounter yet another challenge: the divergent needs and preferences of an increasingly diverse set of users.

Technology often creates emotional and behavioral responses in users that do not accord with designers' wishes.[4] Platform companies, in particular, have been known to make policy and design decisions to advance their own interests at the expense of their users.[5] When platforms enact unilateral and seemingly arbitrary changes to their technologies and policies, users inevitably express anger and frustration.[6] Someone has to respond to these complaints. AllDone elected to delegate this emotional labor to yet another low-wage, mostly female workforce—this time in Las Vegas.

During the second period of my research at AllDone, executives shifted their focus from expanding the user base to increasing revenue in order to keep the company afloat and help it attract a second round of venture capital funding. This generated an organizational problem that I call *trust drag*, which refers to situations in which users' confusion, dissatisfaction, or suspicion of the product jeopardized the company's growth trajectory. Trust drag posed an existential threat to the business. AllDone wanted the sellers registered on its platform (e.g., plumbers, photographers, math tutors) to consistently pay to use its service. When active sellers reduced their activity, or vanished altogether because they felt manipulated or no longer believed that the platform was working for them, the company lost revenue. As AllDone advanced toward raising its second round of funding, trust drag threatened to hold it back at the exact moment when it was aiming for substantial revenue growth.

In this chapter, I move beyond analyses of a platform's policies and algorithms to highlight the human labor that platform companies deploy to aid and persuade their users.[7] AllDone addressed trust drag by developing a virtual call center comprised of workers distributed across the Las Vegas area. Phone agents attempted to counteract trust drag by trying to build users' trust in AllDone when they were confused, to repair their trust after it had been damaged, and to proactively preserve trust when the company chose to alter the platform's rules. Telephone-based customer support agents performed *relational work* by managing relationships with users and helping them adjust to software systems. Economic sociologist Nina Bandelj describes relational work as "the interactional efforts at negotiating economic relations, infused with sense-making, that have implications for power distribution between partners of exchange."[8] All-Done Las Vegas (ADLV) helped the company boost revenue by bolstering customers' trust in the firm and its dynamic software systems.

Using their uniquely human capacity for flexibility, adaptation, creativity, and persuasion, phone support agents generated economic value by helping to integrate users into AllDone's technological systems.[9] Their efforts supported AllDone by maintaining the perceived legitimacy of the platform and securing the ongoing participation of its users.

THE STRATEGIC PIVOT

Tech startups are known for responding to changing conditions by "pivoting," or making sudden shifts in corporate strategy that require organizations to reallocate or restructure their activities, resources, and attention.[10] During the second phase of my research, AllDone's executive team pivoted in its pursuit of VC funding by redirecting its focus from generating growth in the user base to generating more revenue. At AllDone San Francisco's mid-summer quarterly review meeting (described in detail in the preface), the mood was confident and upbeat, but AllDone's leadership also communicated a renewed sense of purpose. Peter and Carter, two of AllDone's cofounders, lauded the recent progress the startup had made. However, Peter also cautioned that "we are not a sustainable enterprise." Adam, the lead software engineer, presented graphs demonstrating that, even as user growth had accelerated, revenue growth was slowing. Peter explained that AllDone was spending more money than it was taking in, running the risk of once again ending up desperate for an outside infusion of cash, just as it had been in the months before executives had raised All-Done's first round of venture capital funding.

Peter emphasized the importance of generating a more sustainable revenue stream so AllDone could survive even if the firm was unable to swiftly secure its second round of VC funding (also known as "Series B"): 'If we have to worry about raising another round, that's bad—Series B is hard to get to.' Yet, while generating more revenue would help AllDone become a self-sustaining company, it would also have the salutary effect of making the firm more attractive to VCs who might offer future rounds of investment capital. "With Series A" funding rounds, Peter elaborated, "you're selling a dream" to investors. "With Series B, you're selling a spreadsheet." Team members nodded along as Peter added, "No one's gonna drop eight figures [on a company] with uncertain revenue," alluding to the fact that Series B rounds often exceed $10 million.

Carter echoed Peter's message, cautioning that startups that secure a second round of VC funding typically 'have to move beyond having a good idea to proving that it works.' Peter announced an ambitious target for the team: to more than double monthly revenue within six months so that AllDone would be taking in roughly as much money as it spent. Demonstrating such rapid revenue growth, he explained, would show VCs that AllDone was worthy of additional investment. Taking in more revenue would also give software developers the "freedom" to pursue projects that they'd been forced to put off while striving to meet the expectations of Series B investors.

At an all-office meeting the following week, Carter explained that everything the company did would now be oriented toward its new revenue goal, which had become 'our motivation, our benchmark for all of our decisions.' Subsequent meetings would begin with a review of AllDone's progress toward this target. To keep the team oriented toward its new mission, Josh, the product manager, integrated it into the office's built environment: he bought a massive roll of paper, and every week he would cut out a banner—about the size of a twin bed sheet—and write the latest revenue figures on it in thick, colored markers. He would then hang it on the balcony above the conference rooms next to the previous week's numbers. All employees had to do was look up from their desks to be reminded of the company's singular focus on boosting its revenue.

TRUST DRAG

AllDone's new orienting principle—prioritizing revenue growth above all else—generated new problems for the organization. These problems necessitated the reconfiguration of the company's product and workforce. AllDone had originally designed its platform to maintain an arms-length and largely automated relationship with its users. The company provided introductions to buyers and sellers, but any transactions that resulted were arranged and completed by users themselves. Executives had decided that AllDone should not process buyers' credit card payments because it would then be held responsible for adjudicating payment-related disputes that arose between users. But managers eventually discovered that if the company was going to grow in the way VCs expected, arms-length relationships with sellers would no longer suffice.

AllDone had reached a point at which it could not extract the revenue it needed from users solely through clever hacks and automated (or seemingly automated) systems. The company's efforts to convert user growth into revenue growth exacerbated instances of trust drag, when users were confused, dissatisfied, or skeptical of AllDone's software systems. Some users had trouble understanding how the product worked. Many others were upset when the quotes they paid to submit to buyers did not yield paying jobs. As one wedding photographer wrote in an e-mail, "I have to say that lately I've become somewhat disenchanted with AD. . . . I feel like I'm spending nearly $15 a pop to give advice to people who are just kicking the tires" and not serious about hiring someone through AllDone. Users who were confused by or dissatisfied with AllDone's service were less likely to become or remain paying customers; worse, some threatened to damage AllDone's reputation, which could endanger the company's future growth.

Carol, ADLV's first contractor, had been hired just before the company raised its first round of venture capital funding. Carter had found Carol through an outsourcing startup called TaskUs, which specialized in providing customer support services to other tech companies. Although he maintained strategic control over ADLV's activities, Carter quickly handed off day-to-day oversight of the team to Veronica, ADP's general manager, so that he could stay focused on developing new projects.

Carol's hiring was one of the many "experiments" emerging from the minds of managers and employees in the San Francisco office. When she first started working for AllDone, Carol spent her workdays calling buyers immediately after they placed a request on AllDone to try to persuade them to submit additional, related requests. (For example, if a buyer had requested a DJ for a party, perhaps she might be interested in hiring a caterer or a bartender as well.) Carter analyzed the data generated from these calls and found that they could boost key metrics by increasing the number of buyer requests and, in turn, the number of paid quotes submitted by sellers. As the months passed, Carol was hired as a contractor working directly for AllDone. She was instructed to recruit nine additional team members to enhance AllDone's efforts to increase user growth by completing request verification calls.

At this time, AllDone's customer support operations were centered in the Philippines. The e-mail support team was designed to process a tremendous volume of incoming messages. Twenty team members would often handle well over ten thousand e-mails per week, and over 70 percent of user e-mail messages received a response in two hours or less. These speedy response times were enabled by the highly routinized nature of AllDone's e-mail support system, which relied on dozens of pre-written responses that team members could select, edit as needed, and send based on the content of a user's inquiry. Some recipients of these messages caught on to the semi-automated nature of the system and complained that a "robot" had replied to their inquiries.

The e-mail support team was thus designed not to engage users in detailed exchanges, but rather to provide them with prompt answers to basic queries. Support agents could "escalate" messages from users in need of additional assistance to Martin in the San Francisco office, who would occasionally ask Carol to reach out to the user via telephone. A handful of ADP e-mail support agents also handled outbound voice calls to the small number of users who managed to locate AllDone's voicemail number (which was not publicized on its website), or who demanded via e-mail to speak with a representative.

Before the company's strategic shift toward revenue growth, the customer support team's limitations had not overly concerned managers in San Francisco. To satisfy investors' prior expectations, AllDone had been focused on growing its user base and increasing market activity rather than on generating revenue. Consequently, the refund policy was incredibly lax: agents were instructed to grant a refund whenever a seller requested one. Thus, sellers rarely found it necessary to escalate their complaints from e-mail to telephone conversations. As AllDone began to seek its second round of venture capital funding, however, the company restructured its customer support operations to help meet the shifting expectations of investors. Growth in user activity was no longer the primary concern; now, members of the San Francisco team were almost exclusively focused on boosting AllDone's revenue. As part of this effort, executives began to devise plans to expand AllDone's phone support operations and to make the support phone number more widely available to the company's revenue-generating users.

Carter determined that it would be best to phase out the phone support duties of the four members of ADP who had been replying to voicemails and to instead rely exclusively on AllDone Las Vegas for the job. As we were walking out of a meeting, he explained his thinking to me:

> Carter says the problem with using AllDone Philippines for phone support is that they're not as conversational as Carol's team in Las Vegas. Filipino workers are more likely to struggle to establish rapport with users—he assumes that most will not be comfortable starting a conversation with a phrase like, "Hey, how's your day going?"

> Carter cites two reasons for this. First, his sense is that Filipino workers are often "culturally trained" to be "meek" and deferential to Americans. I note that just yesterday, Tony (who oversees ADP's small phone team) told me that he directs workers to "over-apologize" in conversations with users. Second, Carter points to the challenges of cross-cultural interactions—he says it's harder to cultivate trusting relationships when you have an accent because you're speaking a second language.

AllDone users could be angry and aggressive in conversations with phone support agents. Additionally, as I had discovered in conversations with Tony, some US-based callers objected to speaking with people with Filipino accents and would demand to talk to an American representative.[11] Whether because of their on-the-job or supposed "cultural" training, or difficulties with the language, Carter perceived Filipinos as more passive and deferential in conversations with Americans. He believed that it would be easier for American workers to form personal connections and build trust with AllDone users.

As AllDone shifted its orientation away from user growth and toward revenue growth, the reorganized and expanded ADLV team became All-Done's primary means of interacting with its customers. In this role, ADLV would directly enhance revenue generation by managing sellers' emotional responses to their experiences with AllDone. When users were confused or upset by AllDone's systems, the phone support team complemented technological systems by helping users adapt to the company's software and encouraging them to accept (or at least tolerate) its policies. These frontline workers regulated their emotional display in an effort to instill particular emotional states in the customers with whom they interacted.[12] AllDone Las Vegas supported the company's revenue growth by managing relationships with sellers, helping to keep them engaged and satisfied with the product.

Like their counterparts in the Philippines, the ten members of AllDone Las Vegas were work-from-home contractors who were paid via oDesk, a digital labor platform. During the majority of my tenure at AllDone, the team consisted entirely of women ranging in age from their late twenties to their fifties, with most on the older end of that spectrum. Some held bachelor's or associate degrees. Team members were hired as independent contractors, and most were paid $10 per hour, without access to employment benefits such as sick leave, health insurance, or a retirement plan. (At the time, the minimum wage for employees in Nevada who did not receive health benefits was $8.25.) Hours were assigned to meet business needs, with some flexibility to accommodate team members' personal preferences. Most averaged close to a forty-hour workweek. Contractors were responsible for providing their own computer equipment and internet connections, but received a $50 stipend each month to help offset the costs of home phone and internet service.

AllDone was a market broker that profited from connecting buyers and sellers of local services. Trust is an essential element of market brokerage. For brokerage relationships to endure in competitive markets, buyers and sellers must believe that the broker is capable of meeting their needs, and that the broker will not exploit its advantageous position to unduly gain at their expense.[13] Emotion management is a key part of this process, particularly for the trust-takers (in this case, AllDone) who are attempting to generate emotional responses in trust-givers (AllDone's users) by signaling their commitment, shared expectations, competence, and integrity.[14] AllDone mobilized phone agents' relational work to solve problems of building, repairing, and preserving trust in AllDone's brand and product—functions that were often impossible to automate, yet integral to the operation of its business.

THE RELATIONAL WORK OF MANAGING TRUST

AllDone San Francisco's strategies for growing its user base left many sellers struggling to understand how to use the website. Because AllDone had prioritized building a nationwide network of users as quickly as possible to impress potential VC investors, its webpages were designed to funnel sellers directly into the signup process, minimizing the presentation of complex information about how the service worked. Once sellers joined AllDone and began to use the platform, some couldn't make sense of core features of the product, including the quoting system, payment structure, and user interface. "Half these sellers I think don't even know how to manage their dashboard," Carol, ADLV's team leader, once advised me over online chat, referring to the webpages sellers used to manage their accounts. "They seriously need a tutorial." Older sellers who had less experience with computers were most likely to exhibit confusion. As Tanya, a phone support agent, explained during an in-person meeting, these users "don't do e-mail." Another agent named Sharon agreed, declaring that "anyone over forty-five needs a live person."

Misunderstandings and mistrust could be exacerbated by software developers' frequent experimentation with the user interface and market rules. To meet venture capitalists' expectations for rapid growth, AllDone's software developers were continually tinkering with various aspects of the platform in an attempt to boost key metrics—as noted earlier, at times they might be running two dozen experiments concurrently. New features were underdeveloped during the testing phase, and engineers frequently chose not to provide affected users with explanations of changes that could be only temporary. Rather than investing limited engineering resources in perfecting experimental product features that might eventually be abandoned, it was far easier for AllDone to, as one manager put it, "throw bodies at the problem," deploying workers in Las Vegas to help users learn about AllDone's rules and systems.

When users required extensive assistance, members of ADLV undertook relational work to help confused buyers and sellers understand the platform's rules and norms. In these cases, members of ADLV taught sellers about the AllDone process over the phone, as in a fifteen-minute exchange that I observed in team leader Carol's home office.

As we're sipping tea at her desk, the phone rings. Carol puts on a smile as she answers on speakerphone. The man on the other end speaks haltingly, asking for Theresa. "We don't have a Theresa," Carol responds, "but can I help you with anything?" After a little back-and-forth, Carol deduces that this seller, Ted, received a request from a buyer named Theresa. Carol explains to Ted that he has received a new request. But Ted doesn't seem to understand what that means, or what he can do with the request. In fact, I'm beginning to get the sense that Ted doesn't even understand what AllDone is.

It was common for sellers to set up an account after receiving a promotional e-mail touting how AllDone could help them find new customers. Yet many of these sellers never actually learned how the service worked.

After a few failed attempts at gathering Ted's account information, Carol is finally able to locate him in the system. Now that Ted has learned what a request is, Carol wants him to look at his queue of buyer requests. "Are you close to a computer?" she asks. "Uhhhhhh" is Ted's hesitant reply. "Or I could go over them [with you over the phone] if you'd like!" Carol offers without missing a beat.

It turns out that Theresa's request for furniture upholstery won't work for Ted: he says he refinishes furniture, but doesn't upholster it. Carol launches into an explanation of how AllDone's system works. "AllDone, as you're unaware of what we do, we're a marketplace for local service providers." She outlines how requests are gathered from buyers and distributed to sellers, and informs him that it's "your responsibility to check your dashboard to see the requests you've been sent."

"In other words, it costs me a dollar ninety-nine [to submit a quote]?"

"Yes, if you'd chosen to respond to Theresa's request."

Finally, Ted says he wants to talk to his colleague Gary about how they'll use AllDone. Carol says that Ted can call her back after he's done so she can "walk you through the whole process and get you up and running and get you lots of business, I hope!"

Carol's conversation with Ted highlights the challenges inherent in AllDone's efforts to rapidly draw a large number of new users to the platform. Carol patiently explained what AllDone was, how the system worked, and how Ted could use AllDone to meet potential buyers. AllDone Las Vegas team members were equipped to explain both formal rules of exchange (e.g., how to reach out to potential clients and the fees they would pay) and informal norms (e.g., how to build a positive online reputation). Team members often went to great lengths to satisfy users—for example, they might offer to upload photos to a seller's profile if the seller was having trouble learning how to do so herself.

Phone agents thus endeavored to alleviate sellers' confusion and leave them confident that AllDone could support them in growing their businesses. Sharon recounted a similar episode during an in-person team meeting:

> "A seller called in—one of those, 'I'm spending money and I don't know what to do, how to turn [using AllDone] into jobs.' He sounded elderly. 'I get annoyed really easily, so forgive me,' he said. I open up his quotes to see what he's saying to people, and he's talking to them like he's talking to us! He'll write, 'I need the buyer to call me to give a price'—but he's talking to the buyer!
>
> I said, 'David, you're not [supposed to be] communicating with us at AllDone—you're communicating with the buyer!' He's like, 'Oh, I shouldn't do that anymore!'" Laughter fills the circle. "I say, 'you wanna throw out warm fuzzies [in your messages].' We were on for almost an hour. 'I promise more fuzzies—I'll be fuzzier, I promise. You are such a blessing to have the patience to stay with me.'"

By educating users on AllDone's systems, phone agents turned potential defectors from the platform into satisfied customers.

When sellers were disappointed with the results of the introductions AllDone provided, their trust in the company could be shaken. AllDone deployed phone support agents to manage the gap between the expectations generated by AllDone's promotional copy—which stated that "there are millions of [web] searches for local services every day—don't miss out on these potential customers!"—and the realities of using a platform on which individual sellers did not always achieve their goals. Members of ADLV attempted to rebuild sellers' trust when market outcomes failed to align with their expectations. Support agents strove to turn detractors into advocates by listening, counseling, reassuring, and caring for individual sellers.

Sellers' concerns ranged from confusion to accusing the company of outright fraud. Those who invested time in creating profiles and then paid between $2 and $15 to submit quotes to buyers tended to expect that their efforts would yield new clients. In many cases, sellers' trust was violated when they did not get hired for jobs, or did not even receive written replies from buyers. Some accused AllDone of brokering in bad faith: of connecting them with people who were just "price shopping" and not committed to hiring anyone, or even of fabricating fake consumer requests to increase revenue.

After receiving no contact from buyers on two quotes, one seller complained via e-mail: "Like so many of these online systems yours is inherently corrupt. And I think you must know this. Neither of these folks are serious. I've wasted a bag of groceries for my kids on false leads." Wedding photographers seemed especially suspicious of the company's methods: AllDone charged them $15 to submit a quote because those who were selected by buyers were likely to make hundreds or even thousands of dollars on a job. One wrote to AllDone denouncing the service as "a SCAM"; others angrily noted that, if five photographers each paid $15 to submit a quote on a bad request, AllDone would have made $75, with the sellers having no chance to realize any returns.

When users' experiences fell short of their expectations—when they complained of feeling dissatisfied, taken advantage of, misled, disappointed, or disillusioned—threats formed that could, on the aggregate, jeopardize AllDone's position as a broker. A recorded phone call from one seller began:

> "Let me tell you: I canceled my subscription to AllDone. I hope you're recording this—you guys are the biggest piece of shit I have seen. It is absolutely, utterly useless. On the one hand, I feel you guys have stolen my money. On the other hand, I never got any responses. I make it a point to badmouth AllDone to other photographers."

The seller's anger is rooted in a betrayal of trust ("I feel like you guys have stolen my money"). These perceptions could be damaging to a broker whose revenue stream relies upon a reputation for making high-quality connections.

Members of ADLV endeavored to repair relationships with sellers who believed that the company was taking advantage of them. Phone support agents performed relational work aimed at what team members called "turning them around," or reversing sellers' sense of betrayal and convincing them that it was in their interest to continue to use AllDone's platform. I observed the following exchange between Carol, AllDone Las Vegas's team leader, and Nancy, the "account specialist" tasked with handling inquiries from AllDone's most valuable users.

> "I have a ticket I want to run past you," Nancy says, referring to a customer support interaction logged in the system, "from Phil, a troublemaker in Miami, shocker. He's having a hissy fit." Phil is upset that he has not been winning jobs and wants to have all of his past payments refunded.
>
> Carol asks for the ticket number, and takes a moment to pull up Phil's file on her computer. Nancy fills the silence, adding, "I know what I would do, but I want an opinion."
>
> "Let's look at his quotes, the correspondence between them," Carol says, skimming the file. "Is he doing what he should do [by personalizing his messages to buyers], or just sending a generic message?"
>
> "Honestly, I think [his correspondence] was good," Nancy replies.
>
> "Give him one month [of refunds]."
>
> A pause.
>
> "The screaming got real loud," adds Nancy, who apparently thought she would have to offer more to satisfy Phil.
>
> "You can win him around, honey," Carol says cheerily. "You can Nancy him!"

When consumers' enchantment turns to disenchantment, front-line workers often face the painful reality of absorbing their anger.[15] Nancy's task was to convince Phil that the company had acted fairly as a broker, and that his experiences with AllDone could improve over time. Team members would patiently listen to a seller's concerns and offer empathy, reassurance, and tips to help the seller succeed in the future ("You can Nancy him!").

Phone agents frequently engaged in expectation management, encouraging sellers to develop more realistic outlooks about their results with the platform. During a videoconference I joined with Nancy and Carol, Nancy recounted an exchange with a general contractor who was upset that the in-home estimates he had given to AllDone clients had not resulted in jobs. "You have to give them a wake-up call," she said, summarizing the conversation. "'I understand [your frustration]—but how's your business outside of AllDone? Do you usually get every job you go on?' 'No, I don't.' 'Well, this is the same thing.' . . . They need to hear this." Such statements were aimed at persuading users not to hold AllDone responsible for their own unsuccessful outcomes.

In the process of adjusting sellers' expectations, team members would also attempt to educate them on best practices. Phone support agents tried to teach sellers how they could improve their performance in the future by demonstrating both their competence and motivation to potential customers.[16] When sellers called because they were upset that buyers were not responding to their quotes, Nancy would often investigate their accounts and see that the sellers had been "really sloppy" with their responses to buyers, sending quotes containing poor spelling or grammar that buyers might find unprofessional. Nancy reported frequently asking sellers to imagine that they were the buyer reading the seller's message. "'Would *you* respond if you received that quote? You have to work on this. The requests will not work themselves.' . . . You have to show them how to stand out from the rest, how to answer in a nice way so people want to respond." At an ADLV team party, Erica, another phone agent, remarked, "I need a button to press to be like, 'you need to work on your profile,'" because she frequently found herself repeating this instruction to sellers.

Phone agents' most effective tactic, however, was to offer sellers personalized attention, sometimes within the context of ongoing relationships. As Carol explained to me during my first visit to her home office, "We have special-needs sellers. You hear all about their personal life: 'my boyfriend,' etcetera. We do therapy, as well, at ADLV! But we give them love. We handle them all the same way, we give them love, and whatever they need." Later that day, as I sat to the side of her desk, I saw Carol lavish attention on an AllDone seller during a forty-five-minute call:

> The phone rings again. This seller is having trouble logging in to her All-Done account for her drapery business. Carol says she's happy to help, and adds some pleasant chit-chat as she looks up the account. "How's your day going so far, Sue? Looking forward to the holiday weekend?"

Sue says she hasn't been receiving buyer requests. "Do you have time?" Carol asks. "We can go into your user page and take a look, see what's going on. Because we generally find the more information you give us, the better we can match you with the requests that come in."

Sue had called because she was having trouble logging in to her account, but she then revealed that the service was not working as she'd expected it to: she had not been receiving requests from potential buyers.

Carol's phone occasionally chirps to signal that additional calls are coming in and going straight to voicemail while she coaches Sue. "Yay!" she cries out at one point, clapping her hands three times. "Good job, honey, you're good at this!" Sue tells Carol about her new iPad and her issues with identity theft. "We'll have to see if we can get you some more business, Sue," Carol says, gently redirecting the conversation.

She adjusts Sue's service categories (her designation in the AllDone database specifying which services she provides) and her travel preferences as Sue describes the parts of Wisconsin where she's most likely to find a market for her drapery business. "My God, can you imagine doing drapery for a mansion that size?" Carol marvels politely. "Goodness me. Well, drapery is a skill, not everybody can do it. What a great talent that is, Sue."

Carol patiently walked Sue through her account settings to improve the likelihood that she'd receive promising introductions. In addition to providing the seller with accurate and useful information, Carol flattered her and engaged her in conversation unrelated to her drapery business. At the end of a long call, Carol promised to follow up with Sue to make sure that everything had worked out. Carol's interventions were aimed at making Sue feel like the company cared about her and wanted to help her business succeed.

When market outcomes violated sellers' expectations, AllDone deployed relational work to help users adjust to its software systems and to secure sellers' ongoing participation in the platform. Each aspect of the task was sufficiently nuanced to require human intervention. Workers assessed users' emotional states, displayed empathy, understood and addressed their needs, and quickly developed relationships that in many cases restored users' confidence and trust in the company. Team members used their interpersonal skills to persuade many sellers to continue their relationship with AllDone by convincing them that, although the system hadn't met their expectations in particular instances, in general AllDone itself was trustworthy and fair.

MANAGING THE FALLOUT FROM EXPERIMENTS

AllDone's pursuit of revenue could also exacerbate users' dissatisfaction, especially when users believed that changes to the platform's rules and features were unfair. In keeping with AllDone's ethos of experimentation, these changes were, by definition, untested before they were unleashed on unsuspecting users. As Josh, AllDone's product manager, wrote to me before one experiment was implemented, "For this test, I don't care about having some people not well served. That's a small price to pay for getting a real answer to a big fundamental question about the best interaction model." Consideration for how experiments would affect the customer support agents who fielded users' angry phone calls was even more rare.

A year earlier, in a bid to incentivize sellers to submit more quotes to buyers—and to convince potential investors that AllDone could connect a high volume of users—the company had created a "subscription" payment option that allowed sellers to send unlimited quotes to buyers for a flat monthly fee, which varied by service category. Quote volume increased dramatically, helping AllDone secure its first major round of funding. But soon after the fundraise, executives worried that subscriptions were limiting AllDone's revenue potential. Analyses showed that even as All-Done's investments in search engine optimization were bringing more and more buyers to the website to place requests (see chapter 3), revenue growth was not keeping pace with user growth. For example, one month's figures showed that users had submitted 26 percent more requests than in the previous month, but revenue had only increased by 13 percent. Sellers who were on a subscription plan were receiving many more requests than they had in the past, but were not paying more to respond to them. In other words, organizational practices developed to solve one problem (user growth) generated new problems at a later time (revenue limitations), in effect sowing the seeds of their own decay.[17]

AllDone San Francisco's product team attempted to address the issue of slowing revenue growth by launching two experimental payment models. In one test, sellers did not pay for introductions, but instead paid a commission to AllDone only when they reported that they had been hired for a job. However, because AllDone did not wish to be responsible for processing consumer credit card payments, it was impossible for the company to know whether sellers were accurately reporting what they owed. In another test, AllDone allowed sellers to offer predefined "products" that buyers could compare and purchase instantly without waiting to receive and review quotes from sellers. (For instance, a one-hour consultation with a resume writer, or four hours of service from a DJ.) This model generated little interest from buyers.

Undeterred, executives continued to develop plans to replace the popular subscription option with a new payment model through which revenue would increase linearly with request volume. Software developers began to test a new system in which sellers would pay to purchase AllDone's internal currency of "coins." For each quote they wished to submit to buyers, they would relinquish a certain number of coins, with the amount varying according to their service category. The more quotes a seller submitted, the more she would have to pay AllDone.

The stakes were high in the company's transition to the coin system. Subscribers accounted for 65 percent of the company's revenue, and AllDone's most valuable relationships were generally with sellers who submitted a large volume of quotes in competitive service categories and locations. Under the new system, some would see the price they paid to contact potential clients increase by as much as ten times. For example, a DJ who responded to twenty requests per month would now pay $100 ($5 per quote), rather than the $15 she'd previously paid for a monthly subscription. A wedding photographer who had previously paid $40 per month to respond to unlimited requests would now pay $15 to submit each quote.

The transition to the coin system would only succeed if AllDone could convince a substantial fraction of its high-value subscribers to remain active on the platform while paying considerably higher fees. If the change alienated too many existing sellers, revenue would plummet, leaving the company's future in doubt. In other words, although executives had decided that the subscription model was unsustainable, a failed transition to the coin model could precipitate an organizational crisis.

Managers in San Francisco first experimented with explaining the change to a small group of sellers via automated e-mail messages. They received overwhelmingly negative responses. As one seller wrote, "Yet again you guys have screwed the pooch completely when it comes to explaining how these changes work. . . . This new change makes it seem like you guys only care about the cash you pocket from these quotes." Adam, the director of engineering, soon sent an e-mail to me and Josh, the product manager, with an idea for subsequent tests: "What if we did the coin transition for the high value subscribers via individual phone call?" Josh replied, "I think it's a great idea." He explained that not only could this method help All-Done preserve relationships with its most important sellers, but also that one-on-one phone calls would allow managers to better understand users' questions and concerns, as the phone team could record sellers' reactions and forward them to San Francisco to help inform the company's messaging around the transition to the coin system. By the end of the day, Josh had asked me to set the plan into motion.

The following week I asked Carol to enlist another team member to help her place nearly a hundred experimental transition calls. She summarized sellers' responses in an e-mailed report:

> Most are very angry at the amount of money it will now cost them to purchase the coins for quotes, versus the cost of unlimited quotes under the subscription price. . . . They think we are being greedy and/or trying to go public (on the stock exchange).

Many of the sellers with whom Carol had spoken felt that AllDone was attempting to take advantage of them, unfairly profiting at their expense.

After Carol and Nancy had finished the experimental calls, Carol arranged a videoconference so the three of us could discuss the results. While both Carol and Nancy remained professional, they were clearly exasperated: unsurprisingly, most of the affected sellers were livid.

"Bloody hell!" Carol exclaims as she joins the call.

"How are you doing?" I ask, my voice tinged with concern.

"Been battered and bruised, but good!" Carol says with a rueful chuckle. "We have to laugh. Otherwise we might cry. When I say it's been brutal the last couple of days, I'm not saying that lightly. It's like guerilla warfare and we're in the trenches."

"Wednesday and Thursday were a frontline battle," Nancy adds. "[Sellers are] really, really upset when you tell them." She shakes her head and continues. "They're insane! People don't like change." Nancy describes what it was like to tell some sellers about the transition. "So many people were like, 'What are you talking about?'" Later, she says, the sellers would read the e-mail AllDone's engineers had sent them detailing the termination of subscriptions "and call up screaming."

As the manager overseeing the transition calls, I was worried about the emotional toll that these calls would take on the team in Las Vegas. After speaking with Carol and Nancy, I wrote in my fieldnotes that "my heart is racing just sitting at my desk. I don't think I'm cut out to be a manager. I don't want the team to suffer by having to make phone calls to tell high-value subscribers about the cancellation." It made me very uncomfortable to hear about the verbal thrashing that Carol and Nancy were absorbing, especially given that, if the test was successful, the entire team would be enlisted to complete this task with thousands of additional sellers. Hoping that I could persuade my colleagues to see the situation the same way, I sent an e-mail to Adam and Josh detailing the results of the initial experiment. I emphasized how "brutal" the calls had been for Carol and Nancy and forwarded a message from Carol detailing their difficulties.

What stood out to Adam, however, was not the abuse that sellers were heaping upon Carol and Nancy, but rather Carol's description of what the team had been able to accomplish under pressure: "We've managed to get most of them to come around and agree to try the coins, but some of these calls are taking a lot of time and a lot of tap dancing, *with jazz hands, of course!*" Carol and Nancy had patiently listened to sellers' concerns and worked to persuade them that AllDone would continue to provide a strong return on their investment. In most cases, a difficult fifteen- or twenty-minute conversation would help to assuage their anger and fears. Adam's reply underscored the critical function of phone agents' relational work:

> My first thought is this is a *really* good use of the phone team if they are able to consistently turn people's anger into trying the new program. At the end of the day we have to convert people to paying 5–10 times as much as they were previously for the same thing, so there is no tap dancing around that issue or tricks we can pull (other than messaging it the best way we can).

It was precisely the fact that team members' one-on-one conversations with sellers were so difficult that revealed just how crucial they would be to a successful transition.

Executives seemed convinced that informing high-value sellers of the transition via an impersonal, automated mass e-mail would be disastrous for the company. One afternoon during the transition process, I noticed Adam meandering toward Peter, AllDone's CEO. Adam took a seat at an adjacent desk and struck up a conversation about the coin tests.

> "One thing I will say is that the calling team has been really useful," Adam remarks. In the first test, he explains, AllDone sent eleven e-mails to sellers letting them know about the change, and immediately received five negative responses. But when Carol and Nancy subsequently called those who had expressed dissatisfaction, "every person is like, 'I'm upset, but I'm going to try it.' . . . You have to figure out how to scale [transition every subscriber to coins] while being as high-touch as possible."

Adam's insistence that the rollout be "as high-touch as possible" speaks to what he saw as the vital importance of maintaining sellers' positive relationships with the firm via personalized attention from AllDone representatives. He continued:

> "To be honest, I don't think the coin rollout is possible over e-mail. [The conversations are] very long because it's complicated. [We first need to tell sellers] what's happening, [then] what they have to understand about what's happening."

The company's head software engineer was convinced that there was no technological solution to the problem. AllDone's software systems alone could not manage sellers' feelings of betrayal amid a radical change in the payment structure. To satisfy investors, AllDone had to introduce a dramatic reworking of the platform's rules. This required the company to mobilize workers who were skilled in preserving the valuable relationships that the change could jeopardize.

Soon Brandon, a member of AllDone San Francisco's marketing team, invited me to a meeting with Josh, Adam, and Carter to discuss AllDone's "messaging" around the transition, or the language that the company should use in its communications with sellers. We were all sitting around a small conference room table when I opened the meeting by again expressing my concern about the transition calls.

> I explain that I've been talking to Carol and Nancy every day. They say they'll do whatever we need them to do, but it sounds like it's been really terrible for them.
>
> Carter, who is seated across the table and to my left, says we have no choice—we can't keep the subscription model, it doesn't work. Once the transition is done, we hope we can keep growing and be on more stable footing. But it will take a lot of really hard work to get there. And these calls will help us keep sellers.
>
> I say I feel bad about what we're asking the phone team to do, and that maybe I'm too sensitive for this job. Carter looks at me and says it's OK to be sensitive. It's good if the team knows I feel bad that it's so hard.
>
> I try one more gambit and say, "We have to give the phone team *something*" that they can tell sellers to make them happier. Maybe we could load sellers up with a bunch of free coins so they don't get so angry?
>
> Josh, who is seated across the table from me, replies, 'Well, we don't *have* to.' He looks at me with a sheepish smile. 'We can do it—even if it sucks.' I wonder if he would be saying this if Carol had been invited to the meeting.

By the end of the meeting it was clear to me that, regardless of the suffering it might cause phone agents to experience, AllDone's leadership was committed to placing them on the front lines of the transition to coins.

The tests continued. Every week or so over the subsequent three months, members of AllDone Las Vegas called dozens of sellers to inform them that their subscriptions were being terminated and to introduce them to the coin system. Phone agents forwarded user reactions to managers in San Francisco, and eventually the product team experimented with additional features designed to appease angry users. Phone support agents began to pitch the new payment model as an opportunity to reduce competition between sellers, with the maximum number of quotes on a buyer's request lowered from ten to five. They also told sellers about AllDone's new auto-refund policy, through which sellers would automatically receive their coins back if a buyer didn't open the quote within four days. But sellers were never pacified.

After four months of testing and refining the program, the product team was confident that the company could safely undertake a site-wide transition to the coin system. AllDone Las Vegas had demonstrated that they could convince many subscribers to pay more to continue to use All-Done. Carol and I began to train every member of the team to make transition calls, and coins were gradually introduced to all subscribers over a period of five weeks. Every week, phone agents called hundreds of All-Done's most active subscribers, announced the change, and tried to persuade sellers to try the new program. In total, they reached out to nearly five thousand high-value subscribers and received calls from many more.

Like customer-support representatives in offline settings, ADLV's female, front-line workers paid an emotional toll in absorbing customer hostility toward company policies to uphold exchange relationships and the accumulation of profit.[18] Team members were battered with insults and verbal abuse for eight hours a day throughout the transition period, and none escaped without being brought to tears. In one instance, a caller who said he was calling the FBI to investigate AllDone screamed into his phone, "You guys are a fucking setup for fucking stealing people's fucking money. *Go fuck yourselves!*"

Although not all sellers were this aggressive, most of the calls were unpleasant and contentious, if not worse. Even sellers who remained relatively civil could still cause team members to lose their composure. On one recorded call, Denise, a phone support agent, began to explain to a seller named Jessica that the subscription program was ending and that it would be replaced by the coin system when she was interrupted:

> Jessica starts to argue with Denise, stating firmly that "my subscription is *not* supposed to be up."
>
> "I was actually going to finish what I was saying, I'm going to get to that in just a second," Denise says, sounding annoyed and impatient.
>
> "Ma'am, I run a business," Jessica says, her voice rising with anger. "I will drop this service if it's so complicated that you cannot explain it to me."
>
> "Wow, ma'am," Denise says with a note of incredulity, "maybe I should have an account representative call you back so they can better explain it to you."
>
> "OK, why don't you drop the tone?"

"I don't feel that I *have* a tone." The line goes dead as Jessica hangs up the phone.

Members of ADLV frequently called Carol for moral support after they fielded difficult calls. "[Sellers are] just pissed off and they want someone to yell at, and it happens to be us," she reassured one team member while I was sitting beside her desk during a visit to Las Vegas. "Deep breath *in*, deep breath *out*! Go to your happy place, go to your happy place!" she added, laughing. "*Oy vey iz mir.*"

Although many sellers were infuriated by the transition to a new payment model, the rollout proved successful: revenue climbed as approximately half of AllDone's former subscribers continued to use the platform despite the vastly higher fees. Years later, executives would continue to view the termination of subscriptions as the most pivotal moment in All-Done's history, unlocking the company's revenue growth and investment potential for years to come. As Carter later reflected in an e-mail, "We absolutely could not have made this critical transition without Vegas." Technology alone was incapable of solving the problems that arose when AllDone sought to profit from using software to administer a nationwide platform. Instead, the company used relational work to help bring users' expectations in line with its software systems.

· · · · ·

AllDone's pursuit of a second round of venture capital funding spurred a strategic pivot from a subscription model to a new, more costly payment system. Sellers reacted with suspicion and hostility. The changes to AllDone's rules and fees left some users feeling bewildered, distrustful, or infuriated. Executives confronted this trust drag with relational work provided by a female, low-wage remote contract workforce in Las Vegas. Phone support agents were increasingly asked to build sellers' trust in AllDone's systems, reactively repair their trust when AllDone failed to meet their expectations, and proactively preserve user trust in the face of changes to the platform's rules.

AllDone's architects had initially assumed that the company could succeed while maintaining arms-length relationships with its users. They soon discovered what economic sociologists have long known: that seemingly cold and calculated economic activity is in fact laden with "hot" emotions, and that the outcomes of transactions are inevitably shaped by social relations. Observing the inner workings of a tech startup sheds new light on how this central insight of economic sociology can be extended to the digital realm. Sometimes AllDone's phone agents facilitated transactions between market participants by making them feel cared for. At other times, phone agents were akin to the "coolers" hired by con artists to handle "marks" after they discover that they have been manipulated or deceived.[19] In these instances, phone agents encouraged users to blame themselves, rather than AllDone, for their troubles, and persuaded many to continue to pay to use the platform.

In a more general sense, AllDone found that it was forced to manage the ways that online relationships disrupted the types of trust upon which service work—and particularly service work performed in homes—depends. Platform companies attempt to create one-size-fits-all solutions that will work for every user, but users' preferences and experiences often diverge from software designers' intentions. As it moved activity in local service markets online, AllDone created a trust crisis between sellers and buyers, as well as between sellers and the platform company itself. After discovering that there was no apparent technological fix, managers mobilized human workers whose emotional labor could generate a sense of closeness through personalized voice calls. Phone agents endeavored to build users' trust in a cloud service by engaging them in human relationships. Low-tech, hands-on work was essential to the success of what was ostensibly a high-tech startup.

This strategy was particularly important for AllDone because venture-backed startups frequently operate in the gray area between legitimate business and fraud. Entrepreneurs are commonly advised to "fake it 'til you make it," or to advance claims about their products that may not yet be entirely true—and, in some cases, may never be—to attract customers, employees, and investors.[20] Venture capitalism incentivizes platform companies to pursue scale by manipulating users. During a platform's earliest stages of growth, investment capital is deployed to subsidize users' activities on the platform, and startups often attract new users by adopting a business model that is not viable in the long term. Users thus develop unrealistic expectations that must be adjusted as the company "pivots" toward generating revenue to attract new investors. This dynamic led some AllDone sellers to view the company as a "scam."

Under the fast-changing conditions of venture capitalism, a human touch may be especially vital in ensuring that technological systems have the effects envisioned by designers. Investors expected AllDone to continually experiment with its product to rapidly increase the firm's valuation. Innovation in AllDone's organizational core (San Francisco) necessitated peripheral workers who provided operational stability (Philippines) and insulated software developers from customer interactions (Las Vegas). As different as their functions were, software developers in San Francisco and computational workers in the Philippines shared a common orientation toward AllDone's users, who generally appeared as abstract representations on computer screens. This was not the case for AllDone Las Vegas's frontline workers, who confronted real people with tangible emotions and immediate problems that needed to be solved. Because they were in continual contact with AllDone's users, the company's ever-changing product was often a source of fear and frustration.

6 Bearing the Burdens of Change

In a popular how-to book for tech entrepreneurs, LinkedIn cofounder and prominent venture capitalist Reid Hoffman argues that startups should adopt practices that "violate many of the [traditional] management 'rules' that are designed for efficiency and risk minimization." He proposes "a new set of rules" designed to help businesses scale at a breakneck pace, including "embrace chaos," "tolerate 'bad' management," "launch a product that embarrasses you," "let fires burn," and "ignore your customers."[1] These tactics, which in other settings would likely be viewed as wasteful and reckless, are directed at helping startups swiftly achieve market dominance at all costs.

If Hoffman had visited AllDone's San Francisco office during my fieldwork—or if he were to read chapter 1 of this book—it's likely that he would have approved of what he saw. Employees operated without long-term plans beyond managing emergent crises and hitting their next strategic benchmarks. Software developers were continually experimenting with new product features and design elements, many of which customers confronted before they had been fully fleshed out. And instead of dwelling on users' complaints or focusing on addressing bugs in the software, employees remained fixated on finding new ways to increase the user metrics that mattered most to investors.

AllDone San Francisco's software developers experienced disruption as exhilarating. Comfortably ensconced in a well-appointed office, they were immersed in the challenging and absorbing work of building a new product and finding creative solutions to organizational problems. They reveled in watching the numbers climb higher, their every success seeming to bring them one step closer to hitting the startup jackpot.

But what do Hoffman's "new rules" for rapidly scaling a business mean for frontline workers? In this chapter, I answer this question by examining how AllDone's Las Vegas–based contractors' experiences of work were shaped by the organizational and structural conditions of venture capitalism. Among AllDone's three work teams, its phone agents bore the burdens of organizational dynamism, or the firm's ever-changing strategies and product features, most directly. While the (almost exclusively) men of AllDone San Francisco enjoyed moving fast and breaking things, the women of AllDone Las Vegas were often left to clean up the messes they left behind.

Phone agents in Las Vegas struggled to keep up with and understand the innovations originating in the San Francisco office. At the same time, they were responsible for advising users who were having the exact same problems they were having in making sense of an ever-evolving product. ADLV contractors struggled to keep up with shifting job tasks, and new managerial directives emphasizing adaptability bred stress and anxiety among workers. These conditions created special difficulties for ADLV's older and more technologically challenged workers, who were already sensitive to the precarious nature of their positions, both within the firm and in the labor market more generally.

AllDone's leaders attempted to import AllDone Philippines' culture of familial love to Las Vegas, but team members did not consistently reproduce ADP's frontstage display of a happy, uncomplaining workforce. Facing relatively low wages, difficult work, and uncertainty about their long-term attachment to the firm, ADLV contractors at times failed to meet performance objectives, violated managerial directives, squabbled with each other, and openly expressed dissatisfaction with managers in San Francisco. Collectively, these conditions and responses contributed to an organizational *culture of frustration*. Because they operated on the front lines of a fast-moving, venture-backed startup, members of AllDone

Las Vegas were asked to absorb the social costs of the continual change orchestrated in the San Francisco office. Yet, because their efforts were neither "scalable" nor easily measurable, managers tended to devalue their work and blame workers themselves for problems that were structural in nature.

THE MANAGERIAL VIEW

Just as AllDone was shifting strategies to attract its second round of funding, I found myself in an unexpected position: I was offered a job in middle management. When I had first arrived at AllDone to start my research as a participant-observer, I was coming in to the office one day per week to help Martin, one of the startup's cofounders, with marketing projects. A month later he had invited me to double my time in the office and join the team in a paid, part-time position. Now Carter, AllDone's president, had asked if I would be interested in working as a full-time employee. On a sunny, warm summer day, we strolled around San Francisco's Yerba Buena Gardens while Carter explained that he would create a new role for me: director of customer support and operations manager, which would consolidate a range of duties currently performed by him, Martin, and Josh, AllDone's product manager. If I accepted this role, one of my primary tasks would be overseeing AllDone's twenty-person e-mail support division in the Philippines and the ten-person phone team in the Las Vegas area.

After our conversation about the new role, Carter forwarded me an e-mail he had recently sent to staffers in San Francisco about his impressions of AllDone Las Vegas. He identified "Personnel Issues" as one of the main managerial challenges pertaining to the team: "We've had more personnel issues on Team Vegas than Team Philippines ever has (and Team Philippines is 20x bigger . . .)." He explained that some team members were "gossiping unproductively"; one was caught trying to "spy" on her colleagues by viewing documents she wasn't supposed to have access to; and there were "lots of general management headaches like team members not notifying Carol [the team leader] when their schedule changes, etc." In light of these issues, Carter concluded his message by stating, "My love affair with the Philippines + pessimism for America's future is only growing . . . :)" Although the position sounded daunting, I was excited about the opportunity to learn more about AllDone's operations by deepening my involvement in the field, and I soon agreed to take the job while continuing my research activities.

Almost immediately after my new role was announced to my colleagues in San Francisco, I discovered that many of them shared Carter's dim assessment of AllDone Las Vegas. Soon after the all-staff meeting ended, I was chatting with Katrina, a user interface designer, while watching two other coworkers' ping-pong match. Katrina told me that she'd been unimpressed when phone agents called her after she placed a request on AllDone. 'I wonder why they're so bad at selling AllDone [to buyers],' Katrina mused. 'Even if they can't fulfill a [buyer's] request, they should be selling the brand—they should be able to talk about the other stuff AllDone can do for buyers.' During a subsequent meeting, Josh, the product manager, echoed these concerns:

> Josh asks Carter how much phone agents actually know about AllDone. Can they handle complicated problems? He says a couple of months ago one of them called him after he placed a request on AllDone. She didn't realize that he was an AllDone employee, so he thought he'd try to test her by asking her to explain various aspects of what the company does. He says she couldn't get very far.

Most members of AllDone San Francisco had little direct experience with members of AllDone Las Vegas, but the prevailing view of ADLV appeared to be focused on the team's shortcomings.

When I met Carol, I learned that she shared some of the concerns I'd heard in San Francisco. Like Carter, Carol drew unflattering comparisons between her team members' attitudes and AllDone's workforce in the Philippines. During my first trip to Las Vegas, Carol told me about catching a phone agent working on her own candle-selling business on company time. 'Look at Team Philippines,' she remarked. 'They have so much gratitude just to have a job. We all should feel that way, especially to have a job we love and a company we love.' A couple of months later, after Carol fired a team member whom she viewed as a troublemaker, she returned again in a phone conversation to the question: "Why can't everybody be like Team Philippines?" Carol believed that some members of her team lacked the "gratitude" that members of AllDone Philippines evinced as they seemed to cheerily go about their workdays. Contrasting ADLV with ADP, she emphasized that "they're *happy*, they're excited about doing the job" in the Philippines. Why, then, did ADLV fall short? Why were there so many "personnel issues" in Las Vegas? Why did team members seem far more disgruntled than workers in the Philippines, who were "happy" even though they "have so little?"[2]

When leaders compared ADLV's struggles with ADP's successes, they frequently attributed differences in the teams' performance not to the conditions under which Las Vegas-based team members labored, but rather to differences in the characteristics of workers. Both Carol and Carter invoked national and gender-based stereotypes in explaining why the contractors in Las Vegas experienced so much conflict. During a series of conversations pertaining to a phone agent named Tanya and her open hostility toward colleagues, Carol exclaimed to me:

> "All girls on a team—bloody hell! It's so *high school*. [Tanya] doesn't like me because I wouldn't fire Cassie; she hates Cassie because she's friends with Tori. It just surprises me that women cannot get along. I don't understand in this day and age why women feel threatened by each other."

> "It's odd," Carol continues says, sounding troubled. "It saddens me that women are like that with each other." She says that when she asks the team for suggestions, such as "where you'd like to go for a meeting—I cannot ask a simple question because it ends up being a catfight! It's not like these women are eighteen years old. I just don't get it."

According to Carol's interpretation, many of ADLV's personnel issues were a natural byproduct of gender relations, given that the workforce was almost entirely female. I heard other members of ADLV echo these sentiments on occasion.

But gender alone could not account for the differences between the two teams—most members of ADP, after all, were also women. Faced with this reality, Carter often attributed the volume of personnel issues experienced by ADLV in comparison with ADP to differences in national culture. In an e-mail, he explained to me "the advantages of Filipino culture (trustworthy, deferential, team players) over American culture (dismissive of rules, individualistic)." After his first visit with the team in Las Vegas, he stated in an e-mail to ADSF employees that members of ADLV had different expectations for their jobs: "Compared to Team Philippines, they are more motivated by 'team' than by 'family.' They are more competitive. They want jobs that have mobility / [are] going somewhere. (Who doesn't?) At least two [members of ADLV] discussed leaving other jobs that were dead ends." Yet Carter's recourse to national culture also falls short of reality, in that it discounts the ambition of Filipino workers, including their obvious interest in jobs that offered opportunities for promotions, raises, and bonuses.

When asked directly, though, Carter acknowledged one likely source of dissatisfaction at ADLV, particularly compared to ADP: The relatively low wages offered to phone agents. In an e-mail Carter sent to me after I accepted my new position working with ADLV, he explained that AllDone was "very aggressive with our compensation" in Las Vegas—by which he meant that AllDone's phone team was aggressively *under*compensated, making ten dollars an hour with no benefits. He wrote that if AllDone were to contract out its customer support operations to an outsourced call center, the company's personnel costs would double or triple to twenty to thirty dollars per hour. Carter said it was important that AllDone keep its customer support costs low for two reasons: first, because "we're exploring opportunities (not committing forever)" to maintaining the team, and second, because "we're cash constrained."[3] ADLV contractors' low pay, he explained, meant that the team would be more difficult to supervise: "This low rate does increase management overhead because we're not dealing with top talent like we do in the Philippines."

In the Philippines, two dollars an hour, on a flexible schedule, at home, with limited supervision, represented a reasonably good option for educated workers who might otherwise spend months in unpaid "internships," relocate overseas, or take grueling overnight shifts in call centers. In Las Vegas, jobs offering ten dollars an hour for fielding customer service calls primarily attracted workers who saw it as a step above minimum-wage work. Only some members of AllDone Las Vegas had college degrees, and some were downwardly mobile, having previously held more stable or remunerative jobs. For example, Sharon had previously run her own payroll company, Emily had worked for a federal agency for over a decade, and Tanya had been employed by the local Chamber of

Commerce. Many had moved to Las Vegas seeking economic opportunity in a booming local economy with a low cost of living. The Great Recession scrapped their plans.

Although Carter believed that offering higher wages would allow All-Done to attract better talent, he did not appear to consider how low pay affected the performance of even the most dedicated workers. As I began to oversee ADLV's operations, I came to understand how team members' precarious financial situations affected their everyday lives. It was not out of the ordinary for workers to ask for a loan or to be paid in advance to cover moving or automobile repair expenses. At least one team member was unable to afford a car, making life in sprawling and public transit-poor Las Vegas exceedingly difficult. Another was evicted from her apartment while working for AllDone. For reasons that ADSF's office manager could never determine, the company's bank frequently failed to disburse wages on time, an obvious source of stress for workers living paycheck to paycheck. According to Carter, some agents received SNAP benefits, or "food stamps." And over time I learned from e-mails and conversations with team members that at least half of ADLV contractors maintained small side hustles, such as selling dietary supplements or weight-loss products, to make extra money. One team member, Cassie, was repeatedly caught spending time on other jobs (usually Amway-type multilevel marketing schemes into which she would try to recruit colleagues) while on the clock for AllDone. The stresses of struggling to make ends meet surely detracted from these workers' ability to focus on their jobs with AllDone.

Because ADLV's contractors worked remotely, their economic hardship also directly affected their working conditions and performance. Sharon told me that she worked in a "little closet" that she had converted into an office, where she would sweat so much that her glasses continually slid off her nose because she "can't afford" to leave the air conditioning on all day in the desert heat. Nancy, who openly joked about her financial liabilities ("If debtor's prison still exists, I'm going to debtor's prison"), said that she worked on a laptop computer from her bedroom. Her husband also worked from home; she explained that sometimes when he was on a conference call, he would barge into the bedroom with their barking dog while *she* was working and ask her to keep the dog quiet. When I visited Shirley's cramped apartment to help her troubleshoot a technological issue,

I found that her computer equipment was so outdated that it was slowing her workflow to a crawl and impairing her interactions with users.[4]
And upon visiting Nicole's apartment, I noticed that a large television set
was switched on in her bedroom, on the same table where she worked on
a fifteen-inch laptop (and where we were interrupted by her five-year-
old daughter). After sustained observation, it was plain to see how contractors' working conditions, exacerbated by low pay, could hamper their
performance and contribute to a culture of frustration. But perhaps most
importantly, phone agents provided customer service within an organization that emphasized technical innovation over user services.

ESSENTIAL, YET EXPERIMENTAL

Carter viewed the Las Vegas area as an ideal site for AllDone's phone
team—in part because he perceived the region as analogous to the Philippines. "Las Vegas is the Philippines of America: Hot, crowded, and affordable," he remarked to Carol, Veronica (ADP's general manager), and
me as we sat down to dinner one night at a restaurant's outdoor patio in
downtown Vegas.

    When I took the helm of ADLV, Carter envisioned that I would trans-
plant the management philosophy he and his deputies had pioneered in
the Philippines to the smaller and more disorganized team in Las Vegas.
'My biggest regret from when I was running Team Vegas,' Carter told me,
'is that I used it ad hoc. I didn't set up a lot of systems or quality-control
mechanisms. We don't know what people are actually saying on the phone.'
I was to establish new customer support procedures, gather and analyze
data on team members' efficacy, and then use my analyses to refine those
processes. At the same time, Carter wanted me to help Carol build managerial infrastructure such as standardized training materials that would
help new hires improve their performance, while also working with her to
record and interpret important metrics so she could track the team's progress toward its goals and make informed personnel decisions. Ultimately,
Carter hoped that under my direction, ADLV contractors could be turned
into flexible and efficient "phone ninjas" capable of taking on a variety of
call projects to meet ADSF's ever-shifting needs.

The realities on the ground, however, were not conducive to such a transformation. ADLV's call center might better be described as a call *de-center* whose contractors worked from home rather than from a centralized office. Instead of following scripts to field deeply routinized calls, workers held unscripted and unpredictable conversations with callers. At ADLV, workers and managers alike scrambled to keep up with escalating customer demand and a fast-changing product.

Only months after Carol had established her group in Las Vegas, the team was being asked to take on new and complex tasks. Carter viewed ADLV as one of the company's many "experiments," born of venture capital's impetus for startups to try anything that might help them swiftly advance their strategic goals. Instead of spending their days calling buyers to solicit additional requests, the team would now shift its focus toward aiding and persuading the sellers whose payments constituted the entirety of AllDone's revenue. Additionally, members of ADSF's product team were beginning to call upon ADLV as a flexible resource to support their own work, much like ADP's "special projects" division (chapter 3).

Because of the uncertainty surrounding where the team figured in All-Done's long-term plans—and because hiring a contractor in Las Vegas cost five times as much as a contractor in the Philippines—leaders in San Francisco wished to keep staffing levels in Las Vegas stable even as user demand and the difficulty of the team's tasks persistently escalated. Executives came to see ADLV as an essential component of the company's strategy for achieving revenue growth, but they nevertheless declined to invest in contractors' pay or working conditions. Workers effectively faced a "speedup" on the shop floor: the same number of people were now asked to do far more than they had done before. Under these circumstances, phone agents found it difficult to adapt to changes in both their labor process and AllDone's product.

Owing in part to staffing deficiencies, Carol struggled to develop the kind of managerial infrastructure that her counterparts in the Philippines had built, and that were common in other call centers. AllDone Philippines had evolved over the previous two-and-a-half years, during which time leaders in San Francisco had hardly enacted any significant changes to work procedures. Over time, early hires were promoted into new managerial positions that allowed them to focus on leadership. They had acquired on-the-ground expertise in the processes they oversaw and had time to create detailed instructions and training videos, built systems to help them monitor workers' output, and led one-on-one coaching sessions with the workers on their teams. While managers at ADSF had no prior experience running call centers, they met with customer-support leads at other startups and learned of a variety of best practices, many of which were similar to those developed by ADP leaders: the company should develop training modules and quizzes that would be updated to help agents learn about changing product features, regularly coach phone agents by offering feedback on recordings of their calls, and build an online "knowledge base" or Frequently Asked Questions webpage so that users could independently look up solutions to their problems rather than calling in.

None of these best practices had been implemented at AllDone when ADLV took over the company's phone support operations. Carol had little time to devote to setting up new systems. Because there were far more calls coming in than ADLV could handle, Carol typically logged twelve-hour days during which she juggled customer support duties—including the toughest calls, which colleagues "escalated" to her—along with answering team members' questions, trying to alleviate the stress and anxieties related to their new workload, planning team meetings and preparing reports, attending videoconferences with managers in San Francisco and the Philippines, and overseeing a variety of other short-term projects.

When Carol did find time to work on developing documentation for her team, the results did not always live up to ADSF's expectations. Although ADSF leadership viewed Carol's "people skills" as unparalleled, her technical acumen and organization skills trailed behind those of the managers they had come to know in the Philippines. Carol's written guides could be difficult to follow, and she was often overwhelmed by the prospect of setting up new technological systems that might help her provide feedback to team members or support them in helping themselves. In other words, Carol's charismatic leadership style did not easily translate into "scalable" processes that could be detailed in documents or delegated to others.

As AllDone's director of customer support, I did my best to help Carol develop the team's managerial infrastructure. But like Carol, I frequently found myself besieged by an ever-expanding workload and unable to

complete the job. My first major task was to implement and train contractors on a new software system that allowed agents to create records
of their interactions with customers. As this was happening, AllDone was
beginning to roll out its new payment model, which resulted in a deluge
of backlash from sellers that I was helping the company manage. At the
same time, I was also responsible for overseeing AllDone's e-mail support
team in the Philippines, which required me to handle the most difficult
customer support cases that had been "escalated" by the team's leader in
the Philippines. And in my role as operations manager, I wrote weekly
messages explaining AllDone's various product changes to members of the
remote teams, while also organizing and transmitting tasks and feedback
between San Francisco, the Philippines, and Las Vegas. AllDone's ever-
changing systems created so many urgent problems that I had little time
to devote to improving ADLV's existing procedures.

The fact that many members of Carol's staff shared her difficulties with
technology amplified the team's already substantial challenges. Given the
demanding nature of contractors' interactions with customers, Carol was
understandably more interested in a candidate's demeanor than in her
technological acumen when recruiting phone agents. My visits to Las
Vegas repeatedly revealed just how baffling and frustrating some team
members found their day-to-day tasks—not only because of the nature
of the work, but also because of their relatively rudimentary working
knowledge of computer hardware, operating systems, and applications.
I witnessed Nancy and Sharon struggling to enter a web address into a
browser, to understand the difference between their two separate AllDone
user accounts, and to use keyboard shortcuts to help them locate information on AllDone's sprawling administrative webpages. Nancy once rue-
fully recounted that when she had purchased a new laptop and brought
it to Carol's house for a training session, neither of them had been able
to figure out how to open it. The embarrassing ordeal ended only when
Nancy called her husband, "an IT guy," who set them straight with no
small amount of mockery. (They had been trying to open the wrong end
of the computer.) AllDone didn't employ any IT staff who could provide
phone agents with tech support.

Many ADLV contractors—particularly those over the age of forty—
struggled to use AllDone's arcane back-end systems. In order to assist a

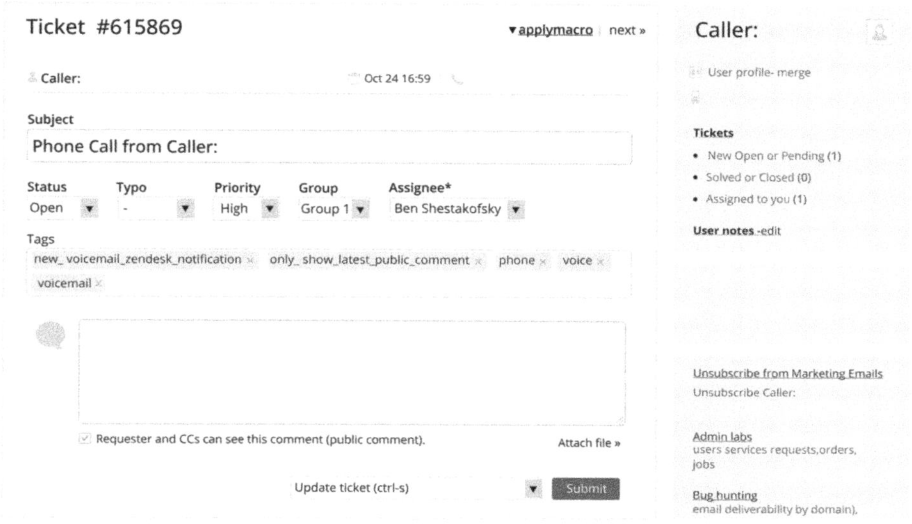

Figure 6. Agent's view of a phone support ticket

user with a problem, agents might have to navigate through some combination of twenty text-based administrative pages to find the right information or make the requested changes. Given the lack of comprehensive documentation, team members typically learned how to navigate these pages through in-person training sessions with Carol; when they returned home to work on their own, they would frequently e-mail or call Carol with follow-up questions about AllDone's systems and policies.

Team members also struggled to use the software that AllDone had purchased from an outside vendor to track their interactions with customers. This, too, proved difficult for agents to navigate. Each customer contact created a webpage with well over a dozen elements with which phone agents might engage (figure 6).[5]

In addition to the deficiencies in ADLV's managerial infrastructure and the range of technical issues confronted by contractors in Las Vegas, the work performed by phone agents was inherently challenging. Members of ADLV experienced real-time interactions with users who brought up myriad problems with AllDone's ever-changing systems that phone agents would have to diagnose and attempt to solve in real time. These customers could be aggressive and abusive.

Although comprehensive scripts can be deadening for customers and employees alike, workers may view them as resources that they can use to manage difficult interactions. Routine, in these cases, can prove a comfort. Certain organizational conditions, however, limit companies' ability to standardize service work. Sociologist Robin Leidner finds that three specific circumstances reduce the likelihood of standardization: when workers' discretion is necessary to produce a customized experience for service-recipients; when interactive tasks are more difficult and complex; and when workers labor without direct managerial supervision or organizational control.[6] All three of these conditions obtained at AllDone.[7]

Unlike their counterparts in the Philippines, ADLV team members frequently used terminology evocative of trauma to describe work episodes. Sellers were "on the warpath today," and contractors were "battered and bruised," engaged in "guerilla warfare" conducted "in the trenches" of a "frontline battle" (see chapter 5). Understandably, some phone agents seemed to truly dread taking on customer support duties.[8] When Emily was asked to answer inbound customer support calls, for example, she cited her diabetes and high blood pressure as reasons why she might not be suited to provide customers with good service. Other team members raised managers' suspicions when they repeatedly cited technical difficulties that kept them from answering live calls from their home computers.[9] ADLV's contractors labored on the front lines of change, serving as a buffer between disgruntled users and the San Francisco–based software developers whose products and policies were responsible for users' discontent.

AllDone Las Vegas was a triage operation. The team lacked the resources it needed to build systems that would support best practices for a call center. Instead, ADLV's phone agents were overtaxed and undersupported, scrambling to manage users' trust as the company lurched from crisis to crisis.

EXPORTING "ALLDONE LOVE" TO LAS VEGAS

As AllDone Las Vegas took shape, its organizational culture was explicitly modeled on AllDone Philippines' culture of familial love. In companies like AllDone, where managers are unable to prespecify each step of service workers' interactions with customers, employers may attempt to cultivate a strong workplace culture to encourage workers to enact the firm's values in their interactions with customers.[10] In AllDone's case, executives believed that promoting AllDone Love in Las Vegas would increase the bottom line by improving the quality of phone agents' interactions with customers while also boosting contractors' morale.

When Carol was hired as ADLV's first contractor, Carter had put ADP managers in charge of training her and supervising her work. Carol was captivated by ADP's online work culture, which matched her own effervescent personality and spiritual outlook. She later recounted to me during a phone meeting what it was like to encounter AllDone Philippines for the first time:

> "From day one, I loved 'em. They're so warm and loving. My first day on the job, it was all I could do to keep up with the [welcome] e-mails I got all day long [from Team Philippines]. I was overwhelmed! 'Who are these people? They're just the most beautiful people!' It was just wonderful! I was really in tears my first day on the job, like, 'Oh. My. God. They're so wonderful!'

> From day one I looked up to Team Philippines—they're *happy*, they're excited about doing the job. I never thought I'd find other people who are like me! 'The pitch of her voice is rising with excitement.' I'm not the only one!"

If any single person was the embodiment of "AllDone, love and joy in motion"—a phrase found in her e-mail signature—it was Carol, a "true believer" who lived and breathed AllDone.[11] Even as she frequently logged twelve-hour days, often including weekends, her enthusiasm for the company long remained unflagging and contagious. She channeled her immeasurable charisma into making phone agents and users believe in AllDone.

AllDone Las Vegas's frontstage feeling rules echoed those of AllDone Philippines, as communications among contractors, and between contractors and managers in San Francisco, frequently emphasized themes of love, family, and gratitude. As Carter told team members during a visit with phone agents, "We're proud of the culture Veronica built [in the Philippines], and that it's living on here in Vegas." And indeed, Carol had copied substantial portions of ADLV's onboarding documents for new hires directly from ADP. Like ADP, ADLV was a work-from-home team, and most team members' interactions with one another were conducted via e-mail, web chat, and telephone. Similar to ADP, ADLV's intra-team e-mails frequently included exuberant professions of contractors' love for their jobs and each other ("I LOVE ALL MY LADIES !!!!!!!!! UP IN HERE ESPECIALLY!!!! SUPER BIG HUG !!!!"); inspirational messages; personal news about family and pets and accompanying requests for prayers; and customers' praise of phone agents or the company. To this they added a fair dose of joking about husbands, boyfriends, and celebrity crushes.

As when Filipino team members met in person, a primary aim of ADLV's monthly meetings (which were mandatory, and for which team members were paid) was to make contractors feel that they were valued members of a work community. In-person gatherings featured numerous conversations about employees' personal lives and stories about interactions with AllDone customers, as opposed to the presentation of data and debates about strategic concerns that dominated staff meetings in San Francisco.

Like their Filipino counterparts, when Carter flew to Las Vegas to visit the team, contractors offered testimonials that highlighted AllDone's positive impact on their lives. During one meeting that I attended, Carter asked team members to introduce themselves, say how long they'd been with AllDone, and tell their favorite AllDone story. Many shared accounts of how AllDone had helped them overcome adversity:

> Eileen, who's been working for AllDone for three months, says she was laid off from her previous job, where she had managed accounts for five years. She was almost out of money when AllDone came along, and it was a blessing. She says she still can't believe AllDone is for real—that a company that cares about its people so much exists.

> Shirley explains that she used to work as a leasing agent, where her boss would yell at her for being patient with people. Now, she says, it's her job to be patient and help people work through things. "I can honestly say, I say it every day to myself. I get up and I love what I do, I love my job, I love All-Done. I've had eleven jobs [in Las Vegas] in seven years; I hadn't had eleven in my entire *lifetime* before I got to Vegas. I've been laid off more than—I go, it's like, 'Oh my God, it took eleven tries to get it right.'"

> Sharon shares that she "was self-employed before AllDone. My business got killed when the economy fell [during the recession]. AllDone was a saving grace because when it's your own business and everything is great, you don't

take other things into consideration, like having a 401(k) and savings. All of a sudden it's gone, so AllDone was a lifesaver. Everybody is amazing. It really was like joining a family, and it still is. I appreciate that every day."

As did their counterparts in the Philippines, ADLV contractors recounted emotional stories of personal transformation enabled by the generosity of a benefactor—the job creator in their midst. The following morning, Carter received an appreciative e-mail from Wendy:

Thanks for the Surprise in being able to see you yesterday! It means so much that you come out to see us You are so Special and Thank You for showing us your gratitude. The feeling is beyond mutual with all of us. We know why we were given the gift of this job. Thanks So much Again and Always, You forever have a place in my heart! Glad to be part of your family!

Wendy told Carter that his expressions of gratitude—indeed, his mere presence in Las Vegas—was meaningful to contractors for whom jobs with AllDone represented a "gift" and provided a "family." As in the case of AllDone's Filipino workforce, of interest here is not the extent to which Wendy's expressions of gratitude were "genuine," but instead how her messages reflected what she believed leaders wished to hear about the impact their business was having on people in need.

Leaders in San Francisco reflected this language of love, gratitude, and family back to the ADLV workforce. Late one Tuesday afternoon I recorded the following interaction in the office:

I see Carter mosey toward the kitchen and I get up to ask him if he's spoken with Carol today. "Yeah," he says, then smiles and chuckles, continuing, "I feel funny saying 'love you lots, too!'" in response to Carol's typical telephone sign-off. Now he's blushing a little bit. "Because I do love her. But it's not something I say a lot around here."

Carter was reluctant to be heard expressing "love" for a colleague by others in the San Francisco office, where such language was out of place, but he did not deny the authenticity of these feelings.[12]

Managers in San Francisco were indeed eager to promulgate the notion that, as in the Philippines, Las Vegas-based contractors believed that AllDone represented a source of opportunity and fulfillment that transcended what typical jobs had to offer. Carter shared workers' testimonials about the trials of finding, and keeping, a good job in Las Vegas in an e-mail to staffers in San Francisco, telling them that "AllDone was 'an answer to prayers' for a couple [of contractors] who had lost their jobs before finding AllDone and were in a pretty tough spot." As with the Filipino workers, Carter invoked a "rescue narrative" in describing AllDone's relationship to its low-wage workers.[13] According to his account, AllDone was making dreams come true for its phone support agents, who were grateful and "excited" to serve in whatever capacities ADSF managers required.[14]

It is true that, despite the challenging nature of their interactions with customers, contractors sometimes described customer support work as a source of meaning, satisfaction, and self-actualization. I introduced myself to Shirley during a lunch break at the first team meeting that I attended.

> After a brief hello, Shirley immediately tells me that what she really likes about her job is connecting with people. Sometimes, she says, you'll talk to someone who really needs help—just two days after the Aurora movie theater shootings, she happened to speak with a woman whose son had survived Columbine. Shirley's eyes open wide, and she looks at me earnestly, continuing: this woman just really needed someone to talk to, and I could be there for her. Shirley says she loves when, at the end of a call, she can tell that "they know they're taken care of."

In an e-mail to the rest of the ADLV team, Wendy expressed a similar sentiment, recounting a conversation with a buyer who wanted to book a taxi service:

> She was using her [friend's] computer and was staying with her because she just lost her home and her car just broke down and that if she did not make it to work she was in danger of loosing [sic] her job. A job that she was being harassed at and they had cut her hours to two days a week.

> My heart hurt for her and all I could say to her was that she had a place in my heart to overcome these issues.

> That made her smile even laugh that someone would reach out and say that.

> She was grateful and knew that I meant it. . . . I told her sometimes the universe brings us in to each others lives to remind her that she is not alone and that there is love around us.

> She then said that I was an angel and that she felt so much better.

This is a reminder why I am blessed to be in my position. What other job can [give] you the blessing of being called on to give encouragement. Feeling so happy and grateful!

Wendy's story exemplifies how ADLV agents could find meaning and dignity in helping AllDone users pursue their dreams or in offering troubled people a patient ear.[15]

Although ADLV's disorganization could be a source of stress for workers, the lack of surveillance and set scripts provided space for phone agents to build meaningful emotional connections with customers. As Shirley once explained during a team meeting,

> "At the end of the day I feel like I made a difference. Even the sellers who start off mad, like, [she raises her voice and furrows her brow, simulating a screaming caller] '*You people!*' By the time we get off the phone, I feel like, OK, I made a difference and somebody's in a better situation because of what we were able to offer them."

These statements were reflected in agents' actions. Some were so devoted to clients that they would transgress company directives. For example, team members frequently provided sellers with their personal phone extensions even though managers advised them not to, so that sellers with whom agents had established relationships could reach them directly the next time a problem arose.[16] Some found that previously disgruntled All-Done users became "attached" and began to call them on a weekly basis. Phone agents often spoke proudly of customers who fell under the sway of the same "AllDone Love" that helped to bind the team together.

Yet, despite workers' and managers' efforts to consolidate an organizational culture of familial love in Las Vegas, an undercurrent of unease, anxiety, and frustration was consistently close to the surface, at times bubbling over into interactions with colleagues and managers.

RELATIONAL BREAKDOWNS

Members of ADLV, like their colleagues in the Philippines, frequently drew on tropes of love and gratitude in their interactions with each other and with ADSF leadership. In Las Vegas, however, a different culture of familial love prevailed—one that included open discussion of workers' needs, an expectation that managers would view their feelings and requests as valid, and expressions of disappointment when those needs weren't met. Contractors did not consistently assume the role of gracious client, nor did management always behave as would befit a benevolent benefactor. Instead, as demonstrated above, managers frequently saw workers as incompetent or unworthy. Workers, for their part, often viewed management as neglectful and unappreciative of their contributions. ADLV's communications with ADSF were at times as likely to include talk of team members' personal struggles and feelings of abandonment as they were to include statements of supplication and gratitude.

If managers in San Francisco often perceived the workforce in Las Vegas as incompetent and insufficiently grateful, workers themselves often viewed managers in San Francisco as out of touch and unappreciative of their efforts. Although ADLV contractors could become exasperated by conversations with abusive customers, perhaps the most frustrating aspect of their jobs arose when systems created by ADSF software engineers placed them in situations that made them feel interactionally incompetent.[17] Minutes into my first meeting with the team, I was bombarded with questions and requests. Team members told me that many aspects of the administrative portals they used to do their work did not function properly.

> Sharon says that what really makes her feel bad is when the system has her call the wrong person or ask them about the wrong thing. There's a bug in the portal agents use to solicit reviews of sellers from buyers over the phone: sometimes it prompts her to call a buyer who has already submitted a review online. In these cases, either the buyer will be upset that she's being asked for a review when she's already submitted one, or Sharon will write up a review for the buyer, click to submit it, and find that she can't because a review of that job is already in the system.

In these instances, AllDone's software provided inaccurate information, creating situations that could leave both customers and phone agents feeling frustrated.

> At another point, Nancy complains that sometimes she'll be forced to call someone to verify one request, when the buyer has actually submitted five.

That means the buyer is getting five different calls in succession, often from different phone agents! Sharon says that when this happens, she always apologizes and explains, 'I'll try to make it so you don't get another call.' But the way the system works, she knows that different phone agents will just continue to be fed different requests submitted by the same buyer. It would be great, she adds, if we could mark peoples' profiles who say, "Don't call me again."

Phone agents were engaged with their work and wanted to provide customers with good service. Sometimes that meant not bothering buyers with superfluous phone calls, as in the above examples. In other cases, team members wanted to offer additional help to those who needed assistance, but felt that AllDone's systems made it difficult for them to do so:

> Emily then turns to me and says she wants the software to let her put a call on hold, or to throw it back into the queue to be called again in a designated number of minutes.

> Nancy agrees: "I hate to say no" when a buyer asks if she can call back, "and I'm like, 'Not really.'"

> Emily jumps in again: 'What would be cool is an admin button for "rush" so a buyer request goes to the front of the queue' when a buyer tells a phone agent she needs quotes as soon as possible.

Phone agents felt embarrassed and frustrated when AllDone's technology forced them to disappoint a customer. When members of AllDone Philippines discovered a bug in the portals they used to complete their behind-the-scenes tasks, they might find it annoying; but because members of AllDone Las Vegas performed customer-facing work, these sorts of technical issues put them in awkward situations that exposed them to direct pressure from customers. VC's pressure for rapid growth meant that software engineers often left both user-facing and back-end systems underdeveloped, leaving phone support agents to absorb the resulting frictions.

In the San Francisco office, leadership instructed software developers to tune out the user complaints that members of ADLV spent their workdays handling. Adam, the director of engineering, once explained during an all-staff meeting that AllDone need not concern itself with users who described their product as terrible, so long as they continued to pay for it.[18]

Although large numbers of sellers might voice their dissatisfaction with the firm—as they did following the transition to the new payment model—they did not leave the platform en masse. Even if members of ADLV experienced their encounters with angry sellers as something akin to going to war, Adam advised, members of ADSF should not allow those negative reactions to distract them from pursuing their strategic goals.[19]

In keeping with this mindset, ADSF's product team rarely addressed issues presented to them by ADLV because they had little immediate bearing on the company's main priorities. During one of Carol's visits to the San Francisco office, Josh, the product manager, joined Carol, Carter, and me in a meeting:

> Carol asks Josh about a bug that sellers have been complaining about that's keeping some of AllDone's e-mails from reaching them. He asks Carol how many sellers are being affected by the problem and she estimates it's around one hundred. Josh nods and explains why a bug like this isn't going to be addressed:

> 'We need to think about which users we'll serve. Do we help one hundred people [with these missing e-mails] or help *everyone* by pushing out a new product?' he says, describing how the product team allocates its resources. 'We send over a million e-mails a day, so one hundred [people being affected] probably isn't a big deal. *We'll only work on bugs that push us toward our top-level [revenue] goal. We'll be under-resourced for the foreseeable future so those are the most important projects for us to work on*' (emphasis added). Josh concludes that 'we're never going to get to' some bugs, and in those cases 'you shouldn't worry about it.'

> Carol nods politely and doesn't question Josh further on the matter. But after Josh leaves, she turns to me and says, 'We run out of things to tell users about bugs. They don't understand the bigger picture.'

From the perspective of software developers in San Francisco, a relatively small number of users' individual concerns could be written off as part of the cost of doing business—they would be sacrificed so engineers could focus on projects that would address the company's top priority of meeting investors' expectations. However, these bugs mattered a great deal to the phone agents in Las Vegas who had to speak with users every day about their problems. As Carol noted, AllDone's users 'don't understand the bigger picture'—that software engineers didn't have time to correct bugs because their primary audience was comprised of venture capital investors, rather than users. In the parlance of venture capital, whereas investors want startups to pursue projects with the potential to be "home runs" that quickly and massively increase the value of the firm, AllDone users were generally more interested in "singles" that would incrementally improve their experiences with the platform. Because users expected AllDone to provide solutions to their problems, engineers' neglect of bugs that were important to them, if not to the company itself, exposed phone agents to emotional strain.

San Francisco–based employees' unwillingness to address issues with the software that affected users—who, in turn, demanded answers from members of ADLV—was a significant source of frustration for phone agents. During one visit to Las Vegas, I met with some ADLV contractors at Carol's house to demonstrate AllDone's new customer support software.

> Sharon takes a seat on the couch looking like she's ready to unload. She sets down a pile of printed and stapled instructions that I had written and e-mailed to the team, as well as her own handwritten notes. She begins to pepper me with questions and suggestions, and I soon realize that she's been recording technological issues as they come up throughout her workdays and retaining these records in case she got an opportunity to talk to someone from ADSF—even if that someone has little power to get bugs fixed himself. . . .

> Sharon brings up another bug in how requests are displaying for attorneys and auto repair, noting that "this has been going on for months." She then turns to Carol, rolls her eyes, and adds, with some bitterness, "I'm sure you forwarded it [to San Francisco] and it got lost."

Resentment among ADLV staffers continued to mount as the issues they identified repeatedly went unaddressed.

Despite their professions of AllDone Love, members of ADLV frequently vocalized their feelings of neglect and their vision of how things should work, as in the meeting described above. Phone support agents felt they had important knowledge that ADSF leaders were missing because they were removed from the immediacy of user interaction and were thus clueless about what users actually wanted and needed.[20] These staffers felt that their input was not sufficiently valued by managers in San Francisco, who at times openly admitted that they prioritized the perceived interests of investors over complaints emerging from users and Las Vegas-based contractors. In the meeting described above, for example, Josh explained to Carol that 'We'll only work on bugs that push us toward our top-level [revenue] goal.'

Team members also felt besieged by the barrage of experiments and frequent product changes that resulted from ADSF's pursuit of venture capital funding. For example, on one occasion ADSF's product team tested displaying the customer support phone number prominently at the bottom of every page on the website as a way to increase user satisfaction, but did not inform anyone in Las Vegas of the change. ADLV immediately found itself on the receiving end of a "call flood" that overwhelmed the team. Among other experiments and ad hoc tasks, phone agents were asked to call sellers to solicit quotes for high-priority requests, place welcome calls to new sellers, call buyers to solicit reviews of sellers, call sellers to deter them from canceling subscriptions (before the transition to coins), solicit sellers to be quoted in press pieces about AllDone, and invite sellers in the San Francisco Bay Area to attend occasional gatherings at the ADSF office.

On another occasion, Josh assigned a project to ADLV that required them to survey more than two thousand buyers by phone. ADLV staffers collectively dubbed the spreadsheet he created for them to document survey responses a "clusterfuck," as I learned during a meeting when the team was seated in a circle in Carol's living room:

> Carol says two words—"Josh's survey"—and the group bursts into groans and laughter. Someone cries out, "You can't work with that thing."
>
> When the hubbub dies down, Sharon addresses me directly: "Obviously, Josh has a brilliant mind. But if you would just do *one* of them yourself—" someone else cuts in, saying the type is so small, and you can't really go through a call like that (asking question after question, presumably about something the buyer doesn't care about).
>
> Shirley then raises her voice above the din, saying that 'you have to do it *your* way.' People are nodding in agreement. 'You have to go through it and understand what [Josh is] looking for, the information he's looking for,' Shirley

continues. 'You can't say it exactly like Josh's script in the spreadsheet. You
have to catch people's attention, keep it moving fast, or they'll take the first
pause and, goodbye, click.'[21]

Not wanting to insult him in my presence, Sharon remarked that "obvi-
ously, Josh had a brilliant mind"—code for an intelligence that is more
theoretically than practically oriented. In this instance, working on a special project required ADLV contractors to figure out for themselves how
to get the results that ADSF managers were seeking. Even Carol, who was
known for her exuberant leadership and positivity, couldn't always hide
her exhaustion with ADSF's experiments. "Oh bloody hell, another test,"
she muttered at a meeting after I acknowledged that AllDone's refund policy might be subject to further revisions.

Frequent product changes made it difficult for support agents to provide accurate information to customers. Each week, I sent team members
lengthy e-mails that typically detailed between six and nine experimental
or long-term changes to the product. The explanations of individual items
varied from one paragraph for simpler changes (e.g., alterations to the text
that would appear on certain webpages) to multiple pages of text and images for more complex projects (e.g., a redesign of sellers' profile pages).
Agents would also have to keep track of which experiments were being implemented on which segments of the user population. "My biggest thing,"
Sharon told me during one meeting as she asked for clarification on a lit-
any of features that were being tried out on users, "is to tell [callers] the
right thing." But, she lamented, "I can't keep all the tests straight."

Carol tried to shield team members from the doubts and anxieties that
came with interacting with unpredictable users, continual changes to the
product, and ADLV's shifting array of projects. As she wrote in one e-mail
to the team:

> As a start up company AllDone is forever evolving and trying new things;
> some work, some do not. So, I know it has been a little crazy lately. hahaha
> lol. But, it is through these changes that we find out what works best and
> what's a keeper.
>
> You are all keepers! 🐢 . . . I'm so proud of our little team; you are all amaz-
> ing women; you all work so hard, and I know how dedicated you are to
> doing the best job possible under any circumstances.

So, please promise me if you are ever feeling worried or un-settled by the changes that are going on, (because there will be more!☺) that you will reach out to me and let me know; because, **I genuinely care about you and your happiness.**

I came to see Carol not only as a supervisor, but also as a counselor for those suffering from the ills of low-wage contract work—both AllDone sellers and phone agents working for ADLV. Carol's work team doubled as a virtual support group for women who felt left out and devalued in a changing economy. Carol would often tell me "I'm putting on my therapist hat" when she was about to speak with a team member to offer counsel on work or personal issues. She was a devoted fan of Oprah Winfrey—and like Oprah, Carol was adept at listening to people's problems and cheering them on, encouraging them to view their challenges through the individualizing glow of therapeutic selfhood instead of questioning relations of production.[22]

In putting on her "therapist hat," Carol was performing relational work with team members, mirroring the outward-facing relational work she provided to disgruntled users. She endeavored to reframe their negative experiences with organizational flux as opportunities for personal growth. As Carol wrote to the team in a weekly e-mail update:

> There are a lot of very exciting things going on at AllDone, and again with that comes change. Which has encouraged me to take a well needed inventory of some of the changes I need to make in my life. So on a more personal note, I hope you will join me in taking a look at the positive aspects of change, so we as a team can be ready to embrace all the wonderful things to come.

She accompanied this message with an excerpt from an online article about how "change, discovering new things, doing things differently is one of the keys to a health [*sic*] brain and also helps fight Dementia and even Alzheimer's." In Carol's telling, contractors' ability to embrace change, rather than fear it, would supposedly contribute to the company's success while also sharpening workers' minds and improving their health.

Yet, in an acknowledgment of the stress that continual change placed on her workers, Carol frequently took on experiments or difficult projects herself rather than delegating them to team members. This strategy was distilled in one of Carol's managerial mantras, which she had picked up from Carter: Keep the team "clueless and happy." Carol felt that she could stabilize contractors' morale by minimizing their exposure to the organizational dynamism that was a product of AllDone's pursuit of venture capital funding. During a phone meeting, Carol told me that "I share only what's pertinent to their job right now. If I share too much, they can get nervous, like, 'Ooh, what's going on?' It can be upsetting because it's change, and some people don't do well with change." Protecting her charges from discomfort, however, left Carol with less time for her duties as a manager, perpetuating the team's habitual disorganization.

An unintended consequence of Carol's propensity to shield team members from change was that contractors sometimes operated in an information vacuum, hampering their job performance in ways that made their work more stressful. During visits to Las Vegas I found that some team members were unable to answer many callers' questions because they lacked an adequate understanding of AllDone's operations. I observed instances in which support agents could not explain basic information about the platform, including the purpose of some of AllDone's webpages and how long buyers should expect to wait for quotes from sellers. The team's work-from-home structure only exacerbated the problem. "When we work remotely," Nancy told me, "we can't walk over to a [colleague's] desk and say, 'this is funny'" after discovering something that seems amiss. "We don't know what's going on." Contractors struggled to understand whether the issues they experienced with the company's technology were caused by bugs in the software or their own confusion about the workings of AllDone's systems. And given that Carol, too, lacked computer savvy, flawed work processes could long remain uncorrected, with workers untrained in how to approach important procedures.

Given the constant experimentation, the lack of communication, and their prior employment histories, phone agents sometimes speculated about whether the company was actually trying out ways to replace them. For example, when Carol asked Tanya to stop working on the experimental task of calling buyers to solicit reviews of their experiences with AllDone sellers, Tanya told Carol she was afraid that this was a signal that her contract would be terminated. "I can't afford to lose my job," Tanya wrote to Carol in an e-mail, "I can't emphasize that enough." Another time, when executives briefly experimented with reviving ADP's defunct phone team to relieve some of the pressure on ADLV, some phone agents became convinced that their jobs would be outsourced to the Philippines. Carol told me that Sharon was "freaked out" and worried that the purpose of my upcoming visit to Las Vegas was 'to make some big announcement that phone support is going to the Philippines and they'll all lose their jobs.' In contrast with AllDone's Filipino contractors, who were told by executives that the company hoped to employ them "for years," Las Vegas–based phone agents openly expressed feelings of insecurity about their place in a fast-changing organization.[23]

In contrast with AllDone Philippines, the "backstage" of AllDone Las Vegas's organizational culture was more visible to managers in San Francisco. Veronica, ADP's general manager, told me that she tried to shield executives from her team's personnel problems. Carol appeared to be somewhat more forthcoming with the issues she faced as ADLV's team leader. Yet ADLV contractors also seemed far more willing to communicate their discontent directly to managers.

Two months into my work with the phone support team, a contractor openly voiced her dissatisfaction with relations between ADLV and ADSF. Tanya sent Carol an e-mail that read, in part:

> I'm a bit annoyed also when I saw on AllDone website under jobs, yeah, they in SF get benefits, they get paid vacation, 401k, and it's insulting at the bottom where it says perks, "Love, inspiration and emoticons from our remote teams in the Philippines and Las Vegas."
>
> What does Las Vegas get?

The contrast in how the two teams' labor was valued by the firm bothered Tanya. The publicity materials that AllDone developed to present an image of a successful, employee-friendly firm to people and institutions in Silicon Valley—including potential investors, technical recruits, and the tech press—underscored the disparities between working conditions in San Francisco and Las Vegas. Members of Team Las Vegas were told that they were AllDoners, yet, when it came to wages and benefits, they found themselves on the outside looking in.

For Tanya, the language of "perks" also rankled. As part of the "onboarding" process for new hires in San Francisco, Chloe, ADSF's office manager, would notify members of ADP and ADLV of the new employee's arrival with the expectation that members of the remote teams would show some "AllDone Love" by e-mailing him or her emoticon-laden welcome messages. The job posting confirmed Tanya's sense that, whatever kind of "love" AllDone Love was, it was short of reciprocal. Tanya's contract was soon terminated after she sent multiple angry and aggressive e-mails to Carol and other members of ADLV, at which point she sent me and Carter an e-mail that ended, "So much for love," referring to what she saw as our betrayal of ADLV's "family" values.[24]

Carol assured me that I should write Tanya off as a mentally ill deviant whose sentiments were not shared by others on the team. Yet, in spite of Carol's efforts to project an image of ADLV as a happy and grateful team to leaders in San Francisco, ADSF managers were far more cognizant of grievances emerging from Las Vegas than from workers in the Philippines, who did not publicly make claims on ADSF employees' time, challenge their expertise, or express disappointment with management's failure to meet their needs. From their position in the national periphery, ADLV workers were closer to core workers in San Francisco than to workers in the Philippines in terms of both geographic and social distance, rendering the structural inequalities between each team more salient.

· · · · ·

The experiences of AllDone's phone support agents reveal the consequences of "moving fast and breaking things" for frontline workers situated between software developers and their customers. Like AllDone's users, phone agents struggled to navigate the chaos that came with the company's efforts to achieve scale at all costs. While members of ADSF could treat dissatisfied customers as abstract data points represented in the company's performance metrics, phone agents in Las Vegas spent their days fielding calls from the actual people who used, and had strong emotional responses to, AllDone's product.

Owing to their structural position within the firm, AllDone's Las Vegas–based phone agents bore the social costs of organizational change far more acutely than did their colleagues in San Francisco and the Philippines. Executives delegated the company's relational work with its customers to ADLV, but these isolated, poorly paid, and inadequately trained workers struggled to keep up with a fast-changing product while simultaneously managing users' discomfort and displeasure with change. Members of ADLV were on the front lines of sustaining users' belief in the company, or their faith that the metaphorical airplane that was still being built in mid-air could actually fly. Both phone agents and the sellers they served paid the price for the speculative logics of finance capital that drove AllDone's corporate strategy—both were frustrated to discover that their everyday lives and livelihoods were in effect someone else's "experiment."

In the conversation that opens chapter 5, Carter remarked that "middle-aged women are what make AllDone work." But it was middle-aged male investors and young male founders and employees who stood to bene-fit most from the labor of middle-aged women. Executives acknowledged that, without the efforts of ADLV, AllDone's strategic pivot—and the in-vestment capital that followed—would likely have been impossible to achieve. Yet, at the same time, ADLV's female workforce was consistently devalued by managers even as the company described their employment relationship in the language of AllDone Love. AllDone devoted consider-able resources to recruiting, compensating, and entertaining its workforce in San Francisco, but executives balked at providing basic benefits or a liv-ing wage for its Las Vegas–based call team.

Like members of AllDone San Francisco, contractors in Las Vegas were told that the ideal worker eagerly embraces risk and change in a fast-moving and flexible work environment; yet, unlike their counterparts in San Francisco, phone agents stood little chance of reaping the rewards. ADLV contractors, for their part, expressed both gratitude for their jobs and displeasure with certain aspects of their work and their treatment by management. A frontstage culture of familial love rang hollow to workers struggling to make ends meet at the same time that they were being asked to manage the increasingly difficult conversations with customers that re-sulted from VC's push for continual expansion and experimentation. Con-tractors were ready to love AllDone, and were frustrated when it seemed not to love them back.

By shepherding sellers through the transition to the new payment model, the team in Las Vegas unlocked a new stage of growth for All-Done. Their very success, however, set in motion a chain of events that ul-timately revealed the fragility of their connection to the company.

PART IV   When a Startup Grows Up

7 Growing Pains

At around 10 p.m. one night, Peter, AllDone's CEO, sends an e-mail informing the staff in San Francisco that the company will be receiving an offer for its second round of funding from Goalpost, one of the most prestigious venture firms in the world. When I arrive at the office the next morning, the excitement is palpable.

Josh, AllDone's product manager, walks by Martin, a cofounder, and startles me by bellowing out a loud "WOOOOO!" As he makes his way back toward his desk, he begins to explain to Antonio, a new product design hire, how VC valuations work. Josh is elated, his face lit up with wide eyes and a big grin. Then Michel, another new design hire, arrives and Josh immediately prompts him to guess the terms of the offer.

A real buzz is starting to build. Josh stands by his desk and cries out, "Does everyone understand how this works?" A circle quickly forms around him. Martin, along with software engineers Brett and Bill, join him in a discussion about term sheets, which stipulate the conditions of a VC's investment. "This is a big day," Martin says. "Remember last year?" he asks, referring to AllDone's first VC fundraise. "Every new meeting [with a VC] was [on] a lower and lower traffic day, lower and lower request day." Yesterday, he says, AllDone reached record highs for visitors to the website and buyer requests.

I hear a loud laugh and turn around to see what's going on—cofounders Carter and Peter, along with AllDone's lead software engineer, Adam, are back from a meeting at the Goalpost office. They immediately start passing the term sheet around the office so everyone can see it. Peter says that the best startups compete for the best deals, and the very best startups *get* the best deals. He adds that a prominent business publication puts out a list of the VC firms that are most successful at bringing startups to IPO, and Goalpost is ranked number one. A circle is forming around Josh's desk again. Carter recounts how during the meeting, someone at Goalpost told them, "Not to sound elitist, but we see ten thousand companies a year and invest in twelve of them."

The buzz dies down after a while and folks slowly drift back to their desks. But soon Josh and Martin return from a trip outside carrying shopping bags brimming with tall, novelty plastic cowboy hats and striped "cat-in-the-hat" style top hats, stick-on moustaches, and plastic bead necklaces. They saunter around the office smiling, laughing, and handing out beads to everyone. Martin puts some energetic pop music on the office speakers. Then Martin, Carter, and Peter retreat to the small conference room.

When they emerge, a brief moment of chaos ensues: Martin runs up to a row of desks and starts spraying silly string around two software engineers, Bill and Sam, who cry out in surprise and then laugh as they throw their hands in front of their faces to protect themselves. Meanwhile, Carter is running around the office dumping confetti on people's heads. When the dust settles, Chloe, the office manager, is pouring champagne into small plastic cups and passing them around. Everyone is standing up now and gathering in a circle near the kitchen. Adam raises his glass for a toast: "Everyone here had a part in this," he says. "Our horizons have shifted—this is the biggest shift in the history of the company."

· · · · ·

This moment is the dream of every Silicon Valley entrepreneur: Their small, scrappy startup had grown from an idea into a business so promising that it earned the validation of an elite venture capital firm. But what comes after the celebration? What happens when a startup starts to grow up?

Theories of entrepreneurship hold that flexible modes of organization are best suited to handle the ambiguity and uncertainty that mark the earliest stages of a firm's development. VC investors tend to push for the most aggressive strategies and riskiest innovations during this period. Personnel policies, procedures, and reporting relations tend to remain relatively informal, and managers favor employees with generalist skill sets. Leaders forego long-term planning as they react to immediate activity in the market.[1]

Over time, however, the managerial practices that support entrepreneurial firms' initial stages of growth give rise to new problems. Once startups have demonstrated that their product is viable, and that a market for that product exists, uncertainty is reduced and production ramps up. Inefficiencies become more costly, informal communication channels become inadequate for coordinating the activities of a growing workforce, and the infusion of capital requires more formalized accounting procedures and more systematic attempts to engage in longer-term strategic planning. Startups in this situation face *organizational drag*, as the structure of the firm limits their ability to meet new investors' expectations. At AllDone, executives responded to this challenge by hiring more experienced leaders to undertake the *managerial work* of building and bolstering bureaucratic routines, systems, and work standards to prepare the organization for a new stage of growth and its escalating potential for profitability.

Venture capital investors help enterprises accelerate processes of professionalization and formalization, aiming both to support a startup's ability to reach growth targets as it continues to develop, and also to build perceptions of the firm's legitimacy in capital markets.[2] In other words, for an enterprise to take its place among the rarified ranks of the "unicorns" (startups valued at over $1 billion), it must shed many of the practices that helped it grow from an idea into a viable business to ensure that it can reliably deliver its product at scale. Leaders develop more bureaucratic routines and procedures, hierarchical communication and coordination systems, and mechanisms for monitoring and controlling employee effort. A firm's division of labor typically expands, with more defined roles taking shape within a more formally delineated organizational structure.

In this chapter, I show how AllDone's second round of VC funding entailed not only an influx of cash, but also new expectations for how the firm would be managed as it faced both exogenous pressures from its new venture capital investor and endogenous challenges associated with growth. Leaders' response to the problem of organizational drag reoriented the company's relationship to its remote workforces, produced increasingly specialized work roles, and elevated new hires with domain-specific expertise and academic or professional backgrounds in business administration to the managerial ranks. At AllDone, workers' ties to one another, feelings of organizational attachment, and subjective experiences of work changed in response to the *culture of rationalization* that accompanied organizational change.

When companies are restructured, workplace cultures may undergo dramatic shifts.[3] Like the venture capital investors whose faith in the firm generates myths and hype, startup workers' experiences of the present are colored by fantasies about what is to come. When AllDone was small, some hoped or assumed that it would always retain the qualities they venerated, while others imagined that joining a growing company "on the ground floor" would eventually transform their present circumstances into an idealized future. Yet, as the consequences of organizational growth became clearer, the imaginative space available to members of AllDone's workforce narrowed. Many found that the futures they had envisioned were in fact fantasies.

Before examining how AllDone changed following its second fundraise, we will first turn to the aspects of the organization that remained the same. Even as AllDone matured, low-wage labor remained crucial to making the venture work.

THE "MAGIC" REMAINS

Following the transition to the new payment model, AllDone's revenue figures had begun to climb steadily. Although the enterprise hadn't quite achieved its goal of taking in as much money as it was spending, its progress was substantial, and AllDone once again appeared to be headed in the right direction. As Adam, AllDone's director of engineering, would later put it, "It's important to have a story for Series B," referring to a start-up's second round of VC investment. AllDone's story was summarized by a simple line graph: since the transition to coins, the revenue arrow was pointing up and to the right, and executives could persuasively argue that, with the new system now securely in place, this trend was bound to con-tinue. Adam recalled sensing the energy that AllDone's story generated in VC offices when executives made their pitch: 'We had a new business model. We were ready to pop. Investors ate it up.' One afternoon, the exec-utive team took three meetings with VC firms; by early the next morning, they had e-mailed the staff in San Francisco to announce that they'd al-ready received two offers, including the one from Goalpost.

There was widespread agreement among leaders in San Francisco that AllDone's remote teams in the Philippines and Las Vegas had played a cru-cial role in achieving this important milestone. After the deal was reached, Peter, AllDone's CEO, reported that investors had been impressed by All-Done's "efficiency." He said the company had become known as the only startup in its market that had figured out how to acquire a high volume of sellers without hiring a costly sales team. AllDone's seller acquisition strategy had been enabled by a combination of software and human infra-structure. Members of AllDone Philippines helped the company identify potential sellers to contact by rating the results produced by a machine-learning algorithm designed to "crawl" the web to find service providers. The "training data," or feedback they provided, helped to improve the al-gorithm's accuracy. According to Adam, this method had allowed AllDone to attract new sellers at 1 percent of the cost that a competitor had spent on its sales staff. It was clear to AllDone executives that AllDone Las Vegas, too, had made the Series B round possible. The successful transition to the new payment model, facilitated by ADLV's relational work, allowed AllDone to meet investors' expectations by demonstrating the company's capacity for continued revenue growth.

When executives had practiced their presentation pitching AllDone to VCs in the office, Carter had called AllDone's use of remote, work-from-home teams "unmatched" by other startups. He claimed that they could scale their teams up to meet new corporate needs at a moment's notice. 'If I came up with a project today, I know I'd have a workforce ready to roll on it next week,' he stated confidently, in keeping with

AllDone's history of deploying low-wage workers to support the company's experiments.

The Las Vegas-based phone agents played an additional role that Carter and other ADSF managers were less eager to discuss. As potential investors were testing out AllDone by placing requests for services, ADLV's phone agents had secretly been responsible for shepherding their "VIP requests" through the system. San Francisco–based software engineers set up a process that flagged user names and e-mail domains that might be associated with potential funders; when these people placed a request on AllDone, it would be forwarded to phone agents in Las Vegas, who would place calls to relevant sellers and encourage them to promptly submit quotes.[4] Augmenting AllDone's matching system with relational work allowed the company to discreetly offer VCs a better experience, enhancing their perceptions of the organization's competence and potential. The remote teams thus played an integral role in the company's ability to secure its Series B funding.

With a second round of funding in the bank, however, the fate of All-Done's remote teams was not immediately clear. The company was now able to expand its cadre of software developers. Although the engineers continued to create new product features, they also began to automate processes that had previously been performed by workers. Members of the organization were forced to confront the possibility that software engineers' efforts could cost scores of Filipino contractors their jobs. Developers were making significant progress toward automating the labor-intensive processes of vetting buyer requests and manually matching requests with All-Done sellers. Executives believed that their efforts would soon eliminate most of the hundred-person unit in the Philippines that performed these tasks: according to an e-mail from Carter, AllDone's president, to Veronica, ADP's general manager, "We should expect for most of the team to be automated (90 percent)."[5] Carter asked Ross, the leader of ADP's matching team, to create detailed plans to prepare for this eventuality. Hoping to cushion the blow of the anticipated layoffs, AllDone's cofounders reached out to executives at other startups in search of a company that might "adopt" the terminated workforce for its own purposes.

ADSF engineers formulated plans to automate other ADP functions as well, including running background checks on sellers and sending follow-up e-mails to apologize to buyers who did not receive any quotes from sellers. At the same time, they began to create systems that would offload some of ADP's labor onto users, such as the process of categorizing sellers in the AllDone database. In an e-mail to AllDone Philippines' four deputy managers, Carter explained the plans and expressed his grief in preparing to terminate so many team members' employment:

> This is not a fun process but I'm committed to having us doing this as effectively and as lovingly as possible. I love our team members more than anything and I want us to do everything we can to keep them on ADP if possible, and if we can't then to let them go in the most loving and respectful way we can.

Yet, to the surprise of executives and managers, even as AllDone's engineering team grew and increased its pace of automation, the company continued to rely on its remote workforce to support and supplement its software. During the lengthy process of teaching, testing, and refining new algorithms, the volume of buyer requests continued to grow, keeping the matching team occupied even though the percentage of matches that they handled was dwindling. By the time automation was complete, ADSF's product team had found new tasks for most of the displaced workers.

The "magic" behind AllDone endured because, with considerable financial resources at their disposal following Goalpost's $12.5 million investment, AllDone's leaders combined the company's two prior strategic priorities: growing the user base and increasing revenue. As in the months following AllDone's first fundraise, managers would prioritize building the company by hiring more software developers while simultaneously increasing key user metrics by bringing more buyers and sellers onto the platform. This time, however, expansion would occur within the revenue generation framework that had been established with the transition to AllDone's new payment model. The dual goals of expansion and revenue generation existed in tension with one another. On the one hand, AllDone sought to draw more users to the platform and convert them into active, paying customers. On the other hand, the company's attempts to monetize their activities could spur user dissatisfaction and exit. As the firm grew, AllDone continued to confront valuation lag, or the temporal gap between investment and the realization of returns; technical drag, or the gulf between software designers' vision and the limitations of algorithmic systems and organizational resources; and trust drag, or users' dissatisfaction with the company's ever-changing software systems. Under the conditions of venture capitalism, which spurred rising customer demand and perpetual flux in the platform's features and policies, these drags did not disappear, nor were they permanently "solved" as AllDone acquired additional resources.[6]

It was now clear to AllDone's founders, and its investors, that computational work and relational work would remain crucial elements of AllDone's operations for the foreseeable future. The question, then, was how best to organize it. At the behest of their new backers, AllDone's leaders set in motion rationalization processes that would fundamentally alter the outlooks and experiences of its workforce. Although members of each team expressed feelings of disappointment, loss, and even betrayal amid the firm's reorganization, workers' structural position within the firm determined how dramatically they were affected by the company's evolution. Phone support agents in Las Vegas remained the most vulnerable to organizational change—over the course of a year, the team's management and procedures were revamped before team members' jobs were eliminated, replaced by a much larger and more professionalized operation in Salt Lake City. After devoting years of her life to the company, the leader of AllDone Philippines also discovered that there was no longer a place for her in the organization, leaving her embittered by what she perceived to be the company's violation of an implicit bargain of mutual commitment and familial love. Venture capitalism created massive rewards for those sitting atop the organizational hierarchy while rendering some below newly disposable, revealing the ephemerality of the arrangements and understandings that had come before.

OVERHAULING THE ORG CHART

AllDone San Francisco's leaders told staffers that, with the support of a VC firm like Goalpost, the outlook for a highly profitable "exit" had improved dramatically. AllDone's first funder had been an investor of relatively modest reputation, whose offer the cofounders accepted after having been turned down by over forty others. Goalpost, on the other hand, had provided early funding to some of the biggest and most successful companies in tech. As Adam explained to attendees of a meeting the afternoon Goalpost extended their offer, top VCs 'don't want you to sell for $100 million. They don't give a shit about that and they won't encourage any thinking about that. They want an IPO.' In another meeting, Josh, the product manager, called the offer 'as good an indicator as any that AllDone has traction,' while Carter relayed that, 'according to Goalpost, we're in the top 1 percent of their entire portfolio in terms of our ability to execute. So they have a lot of confidence in us.'

After the deal was finalized, Carter e-mailed the staff in San Francisco:

> Six weeks ago we weren't thinking about raising money or anything other than our $350k [monthly revenue] goal and what A/B test might get us there. And today we have *the* best investor in Silicon Valley behind us, [and] another $12.5mm in the bank.

> I remember when we first started AllDone someone asked me "what do you think the chances are that AllDone becomes a billion dollar company?" I responded "maybe 1%?" That was generous. We had no product, no team, no momentum, nothing.

> If someone asked me that question today, I would say "certainly far from certain . . . but we've got a really damn good shot."

As Adam pointed out to colleagues in an e-mail, "Once your company gets to a certain size where people like Goalpost have invested . . . they really do a lot of things in their power to help you succeed." Goalpost's investment thus represented validation that AllDone had taken an important step toward joining the pantheon of tech giants.

Employees soon discovered that taking this step would require them to change the fabric of the organization. A comparison of AllDone San Francisco's hiring practices following its Series A and Series B fundraises illustrates the increasing salience of organizational drag and managerial work for the company's executives. Just as they had done after securing the company's first round of VC funding, AllDone's leaders again planned to quickly increase the size of the staff in San Francisco by 250 percent—this time from twenty to fifty employees. (During the previous hiring spree, the headcount had grown from eight to twenty.)

Following the Series A investment, executives had sought "smart" and resourceful talent to fill nontechnical roles—people who could be trusted to take on a broad range of unanticipated issues and quickly find workable solutions.[7] Paul and Brandon, both friends of AllDone cofounders, had been invited to join the marketing department. Both took on roles that were largely unrelated to their previous work experience, and both held elite credentials: Paul had just completed a JD at an Ivy League institution, and Brandon came from the world of Washington, D.C., politics.[8] I, too, began my position as director of customer support and operations manager with some prior managerial experience, but no expertise in those areas. When Carter had offered me the job, he asked if I had any concerns. I told him that my main concern was that I had no background in customer support. Carter was nonplussed. 'It doesn't matter if you're not great at customer support,' he told me, explaining that Martin, another of AllDone's cofounders who was currently heading e-mail support, 'gets so angry when he's e-mailing users! What's important is that you're a good manager.' Like Paul and Brandon, what I had possessed was the cofounders' trust; they believed that I was a hardworking thinker who could scale up solutions to a diverse array of problems.[9]

The hiring strategy that followed the Series B round reflected a new set of assumptions pertaining to organizing for a new, more mature, stage of growth. After the funding was secured, AllDone executives began to meet regularly with Tom, AllDone's lead advisor at Goalpost, who had assumed a seat on AllDone's board of directors. Carter shared notes with the ADSF team from the first such meeting, which covered what Tom said were "the things that we tell every Goalpost company to expect" after receiving a Series B round.

The first section of his notes expounded on how AllDone San Francisco's growth would affect its organizational structure. Tom emphasized that employees should prepare to operate within an expanded division of labor that would increasingly be directed by individuals with specialized expertise. Broad organizational roles would become more focused. Tom advised that current employees should grow accustomed to "delegating" decisions that they had previously had a hand in making, and should also "com[e] to terms with the fact that as we grow it's impossible for us each to know exactly what is happening in all parts of the organization," as staffers had learned to expect when the company was smaller. For AllDone to have a shot at becoming the next Amazon, each employee would have to accept a smaller role within a larger organizational structure.

Second, as the company grew, "senior hires" whose "pay ranges are bigger" would in some cases be inserted toward the top of the burgeoning organizational hierarchy.

> It's always better to promote internally if possible. But we will certainly have to promote externally as well and over the next year we should expect to bring in new team members who are sometimes above us, sometimes next to us, sometimes below us.

Not only would ADSF employees have to accept narrower roles, but some would also find that they had new bosses with little prior knowledge of how things worked at AllDone. Because AllDone would be competing with other tech companies for top specialists, Tom recommended that the company hire a public relations firm for "help with building your profile within the tech / business community and [to] drive exposure for recruiting purposes. [You] need to think about what potential candidates will be most impressed by." Goalpost would lend its connections and cachet, as well as its capital, to help AllDone compete for experienced professionals who could shepherd the firm toward a potential IPO. These changes to AllDone's organizational structure, Tom emphasized, were not temporary, but would remain in effect throughout the company's subsequent development: "This transition will continue forever as we grow to 50, and then 100, and then 1000."

Soon after the new funding was announced, I informed Carter that, as we had originally planned, I would be leaving AllDone in less than four months to return to my PhD program full-time. As noted above, less than a year earlier, I had entered my position as director of customer support and operations manager with a generalist's skill set. Now, Carter sought my help in finding and selecting my replacement. This time, however, he aimed to bring in a specialist who would bring considerable managerial and domain-specific expertise to an expanded role directing the entirety of AllDone's distributed operations in the Philippines and Las Vegas.

Carter enlisted professional recruiters to locate candidates with prior experience in growing large customer support teams. In interviews, Carter and I asked applicants to demonstrate their expertise by telling us about how long they'd worked in the industry, how many team members they had managed, which support "channels" they had been in charge of (e.g., e-mail, phone, live chat), which employee performance metrics they felt were most important to track, and how they would approach conceiving of and launching AllDone's live chat channel. Dana, who was hired to replace me, had previously led operations for another tech startup; before that, she had completed an MBA and then worked at a prestigious global management consulting firm. As AllDone's new "director of people operations," Dana took over day-to-day control of the company's vast remote workforce, assuming my roles as well as Carter's duties overseeing AllDone Philippines.

Other ADSF employees began to take on increasingly specialized domains in an expanded division of labor and thickening organizational hierarchy. Within a year after I left the company, the team had more than doubled in size and moved into a luxurious four-story loft office featuring large windows, reclaimed hardwood floors, and an expanding array of perks to please a growing workforce. A year and a half after that, AllDone employed fifty software engineers who were divided into specialized teams, and within less than a year that number had doubled. Three-and-a-half years after I left the field, AllDone San Francisco totaled about 275 employees, with the workforce having become far more gender-balanced and racially diverse than it had been during my tenure.

In the Philippines, too, the new infusion of VC funding spurred a process of professionalization. Eight months after Dana took over as AllDone's head of operations, she and Carter moved AllDone Philippines' general manager, Veronica—ADP's first contractor, who had led the team since its inception nearly five years earlier—into a newly created position as ADP's "director of culture." ADP received a new executive general manager named Bin, who held an MBA and had prior experience helping American companies establish and improve business process outsourcing operations in the Philippines. A year after my departure, ADP had grown from 200 to more than 450 contractors, expanding in another year to about 800. Six hundred were in a subgroup responsible for writing keyword-rich text to boost AllDone's standing in search engines; when that group was halved, the Filipino workforce dropped back to around 450.

Consistent with the priorities advocated by Goalpost, Dana and Bin worked to further rationalize and professionalize ADP by creating new processes aimed at boosting efficiency. First, they increased the division of labor within each of ADP's departments and oversaw the development of a skill-based progression program that allowed ADP staffers to move between departments, thus reducing tedium and expanding career ladders. Second, they increased the number of in-person meetings for workers in the Philippines and added special training sessions for team leaders. The nature of in-person meetings changed as well: gatherings were now geared toward work-related topics and sharing information about the business with team members, rather than simply consisting of morale-boosting festivities. Bin also instituted new procedures for ADP's department leaders. Previously, managers had set their own schedules; now, they were required to be online and available to team members at prespecified times. Finally, Dana and Bin also revamped how ADP recorded, tracked, and assessed contractors' performance metrics.

The consequences of professionalization were more dramatic in Las Vegas, a site of perpetual frustration for managers and workers alike. During the transition to AllDone's new payment model, Carter and I had begun (at his behest) to seek a new co-team leader for AllDone Las Vegas who would share that role with Carol. Carol would continue to handle the "soft" aspects of the job at which she excelled—building camaraderie, sharing her insights into managing users' feelings, and handling what she often called "drama," or the emotions of team members. The new hire would, I came to realize, take on the job that I had been tasked with as director of customer support, but had failed to fully implement from afar amid the chaos of ADLV's evolving systems and escalating workload: rationalizing operations in Las Vegas.

After the transition to the coins model was completed, Carter selected Mike, an enthusiastic man in his late twenties who had previously worked at Zappos (which was headquartered in the Las Vegas area), to become ADLV's "data person." Mike's projects would include developing metrics to assess business needs (e.g., categorizing the reasons users were calling), tracking team member performance, building training and coaching programs, expanding ADLV's division of labor, and identifying and remedying inefficiencies (e.g., shortening call times and better allocating worker schedules to match customer demand). However, he made little headway on these tasks before Dana was hired a few months later and set about re-organizing the team's operations.

Once Dana joined ADSF, she began to centralize authority over cus-tomer support (now renamed "customer operations") in the San Francisco office. Within months, Dana was overseeing a staff of eight customer opera-tions specialists in San Francisco, who took charge of a variety of tasks pre-viously handled by Carol and Mike, such as training new ADLV hires. Dana also introduced procedures designed to improve the execution and assess-ment of new projects, including a checklist detailing the processes to be fol-lowed before and after what had previously been ad hoc product launches. ADLV's success in introducing sellers to AllDone's new payment model had convinced executives of the value of workers who could build and bolster users' trust in the company. But while ADLV's performance may have been good enough for the cofounders—generalists with no prior experience in customer support—Dana was dismayed by the team she was handed.

As AllDone acquired a third round of venture capital funding ($30 million) less than a year after my exit, Dana reorganized the company's call center operations. Instead of expanding and training its small, work-from-home team in the Las Vegas area—which even some inexperienced managers had long viewed as dysfunctional, if productive enough—the Las Vegas team was terminated. Its functions were transplanted to a well-appointed office near Salt Lake City, where AllDone brought on an ex-isting, experienced phone support team just as it was being laid off by another startup following its acquisition by a competitor.

AllDone Salt Lake's managers organized a more highly trained staff that operated in a more expansive division of labor and received more rigorous oversight and guidance than had ADLV. When the team was launched, customer support agents were hired as full-time employees making $12 to $16 per hour, and received benefits, including health in-surance and paid parental leave. Eventually they were also offered perks like free snacks and lunches. Reflecting the importance of relational work to the tech company's future, the new phone team quickly grew to over one hundred employees, and eventually totaled around seven hundred. Although the composition of the phone support team had changed, many of its functions remained similar to those that ADLV had handled: phone agents would educate users about the product, repair relationships with disgruntled users, and work to preserve users' trust in AllDone amid ADSF's continual experimentation with the rules and software systems that structured market activity.

Across all three of AllDone's work teams, the company's acquisition of a second round of venture capital funding triggered significant and enduring changes in the structure of the organization. How, then, did AllDoners respond to these changes?

CULTURES OF RATIONALIZATION

As AllDone rationalized operations across its three teams, workers' affective ties to the organization began to change. On each team, friction arose between the new leaders who were brought in to advance the agenda for growth established by Goalpost, and the longer-tenured employees who resented or resisted their efforts. Executives attempted to transform cultural practices and labor processes to which workers had become accustomed, and people across all three work teams reported feelings of disenchantment with—and even betrayal by—a growing company that was taking on an increasingly "corporate" mien. In San Francisco, the Philippines, and Las Vegas, employees and contractors alike decried shifting company values, inequities in compensation, and the diminishment of the autonomy and sense of community they had previously enjoyed on the job.

When I spoke with former colleagues from AllDone's San Francisco office following my departure from the field, many expressed dissatisfaction as corporate routines and structures evolved to accommodate a larger and more complex operation.[10] Some long-standing employees worried that newcomers were eroding the organization's values. Over brunch at a Vietnamese restaurant in downtown Oakland, Chloe, the office manager, bemoaned the lack of "diversity of opinion" in the office as a slew of "one-percenters"—MBAs with previous experience in management consulting—were hired.

Differences between team members also became more salient as some began to exercise their stock options and sell equity to AllDone's new venture capital investors, revealing vast inequalities in employees' grants. Within a year of my departure from the field, AllDone had already raised two additional funding rounds, adding $130 million to its coffers at a valuation of $650 million. Employees began to watch as AllDone's founders and some of the early hires alongside whom they worked sold portions of their equity to the new investors and became millionaires.

Chloe was upset to find that her stock 'isn't worth anything.' When I caught up with her one night over dinner at a restaurant near the office, we determined that, although she was hired before I had become a full-time employee, her stock-option grant had been one-fifth the size of mine. Chloe concluded that AllDone's executives 'will get away with whatever they can,' offering as little equity as possible to employees. Brett, a software engineer, also told me over dinner that 'I'm kind of pissed knowing how little stock I was given now that some people are making a ton [of money by selling theirs]. I get that that's how it works, but still. I don't like how opaque it is.' Now that owners of equity were able to "cash in" their shares, employees who had harbored the fantasy that AllDone's ascent would yield life-altering wealth discovered that their ability to capture a slice of the returns produced by their labor was far more limited than they had imagined.

In their everyday work lives, ADSF employees experienced an array of growing pains common to maturing organizations. When AllDone was a smaller company, employees had viewed the office as an open environment that fostered the exchange of ideas. Two years after my departure, Sam, an ADSF software engineer, told me how quarterly review meetings had changed. In the beginning, quarterly reviews were highly anticipated events that brought team members together to discuss the company's progress and debate its strategic direction. Now, Sam explained, AllDone livestreamed the presentations, which employees could either attend in person or watch online from wherever they preferred to be. He remarked that he had viewed the last quarterly review from his desk upstairs in the office—if he wasn't actively participating, he saw no reason to sit in a crowded room behind people who might obscure his view. "It's a tight ship," he said—there was no longer time allocated for employees to ask questions of the presenters. "We're a big company now." Whereas in the past quarterly review meetings had provided ADSF staffers with an energizing collective ritual, Sam described a noninteractive experience that he could passively observe from his desk.

During my stint at AllDone, the entire team had gathered around a communal lunch table every day for meals and conversation. Now, Brett told me, "people don't really hang downstairs" where lunch was served, with most choosing instead to take food back to their desks. Brett was becoming frustrated with the proliferation of meetings he was asked to attend, which sometimes stretched well into the evening. As the team expanded rapidly, members of the old guard had to adjust to not knowing the names of many of their colleagues or what members of other departments were working on. At the same time, an increase in voluntary turnover—which had been virtually nonexistent during my tenure with the company—meant the loss of old friends and familiar faces.

Many found that the passion they had previously felt for the company and for their jobs was waning. Some who had previously experienced far more autonomy now complained that executives were exerting unwelcome influence over their projects. One evening I met another software engineer, Vince, at a pub and caught up on how our lives had changed since I left AllDone:

> I tell Vince how all-consuming life as a grad student can be, how it feels like there's always something else I should be working on. I ask if that's what it was like to work for AllDone in the early days.
>
> Vince says, 'Yeah, at the beginning we didn't even think it would work, but we were all throwing ourselves into it. But as AllDone gets bigger, different people want different things out of it, and it wants different things out of you.' Now he has to do work that doesn't interest him as much, and he's also responsible for managing other people, which he doesn't enjoy. His work for AllDone is "no longer an obsession."

Vince's story is a classic tale of bureaucratization and disenchantment. AllDone's early employees had reveled in the thrill that came with seeing their hard work change the trajectory of the product and the organization and, potentially, their fortunes. But as the firm grew, they found that All-Done was becoming an entity that was increasingly independent of, and exerting control over, the people who had created it.[11]

WHERE'S THE LOVE?

Like their counterparts in San Francisco, the events following AllDone's second round of VC funding unsettled off-site contractors' relationships with each other and with the company. Dana, in particular, who brought in what Carter referred to as a "super-aggressive" management style, seemed to have little patience for ADP's and ADLV's sentiment-laden organizational cultures. Members of ADP told me that AllDone had begun to feel less like a "family" and more like just another job in the Philippines' booming business process outsourcing industry. Less than a year after I left the field, I spent an afternoon catching up with David, Rebecca, and Natalia—ADP managers with whom I had worked closely—during their first visit to the United States. Almost immediately, the three began to discuss their recent meetings at the ADSF office with Dana and Ken, the leader of the new team in the Salt Lake City area. Rebecca turned to me to explain, her brows furrowing as her face took on a look of concern:

> Ken came in talking about how "we're a sports team, not a family." This didn't sit well with the crew from ADP: 'We've been at AllDone for a long time, and it's always been like a family for us,' Rebecca says, adding that after the meeting she took one of Dana's new ADSF hires aside and told her that 'It's important to maintain the culture.'

For years, Carter had told ADP staffers that the most important thing they could do for the company was to nurture and protect the culture of All-Done Love as the firm grew. Now, ADP team leaders felt that new managers who did not understand the value of their team's culture were trying to "standardize everything" across AllDone's three teams, eroding the qualities that had made ADP feel special.

Two years later I spoke with Jasmine, an ADP associate manager, over Skype. I asked Jasmine how things were going at AllDone and whether the company had changed in the years since I had worked there.

J: We did a big shakeup since the days of Veronica [AllDone's previous general manager, who had been replaced by Bin]. When she left, it was horrible. Especially for those of us who started out with AllDone as something that is—for me, I started out with AllDone just so I would have something to do during home time. I started out working with Veronica, Rebecca, Ross—it [was] a hobby [laughs and smiles]. We *never* considered it as work. With the new setup it's really not the same thing.

B: Is it that there are more performance metrics now?

J: We have more accountability I guess, more change in processes and all that stuff. I think for me the hardest transition was that more new people were placed in upper management and then [we] had to do transfers [to different departments] and all that. A little bit of the old still remains, but it's more [a case of the] old culture adjusting to the new one.

B: What do you mean by that?

J: We kept telling ourselves, 'Well, AllDone is a big thing which used to be a dream. Maybe we need to grow up a bit.'

As we continued to talk, she explained how the team had become "very, very structured" as more specialized departments and job functions emerged. Among the many new employees were "more BPO [business process outsourcing]-experienced people" and new layers of upper management. In the past, working for AllDone had felt like "a hobby," and "a housewife" like Jasmine without prior experience could work her way up the ranks to become a team leader. Now, Jasmine's job with AllDone felt indistinguishable from one with any other company in the global business process outsourcing industry. Without the relational work that made Jasmine's time on the job feel like spending time with friends and family, working for ADP had become something much more mundane.[12] Contractors who had been with AllDone since the early days found that their preferred vision of the company clashed with new realities.

During a visit to the Philippines less than a year after I left AllDone, Veronica echoed these sentiments, explaining that her new supervisors now expected her to demonstrate a higher level of organizational acumen and accountability.[13] In her new role as "director of culture," Veronica had planned two dinners with team members that she invited me to join. She told me that Bin had asked for her "agenda" for the dinners. 'Carter never wanted a dinner agenda,' she told me, explaining that Carter had seen value in hosting a team get-together simply for the sake of building camaraderie. "I was spoiled by Carter," she concluded. Veronica also told me that Dana had chided her for occasionally letting important e-mails go unanswered for more than twenty-four hours, which Dana viewed as unacceptable. Dana had told her, 'We're a big company now, so we can't be as laid-back about things as we were in the past.'

As we shared a taxi following the second dinner that I attended, Veronica wistfully told me that she missed the old days when Carter and others from ADSF would visit the Philippines for team meetings and then spend an extra week or two traveling to vacation spots around the country with her and other team members. 'Now Carter comes and wears a collared shirt' to meetings, rather than the T-shirts he wore in the past, she told me. 'People aren't used to it. Jasmine said he looks different. He doesn't have time for fun now when he visits. It's all business.' Like Jasmine, Veronica noticed that Carter had backed off of the relational work that had made ADP staffers feel that they were not only his workforce, but also his friends.

ADP managers were surprised to find that their new supervisors not only eschewed the language of love, but also expected them to independently articulate matters pertaining to their departments in the language of business that had long prevailed in the San Francisco office. Rebecca, David, and Natalia described their meetings at the ADSF office: after each of the ADP leaders delivered their presentations, they told me, Ken had asked what they viewed as tough—and, to their minds, irrelevant—questions. One example of such a question was, 'How long does it take for a new recruit to become an expert?' The fact that they viewed this as an irrelevant question shows how ADP managers had grown accustomed to meetings as venues for building morale and sharing praise, rather than for developing business strategy. Indeed, during my time at AllDone, ADSF staffers had generally refrained from quizzing Veronica and Carol on the strategic implications of their teams' performance during their rare visits to the San Francisco office. The new standards of professionalism that accompanied the Series B fundraise thus drove important organizational changes that impacted team members' experiences and outlooks.

At the same time that they were grappling with significant changes in their team's organizational culture, ADP's managers were confronting the same mundane issues of corporate growth that troubled their colleagues in San Francisco. When I asked the three managers to tell me about the biggest changes in their work as ADP had more than doubled in size, Rebecca said, 'I used to personally know all my team members. Not anymore.' David, who headed e-mail support, said, 'It's become a lot more complicated, there are a lot more layers of people to go through' when consulting on decisions. Depending on what type of question he had, he might have to approach one of five different members of ADSF: one was in charge of questions about bugs in the software; another handled legal inquiries; another coordinated social media, and so on. Previously, he had sent his questions directly to the top of the chain (to me); now, he had to go through additional levels of management before he could get a question to Dana. The managers cited rigorous new performance goals, metrics, and demands that they, personally, propose improvements to their teams' workflows. In effect, Bin was instituting a speedup, insisting that ADP's workers pick up the pace on their digital assembly line. The managers seemed overwhelmed by the new demands that had arisen since AllDone had begun to mature into a later-stage startup.

With all the new money flowing into AllDone, some members of ADP—like many of their counterparts in San Francisco—increasingly questioned why they did not seem to be sharing in the wealth. During my final visit to the Philippines described above, shortly after Veronica had been moved into her new role as director of culture, team members' conversations at one of the dinners frequently shifted from English to Tagalog and back. In our taxi ride back to the hotel where I was staying, Veronica confirmed that one major component of the discussion had centered on team members' desire for the benefits that would come with being recognized as full employees rather than independent contractors, including office space where they could work when rainy weather caused internet disruptions and brownouts in their homes.

> 'Especially with all this [Series C] money—we keep telling the team that we have all these investors, and they are asking, "What does this mean for us?" I know we need engineers [in San Francisco], but I don't see why we [in the Philippines] can't have this too.'
>
> Veronica goes on to explain that there's someone who works at her co-working space who has helped lots of American companies incorporate in the Philippines, and that it would be easy for AllDone to do. I ask her what that would mean for the company. Veronica presumes that AllDone would incur additional costs in the form of taxes paid to the Philippine state, plus costs associated with providing employment benefits for workers.

As AllDone raked in VC funding and began to feel more like a typical corporation rather than a "dream" or a "family," the material gulf between Filipino contractors' circumstances and those of AllDone San Francisco became more salient. Team members increasingly asked why such a successful company refused to improve wages and conditions for its Fili-pino workers.[14]

Veronica would soon feel betrayed by the company to which she had given so much of her life as general manager for nearly five years. Soon after Dana was hired, Carter told me that Veronica had begun to resist the new arrangement by slacking off and expressing more entitlement than gratitude. During Veronica's visit to San Francisco a year after I had ended my fieldwork at AllDone, after Bin had been installed as executive general manager, I invited her to my apartment in Oakland for dinner. When I re-marked that she seemed distressed, Veronica told me that she had been having anxiety attacks and had become consumed by her fear that she would be ousted from the company. She said she had been 'sobbing most of the time.' Long ago, Martin had promised her that she would 'always have a place at AllDone.' But now, with so much change, she no longer be-lieved his assurances.

After years of service to AllDone, and after receiving countless plau-dits from executives about her importance to the company, Veronica had begun to question whether what they had said in the past mattered anymore.

> Veronica says she feels like she has no certainty about the future. 'I'm still an independent contractor after five years,' she adds. She worries that things could change for her at any moment. 'I feel like they're moving me toward the door and I'm really close, they're just waiting to make the last little push.' She says she's in the dark on a lot of things at work—people leave her out of conversations that in the past she would have been a part of. For the first time, Carter didn't come to meet her at the airport when she arrived in San Francisco for this visit. 'AllDone was my life for four and a half years,' she says. 'I gave everything else up,' including dating and television. Now she feels "abandoned" and "betrayed."

Veronica's new title, "director of culture," only exacerbated her concerns. She believed that Carter was reluctant to terminate her because he didn't want the team to find out that she was being forced out of the company, but Bin's appointment as general manager confirmed her suspicion that her work was no longer valued. Carter ultimately helped ease Veronica out of the organization while saving face publicly by encouraging her to pursue her dream of earning an MBA abroad at AllDone's expense. While

grateful for the opportunity, Veronica observed that Carter had long resisted this idea when he was more reliant on her leadership. In public
speeches, Carter would later use Veronica's story as an example of how
AllDone helped make Filipino workers' dreams come true, excluding the
fact that she left for business school only after having been forced out of
her role as general manager.

In Las Vegas, AllDone's push toward professionalization would have
even more dramatic consequences than in the Philippines. During the
year I spent working directly with AllDone Las Vegas, the nature of team
members' jobs had changed significantly. Agents were working harder
and more flexibly, handling tasks that required greater levels of skill and
that caused workers far more distress, and creating more value for All-
Done. The events surrounding AllDone's Series B round generated two
additional sources of stress and frustration for the team: a failed leadership transition and static pay, despite their more difficult workload and
AllDone's newfound wealth.[15] Amid these developments, ADLV team
members—and even team leaders—gave fuller voice to their feelings of
neglect and betrayal.

The first problem—at least in ADLV team members' telling—was Mike.
ADLV staffers told me that they had initially been suspicious of me when
I had joined the team, but that they had come to "love" me because I "listened" to them.[16] Mike was another story. Contractors complained that
he was arrogant, that he lorded his knowledge over them and imposed
rules arbitrarily. Mike may have known the Zappos way inside and out,
but some team members resented him. He seemed uninterested in learning how things worked at AllDone, and they felt that he devalued their
decades of work experience. Few of the phone agents felt a personal connection with Mike, and personal connection was the currency of the team
culture. This placed a greater burden on Carol, who struggled to support
disgruntled workers without undermining Mike's authority. I, too, found
Mike difficult to work with. He seemed to struggle to sustain focus on
tasks like analyzing spreadsheets, writing reports, or developing and implementing new processes. I leaned on Mike to research and accomplish
things that I didn't know how to do, but he was often unable to deliver. As
a lame duck on my way out the door, I felt little incentive to hold Mike's
feet to the fire.

Morale in Las Vegas soured further after AllDone secured its $12.5 million Series B funding round. To share the news with ADLV contractors, Carol and Mike gathered the team for a lunchtime celebration that stretched into the afternoon. When team members were told about the new funding, Mike told me, "they went bananas." They expected that some of the funding would be funneled into wage increases. They believed this, in part, because of Carol's recruiting pitch to new hires: "When they took this job," she once told me, "I said, 'This is the price: ten dollars an hour, and there it is. AllDone will grow and other things will come. As of now, this is what it is.'" Any time team members asked about pay increases, Carol would return to this mantra, implying that management would reevaluate their compensation when the company's financial outlook improved. The Series B investment appeared to indicate that this time had come.

The contractors' excitement quickly turned into disillusionment. Soon after the funding was announced, I began discussing the possibility of increasing ADLV's compensation with Carter. Around the same time, however, executives also received word that Tanya, a former ADLV phone agent who had been fired, had filed a complaint with the Internal Revenue Service about AllDone's employment practices. Her unemployment claim had been rejected because she had worked as an independent contractor rather than as an employee. Tanya subsequently argued that she had been misclassified—an assessment shared by AllDone's legal counsel.[17] Before AllDone could increase ADLV's wages, Carter told me, the company would first have to find a way to transition ADLV contractors to full-time employee status to comply with federal labor law.

Moving forward, ADLV team members would be classified as employees, but their employer of record would be an outside shell company rather than AllDone itself. The firm pursued this strategy to preserve the benefits differential between the phone agents and ADSF staffers: if ADLV employees were on company payroll, AllDone would be legally required to offer them the same benefits as its other full-time employees, and executives had no intention of doing so. ADLV employees were now offered the option of purchasing health benefits, albeit at a prohibitive cost. To avoid potential future legal issues, AllDone also provided back overtime pay to current employees who had worked over forty hours a week or over eight hours a day in the past. (Employees were not let in on the reasoning behind that move.)

These decisions reduced AllDone's legal liabilities, but they increased costs. AllDone now had to pay administrative fees to the shell company that was serving as ADLV team members' employer of record, and All-Done was also now responsible for paying half of employees' Social Security and Medicare taxes, which had previously been shouldered by the workers themselves when they had operated as independent contractors.

It was in this context that Carter declined to provide the phone agents their long-promised raise. For weeks, I tried to steer Carter toward dipping into the $12.5 million to bump the team's starting wage from $10 to $12, but he would often delay these conversations or brush them aside. I protested that, with mandatory tax withholding, employees' take-home pay would actually *decrease* if AllDone didn't give them a raise, which would surely anger team members. Carter proposed that I could still pitch this as a raise because employees' overall tax burden would be reduced, as they would no longer be paying self-employment taxes. None of my arguments seemed to make any difference.

I was dismayed by the situation, which highlighted the stark contrast between how workers in San Francisco and Las Vegas were valued by the company. Management had just sprung for a lavish post-fundraise celebration for San Francisco–based staffers, who piled into a party bus for a trip to wine country. In addition to treating employees to some fancy tastings, Peter, the CEO, had handed each person an envelope containing $500 in cash. I also worried about the strain that this episode was causing for Carol. She sent me an e-mail in which she expressed her concerns:

> When we first started this team and offered $10.00 an hour. I was able to explain that we are a start up and we don't have the money right now to pay more. That's not going to fly anymore! :) At that time, even though the team members could have taken other jobs that paid more, they accepted the job we offered. And they did that because they believed in us and they trust in us! We can't now turn around and betray that trust, loyalty, dedication and commitment they made to us and AllDone.

According to Carol, AllDone executives could no longer present the company to phone agents in Las Vegas as a small, cash-strapped startup. Team members had placed their trust in Carol that their sacrifices would be recognized when AllDone's coffers expanded, and that they would share in the gains generated by AllDone's growth.

Carol's message continued by reminding me of the value the team's relational work provided the company. She wrote:

> I wonder, did everyone forget about the coins rollouts? The unrelentless work this team did making call, after call; while taking the bombardment of abuse—every day! It was heartbreakingly difficult to hear people say the hateful things that we heard about the company we love. But, they did it! And they did it because they believe so much in AllDone. I know our task was only a small part of a bigger plan. But, without our part the increase in revenue, directly thereafter, would likely not have been possible. . . .
>
> And lets not forget all [the] project[s] we are always excited to take on and least of all the buyers we connect with. Some, by touching their heart, we make a difference in their life and create a user experience they will never forget.
>
> The value in these things is greater than any metric and is something you can't put a price on!
>
> We understand the financial cost involved to switch the team to salary. But, lets not lose sight of the value we bring and just one of . . . the ultimate goals, which is to provide the absolute best customer experience possible.

Carol recognized that it could be difficult to measure the precise impact of ADLV team members' activities on the company's revenue. Nevertheless, she was asking that the value of her team's contributions to the firm be recognized.

Even Mike, the new co-team lead, worried that ADSF underestimated ADLV's value. In an e-mail to me and Carol, he wrote:

> The team members may not build products, create marketing campaigns, or make the website look really cool, but they do something that in my own personal opinion is much more important. At the most basic level, they make the people giving us money, feel good about giving us money.

Whereas Carter had previously stated that the phone team should deliver a measurable "return on investment," Mike echoed Carol's assessment that the team contributed to AllDone in ways that were more difficult to quantify. Although ADLV's tasks were less glamorous than the engineering work that occurred in the San Francisco office, Mike argued, phone agents' ability to manage users' emotions was just as crucial to the company's success.

The issue finally came to a head a couple of weeks before I left the company. Dana had just assumed her new role as AllDone's director of operations, and Carol and Mike were visiting the ADSF office to talk with her about ADLV's future. When I arrived that morning, I found Carol in tears in a conference room because Nancy, her most trusted team member, had just threatened to quit. "These girls do so much," she explained, exasperated. Carol broke down again in an afternoon meeting with Dana and me, and as she cried, she pleaded her case to Dana:

> "Nobody knows how hard these girls work. They're doing it because we've asked them to, to be patient. They don't feel appreciated or valued. To get us to do all this [new tasks Dana had proposed], how do we do it without exceptional people? The exceptional people we [already] have need to be compensated fairly. It's not fair! It's not just money—show them appreciation and recognition for doing an amazing job. Fucking A! All the stuff they do every day, Dana, *I'm* the one they come to. They take it, they take it, they take it all day long for AllDone! You've been stringing them along!"

Carol lamented what she saw as ADSF's underappreciation and mistreatment of her team. AllDone's refusal to fulfill promises she had made on the company's behalf put her credibility on the line. She had long been a true believer in AllDone. Carol's colleagues frequently observed that AllDone was her life—she appeared to log longer hours than anyone in ADSF (twelve-hour days and weekends were the norm), and worked tirelessly to keep her team members motivated when they believed they were being mistreated. And now she felt that AllDone was throwing her under the bus.

As Carol and others on the team would later tell me, most ADLV staffers were now working out of loyalty and allegiance to Carol, rather than to AllDone. Dana, with her commitment to hierarchy and procedure, seemed less concerned by the potential consequences of humiliating Carol. 'I have a lot of un-PC thoughts about that kind of maternal personality,' she told me during one meeting. 'Someone who needs to be needed—a symbiotic relationship with team members. But, for better or for worse,' she added with a knowing nod, 'we're getting a lot of value out of that.'

The meeting proved a turning point, but it also spelled the beginning of the end for ADLV. Afterwards Dana sat down with me in the office's small conference room, where I showed her a spreadsheet of the phone agents' wages. Something about the stark reality of the numbers moved Dana, who asked me, "How do they live on this?" After determining that ADLV's best-paid phone agent made $500 a week, she said, matter-of-factly, "That's really bad." After crunching some numbers, Dana determined that the cost to the company of increasing the workers' pay to $12 per hour was "peanuts." Carter had consistently brushed aside my input on this topic—perhaps believing I was too emotionally invested in the workforce—but he immediately capitulated to Dana's judgment.[18] The phone agents, now employees, would make a minimum of $12 per hour.

Within months, Dana and Paul, the head of ADSF's burgeoning sales team, began exploring alternatives to the Las Vegas-based workforce. They launched an experimental phone team in the Salt Lake City area to try out a new set of sales-oriented tasks. By this point I had left the company, so I asked Carter about the move the next time I saw him at an AllDone event. He contrasted the labor pools from which AllDone's phone agents were drawn, describing Salt Lake City as 'the kind of place Stanford MBAs come back to after graduation. People move there to be with their families, not to go to bars,' he told me. 'It's better for the business. Fewer distractions.' Carter believed that phone agents in Salt Lake City were better educated and more capable than those in Vegas, and that the area's prevailing Mormon culture would translate into less "drama" and more docile workers.[19]

On a visit to Las Vegas to inform the team of the AllDone Salt Lake (ADSL) experiment, Dana told them that the company didn't yet know whether ADLV, ADSL, or both would survive. Soon after Dana's announcement, Chloe, ADSF's office manager, invited me to join her as a surprise guest at a party in Vegas, at AllDone's expense, to help cheer the team up. Dana was not coming because as she, Chloe, and Carol would all tell me independently of one another, team members would have assumed that she was there to fire them.

My former colleagues seemed happy to see me, but the mood was bittersweet. Mike, Carol, and the rest of the team were chafing under

Dana's direction. Dana had centralized decision-making in San Francisco as she hired deputies to help her oversee the remote teams, and ADLV team members felt that the new managers in San Francisco didn't listen to their input or respect their intelligence. "They talk to us like we're stupid," Carol told me. "They seem to have this elitist attitude. We have no respect at all." As usual, Carol's ability to read people was spot on: In a conversation with Dana about whether AllDone could present the change in employment status as a "pay increase" without offering an actual raise, Dana had remarked to me, "They *are* pretty stupid." (I replied that one phone agent, Sharon, had previously run her own payroll company.)

Most of all, however, the team members resented the metrics. They felt that focusing on answering a high volume of calls and meeting goals for shorter call times would detract from their ability to give users a good experience, which had long been a point of pride for phone agents. As Wendy put it, her eyes opening wide with sadness: "I work from the heart. Carol hired us for our hearts!" The "heart" and "love" that had previously motivated team members and provided a language through which to understand their activities—undergirded by the promise that ADLV's fortunes would rise along with the company's—were disappearing. AllDone's new leadership style highlighted the gulf between contractors' expectations and the actual opportunities available to them. "I believed in AllDone, and I made the team believe," Carol told me. "I feel like I sold them a bill of goods."

The introduction of ADSL—and the threat to Las Vegas–based employees' jobs that was raised by this development—intensified team members' disillusionment and dread. Yet, in spite of the team's insecurity, few were looking for new jobs. Mike, who was younger and had prior experience in the tech world, quickly used his connections from working at Zappos to find a new job at a local startup. Carol, for her part, vacillated between criticizing Mike for his lack of loyalty to AllDone and criticizing Carter and AllDone for its lack of loyalty to ADLV. Most of the remaining members of ADLV with whom I spoke shared Carol's ambivalence: they were disappointed and angry with AllDone, but at the same time, they were holding out hope that executives would find a reason to keep them around.

It was clear to Chloe, Mike, and me that ADSF leaders had already made their decision. (Chloe speculated that Dana and Carter had okayed the party "because they know what they're doing is shitty.") Carol was soon stripped of her duties as ADLV team leader, and day-to-day management shifted to two operations managers working under Dana in San Francisco. Carol angrily told me that she was no longer putting in "twelve-, fourteen-, sixteen-hour days" because "it doesn't matter anymore. I'll never put this [much] energy into a job again. *Ever*."[20] Dana asked Carol to spend a few weeks at the Salt Lake City office as an "Ambassador of AllDone Love," tasked with transplanting ADLV culture to ADSL. "Is that all I'm good for?" she said to me bitterly. "They'll use me to make them happy, and then, 'see ya.'"

ADLV was finally shuttered a year after Dana had taken over leadership of the team, supplanted by the fast-growing phone team in the Salt Lake City area. Carol described the team in Las Vegas as (and clearly herself felt) "devastated" and "heartbroken." She recounted to me an e-mail she'd sent to Carter: "People are not disposable. Family is not disposable." Carter had previously assured Carol that she would always have a place at All-Done, and he proposed installing Carol in a new "life coach" position as a member of ADSL's human resources department. However, Ken, ADSL's team leader, didn't seem to want her there. Carter claimed to be unable to intervene further on Carol's behalf, and she was ultimately not offered a position with the team in Salt Lake City. Carter tried to make things right by increasing Carol's employee education allowance and allowing her to use it to get training as a life coach as part of her severance package.

Both Carol and Veronica—the women who had made tremendous personal sacrifices to build AllDone's remote teams and infused them with sentiment-laden organizational cultures—had been replaced. The strategies and personnel that had fueled AllDone's earliest stages of growth, allowing it to capture its first two rounds of venture capital funding, would no longer be needed. With new investors on board and their new expectations for how a later-stage startup should scale up, early leaders were replaced by formally trained and experienced specialists. Carol and Veronica had bought into the company's rhetoric about love and family, but discovered that AllDone was in fact a business, first and foremost.

ADLV agents' loyalty to the company had not been rewarded—they had not been the "venture laborers" that some had thought or hoped they were becoming by working for a startup.[21] Owing to a misrecognition of their position within the startup economy, some ADLV phone agents seemed to have believed that they were in line to capture a portion of AllDone's skyrocketing valuation. At a party at Carol's house shortly before I left AllDone, I spoke with a new ADLV team member—the only man who worked as a phone agent while I was helping to lead the team. 'I'm convinced it's gonna be huge,' Rodney told me. 'I think AllDone is gonna be the next Google. There's gonna be receptionists who become millionaires.' If receptionists could strike it rich in Rodney's imagination, he may have dreamed that phone support agents, too, would share in the bounty.[22] On the anniversary of Amazon's founding, another phone agent named Wendy sent the team an e-mail that compared AllDone to the tech giant: "Since we work for a company that is going to have this success . . . Where will we be in 18 years. . . . Oh the Places WE are heading for!!!"

Now, things were going well for the company, but not for the team in Las Vegas. ADLV staffers found themselves in a position similar to that of the AllDone sellers whom they counseled. Both phone support agents and sellers were integral to the company's success, but many were excluded from the rewards that resulted from AllDone's growth. Both ADLV team members and AllDone's sellers discovered that their relationship with the company could be instantly destabilized by the whims of managers in the San Francisco office as they shifted the company's strategic direction to meet the expectations of venture capital investors. After three years, the AllDone Las Vegas experiment had outlived its usefulness for the firm, and its members were discarded; their fantasies had frayed and the experiences of self-transformation that they had envisioned would never be realized.

· · · · ·

Venture capitalism generates value by raising expectations. Startup workers collaborate to boost perceptions of a firm's potential. Companies that demonstrate precipitous and continuous growth receive attention from investors who bid up the price of equity in the firm. Investors can reap windfall profits when the most successful startups are sold for billions of dollars. As a high-growth tech startup, AllDone's success was predicated on the organization's capacity to capture the imagination of users, workers, and investors. The logic of venture capitalism was internalized by the firm and by members of the organization. The structures and strategies of the fast-growing, venture-backed workplace shaped workers' expectations, experiences, and identities.[23]

The members of AllDone who labored to enhance the company's prospects and prove its promise were drawn into an economy of anticipation. As participants in venture capitalism, workers were invited to project their dreams and desires onto the firm's future. Some hoped that working for AllDone would make them rich, while others simply imagined a pathway toward upward mobility. Some saw in AllDone a refuge from alienating jobs and the bureaucratic norms of the working world. Many shared a sense that they were a part of something special, and that as the company grew and changed the world, their lives would be transformed for the better.

AllDone's Series B investment presented executives with the imperative to restructure the organization to meet funders' expectations for how the company should prepare for its next stage of growth. AllDone's executives installed new leaders across all three of AllDone's teams to rationalize and professionalize the company's operations. Workers found that old ways of getting work done and of relating to colleagues and the company were being replaced by more impersonal and hierarchical systems. As AllDone was transformed, long-standing members of the organization grappled with the feeling that they had in some way lost ownership over their work and workplace culture. Exploitation that had previously been obscured by the rhetoric of "family" became increasingly visible, and dreams began to seem more like deceptions.[24] Many of those who had previously believed that working for AllDone was "more than a job" became disillusioned, and some found themselves unemployed.

When the profits started to flow, existing inequalities within the firm intensified as the bulk of the benefits accrued to those who were already most privileged. The startup's investors, cofounders, and a handful of early employees began to reap millions from selling their equity in the company. Others were disappointed to find that their expectations for financial gain had been unrealistic. And members of AllDone Las Vegas discovered that their dreams of sharing in the wealth they had helped to create had been nothing more than "cruel optimism."[25] Instead of ascending with the "rocket ship" they had helped to launch, ADLV contractors found themselves left behind, looking up from the launchpad.

Conclusion

REORGANIZING INNOVATION

Will was a web designer living in Los Angeles and supporting his wife, an aspiring actress. He couldn't shake the idea that he, too, should be pursuing his passion. When he heard about AllDone, he decided to try using it to set up a side business. He created a profile on AllDone to offer online guitar lessons, figuring he could make some extra money in his spare time by applying his lifelong love of music and his experience playing in bands. Will soon landed a couple of clients and signed up for a subscription, which allowed him to respond to all the requests he received from potential clients for a flat fee of $20 per month. Soon he was replying to dozens of inquiries from across the country every month. A small but meaningful number of the people who signed up for an initial lesson stuck around, leaving him with a slowly expanding roster of students.

By projecting his business's costs and growth rate into the future, Will realized he would soon be able to dedicate himself to teaching full time. 'I put together a business plan and I finally convinced my wife to let me give up web design and do guitar lessons instead,' he later explained. Money may be tight at times, but he'd be doing work that he found meaningful.

One day, Will got a call from Carol, AllDone's phone support lead. She had bad news: AllDone would no longer be offering subscriptions to guitar teachers like Will. He would now have to pay a separate fee to contact each potential client. If he wanted to respond to the same number of people as he had before, it would cost him hundreds of dollars a month. Will panicked. "Since both closing AND getting the right kinds of students are things with unpredictable variables," he later wrote in an e-mail to AllDone customer support, "and with consideration to the volume of students I need to both procure and *maintain*, the only viable way is to have the ability to respond to every inquiry. The cost of doing that [now] is simply too high." The next time Will spoke with Carol, he pleaded with her to let him keep his subscription. When Carol said the decision had been made by management and that there was nothing she could do, Will cried out, "You guys have shattered my dreams!"

The day after Carol told me about Will's troubles, I recounted his story to Josh, AllDone's product manager. I told him I felt bad about what had happened to Will. 'It's not that sad,' Josh replied, betraying no emotion. 'He must have gotten a lot of business through us. He can do what he wants to do.'

There are many ways in which this episode epitomizes the disconnect between the Silicon Valley elite and the millions of workers whose livelihoods are affected by their decisions. If AllDone's cofounders and early employees ever managed to cash out, their riches would come at the expense of some of the sellers who relied on their platform. Drivers and delivery workers who generate revenue for companies like Instacart and Doordash have voiced similar complaints. In 2017, dashcam footage of an Uber driver sharing his frustrations with the company's CEO, Travis Kalanick, sparked nearly four months of negative news coverage about Uber that ultimately cost Kalanick his job.[1]

I would draw readers' attention to another aspect of Will's complaint. He had invested in his business under one set of rules, only to find that they had been suddenly and unilaterally altered, undermining his ability to make a living. In fact, when Will's subscription was eliminated, AllDone's managers didn't even know whether the change to the company's fee structure would become a viable business model—guitar teachers were among the first categories of sellers to be subjected to that experiment. Whenever software engineers rolled out major changes, they counted on AllDone's workers in the Philippines and Las Vegas to smooth things over.

Why do the working conditions generated by tech startups like AllDone seem to be constantly in flux? Is it because of the unique vision—or, perhaps, incompetence and heartlessness—of their leaders? Is it because of the nature of "cloud"-based software itself, which allows programmers to push out instantaneous updates and revisions? Is it because platforms are often designed to encourage workers to view their work as a "game," rather than a stable source of income?

This book has advanced an alternative view. I have argued that venture capital compels tech companies to engage in relentless experimentation to facilitate rapid growth aimed at increasing the firm's valuation in capital markets and generating windfall returns for investors. Although gig economy workers like Will are subject to the authority of tech CEOs, startup executives are themselves disciplined by a small but deeply influential community of investors. For entrepreneurs like AllDone's cofounders to have any chance of "disrupting" a market and "changing the world" with technology, they must first mold their organizations to meet the expectations of the institutions whose funds can help transform ideas into billion-dollar companies. When we villainize individual actors or companies, we draw attention away from the system that incentivizes them to treat everyone and everything in their environment instrumentally. A venture-backed startup's workforce is ultimately a number on a spreadsheet that can be brought in, tested, and let go as part of its quest to achieve the rapid and precipitous inflation of the company's value as an asset.

HOW FINANCE CAPITAL IS SHAPING FUTURES OF WORK

Digital platforms are altering the nature of work and employment for millions of people around the globe. Scholars have noted how the rise of platform-based gig work is consistent with broader structural shifts in the economy that have increasingly offloaded economic risks onto workers.[2] In this book, I have made the case that shifting our focus from the workers who *use* platforms to find gigs to the workers who *build* the platforms themselves can help us deepen analyses of work, technology, and society. Instead of viewing financialized capitalism as the background or context in which the platform business model has taken root, observing the inner workings of an emerging platform company allows us to center the role of particular financial actors—along with their specific interests and motives—in influencing the shape of technological change.

I have examined the causes and consequences of venture capitalism, an investor logic that pushes promising tech startups to deliver massive returns by quickly and exponentially inflating their valuation. Startups attempt to achieve this end by engaging in relentless experimentation with their products, production processes, workforces, and even business models. Despite their association with machine learning and AI, this process inevitably requires forms of labor that rarely feature prominently in public accounts of startups—which at AllDone included overseas information-processing work and off-site customer support.

As they try to "disrupt" the markets in which they operate, VC-backed startups simultaneously disrupt the lives of many of the people whose livelihoods are tied to their products. Venture capitalism's effects begin inside the companies that constitute the locus of technological innovation in our contemporary economy, radiating outward to the far-flung contractors who perform the computational and relational work that allows these firms to function, onward toward the workers who use digital labor platforms, and ultimately seeping into the fabric of the societies in which new technologies are deployed.

A startup's pursuit of venture funding generates drags, or organizational problems that must be solved swiftly to transform aspirations into realities. The case of AllDone shows how, within the context of imperfect AI and limited resources, managers address problems by mobilizing particular combinations of technological systems and human labor. Software developers explored new horizons of value by generating continual change. Computational workers performed routinized, behind-the-scenes labor to provide a stable substrate on which developers could experiment. And relational workers interfaced with users who were trying to make sense of and take advantage of the software.

The coordinated activities of startup workers in turn affect all the people who rely on emerging digital labor platforms. At AllDone, the *internal* instability generated by VC rippled out to affect hundreds of thousands of *external* workers who used the platform to find work. The changes orchestrated in the San Francisco office, and supported by contractors in the Philippines and Las Vegas, subjected local service providers to a series of ever-shifting policies and pricing schemes. Sellers who invested their time and energy in establishing a profile on AllDone and learning how to benefit from its services discovered that their success with the platform was subject to the whims of software developers who were ultimately accountable to investors rather than to the workers whose livelihoods they were reshaping.

Venture capitalism represents an extreme manifestation of the financialization of the economy. But the story of AllDone and its ilk shows that financialization doesn't just operate at the level of firms and financial markets. Instead, it has penetrated into the core of our everyday lives. When you hire a house cleaner on a platform like AllDone, you aren't just helping her pay her bills. To connect with customers like you, your house cleaner has to line the pockets of an ultra-wealthy investor in Silicon Valley. From this perspective, AllDone has essentially replaced the Yellow Pages while making a small number of rich people richer—not exactly "changing the world."

By shaping the internal organization of tech startups, their ties with external contractors, the products they develop, and the global labor market more broadly, venture capitalists profit from destabilizing work and employment relations. It is time for the logic and influence of finance capital to take center stage in our conversations about technology and futures of work.

CENTERING CAPITAL, RECONSIDERING WORK AND TECHNOLOGY

This book contributes to research at the intersection of economic sociology, with its interest in examining the increasing influence of financial actors in our economy, and the sociology of work, which has long been concerned with how work is organized and how people make sense of what they do on the job. Economic sociologists have documented how powerful investors compel managers to restructure firms to reduce costs and increase strategic flexibility. However, there is a dearth of research on how shareholders extract value from firms outside of large, publicly traded corporations.[3] Inside VC-backed startups like AllDone, researchers can directly observe the pressures investors place on firms and their consequences for organizational design. This makes tech startups ideal sites in which to examine how financial logics impact workers on the ground.

There is a long and enduring tradition of scholarship analyzing how the interests of capital shape the relationship between work and technology in firms.[4] The dominant narrative suggests that owners and managers use new technologies to enhance their control over labor and increase productivity. The introduction of the moving assembly line, for example, allowed managers to reduce labor costs by expanding the division of labor, increasing output, and making individual workers more interchangeable. The contemporary economy continues to present us with examples of this phenomenon, from electronic devices that monitor and direct Amazon's warehouse workforce to software that tracks keystrokes and rates the productivity of white-collar workers.[5]

The case of AllDone, however, highlights the fact that the interests of capital cannot always be distilled into the drive toward efficiency. As sociologist Ching Kwan Lee has argued, there are in fact *varieties* of capital—each of which might advance the particular interests of owners and respond to incentives in unique ways.[6] Venture-backed startups are likely to adopt different approaches to technological change than publicly traded tech companies. VC investors build portfolios of high-risk and potentially high-reward enterprises, expecting that most will fail but that a small number will deliver exponential returns. Instead of pursuing steady expansion derived from a profitable product and efficient business practices, startup managers are fixated on rapidly, repeatedly, and precipitously inflating the company's perceived value—regardless of the waste or inefficiency that may result. Nearly every aspect of an organization and its product is provisional and can be altered at a moment's notice.

Inside of firms, the structural constraints imposed by financiers are filtered through managerial initiatives and technology choices that generate pressures and opportunities for workers. At AllDone, the burdens associated with "moving fast and breaking things" were unequally distributed across the organization. Software developers in San Francisco found it engrossing and exciting to engage in continual experimentation. Because they served as the company's behind-the-scenes computational infrastructure, workers in the Philippines experienced far less instability in their daily work lives. Frontline customer support workers in Las Vegas, on the other hand, frequently felt fearful of and overwhelmed by the changes that developers were constantly setting into motion.[7]

This suggests that when the imperatives of financiers are driving innovation, workers' degrees of *exposure to* and *control over* that change become important axes of organizational inequality. This insight applies to both the workers who rely on platforms to find work *and* to the varied types of workers supporting the platform economy's operations.[8] In the Philippines—where observers typically assume that digital labor is precarious, short-term, and even exploitative work—AllDone constructed relatively stable, well-paying jobs underpinned by a culture of familial love in order to overcome limited engineering resources and the shortcomings of AI. At the same time, workers in the Las Vegas area, who were directly exposed to organizational flux yet had little control over its form, felt besieged by management's demand for flexibility.

Each of these teams was constructed to manage the consequences of venture capital's demand for quick and precipitous asset price inflation via continuous innovation and experimentation. The consequences for workers depended on their relationship to that flux. Ethnographic research can deepen our understanding of how financialization is changing work by uncovering variation in what investors want, how they go about achieving their goals, and the consequences for workers with different roles within, across, and even outside of organizations. Efforts to improve working conditions should be based on fine-grained analyses that account for divergent experiences of work.

The case of AllDone also shows how financialized logics can capture the imagination of workers across an organization—even among those who do not hold equity in the company.[9] In its quest to captivate investors, AllDone mobilized workers' dreams. Some hoped for an alternative to laboring in traditional corporate bureaucracies; others saw in AllDone a path to the middle class; and many fantasized about sharing in the immense wealth that the company was creating. Implicit promises of jobs for life or deferred compensation impelled independent contractors to dedicate themselves to a company that existed to serve the interests of investors above all else.

My point here is not that AllDone's business practices were uniquely harmful, manipulative, or inhumane in comparison with those of its competitors. Capitalism is rife with contradictions, and venture capitalism is no exception. As I have noted, members of AllDone's remote workforce in the Philippines and Las Vegas generally appeared to view their jobs as superior to most of the alternatives available to people like them. At the same time, it was also true that at the time of my research, these contractors comprised 92 percent of AllDone's workforce, virtually none of whom would directly share in the wealth they were helping to create. Instead, the vast majority of those gains would be siphoned off by investors and the company's cofounders.

The actions of AllDone and its leaders were guided by the structure of the venture capital system. Technological innovation is deeply implicated in our visions of a better life. Yet companies whose express purpose is innovation are deliberately designed to enrich a small cadre of investors and early employees, rather than to support the hopes and dreams of a firm's broader workforce or the millions who come to rely on new technologies to generate income. As regions around the globe try to boost economic development by emulating Silicon Valley, we must ask ourselves whether we really need more innovation that erodes labor rights while minting billionaires. How can societies enjoy the benefits of technological change while sharing the gains more broadly?

THE SOCIAL COSTS OF VENTURE CAPITALISM

Technology has long figured prominently in our imagination of the future. Some envision it as a force that can liberate us from dangerous or tedious work, elevate our skills, level inequalities, and help us realize our potential as human beings. To others, technology promises to degrade our experiences of work, rob us of our livelihoods, amplify inequalities, and alienate us from ourselves and the world around us.

Tech entrepreneurs commonly claim that they are motivated not by the pursuit of profit, but by an altruistic desire to change the world for the better. There is no disputing that technological innovation can elevate living standards, improve health and safety, and provide us with novel goods and services that we soon can't or won't live without. Champions of the tech industry celebrate the centrality of venture capital to the innovation ecosystem, arguing that it creates a marketplace in which the best ideas can be nurtured and supported.[10] But the ideas that are best for capital markets are not necessarily those that are best for societies. VC-backed companies may indeed be changing how we live and work. But venture capitalism serves the status quo insofar as it reproduces a variety of deeply entrenched inequalities in need of "disruption."

Even casual observers of the tech industry are aware of its troubling track record on racial and gender inequalities. The problem of algorithmic bias is widely acknowledged.[11] And corporations have long relied on low-wage, feminized, and offshored workforces to reduce costs and increase profits. As Carter, AllDone's president, noted in reference to the company's support staff in the Philippines and Las Vegas, "Middle-aged women are what make AllDone work." But women and people of color are rarely among the ranks of those who benefit most from venture capitalism.

The racial and gender disparities begin at the top of the VC ecosystem. Venture capital firms' principal investors—known as partners—receive a proportion of the profits generated by their funds. A recent survey of US VC firms revealed that 78 percent of partners are white, with 4 percent listed as Hispanic and 3 percent as Black. Only 16 percent of investment partners are women.[12] And the founders who receive funding generally look like VCs. According to an industry report, 91 percent of VC-backed startup founders are men, and 77 percent are white.[13] Companies founded solely by women received only 2.2 percent of the total capital invested in VC-backed startups in the United States in 2018.[14]

Employment discrimination in the tech industry is pervasive and well documented.[15] In chapter 2, I quoted an AllDone engineer who argued that the resource-constrained company couldn't afford to compete with Silicon Valley tech giants for underrepresented talent. But even firms with the most lavish recruiting budgets and stated commitments to increasing diversity have failed to make a significant dent in the problem. For example, in 2020, nearly 94 percent of Google's US employees were either white or of Asian descent. Men held 73 percent of leadership roles; Black and Latinx men and women *combined* held only 2.6 and 3.7 percent, respectively, of top jobs.[16]

Workplace cultures in VC-backed firms, as in all workplaces, are suffused with gender and racial politics. At AllDone, workers' race, gender, and geographic location were inseparable from managers' judgments about and justifications for how particular types of work and workers should be valued and rewarded. The team in San Francisco celebrated AllDone's second round of VC funding with a lavish outing at a Napa winery, while the team in Las Vegas was told that there wasn't money for a raise. Managers rationalized massive disparities in compensation by figuring themselves as benefactors and extolling the difference that $2 an hour made in Filipino workers' lives. These ways of understanding what people's efforts are worth underlie a global system of labor that systematically separates certain types of workers from the massive profits they help to generate. Nothing I saw in this study suggests that venture capitalism is particularly well equipped to ameliorate these long-standing inequalities.

Among the most glaring social problems associated with venture capitalism is its role in reproducing vast disparities in wealth. Tech companies are generating previously unimaginable returns for shareholders in today's economy. At the end of 2019, the combined market value of Facebook, Alphabet, Amazon, Microsoft, and Apple was $5 trillion. One year later, after the emergence of the COVID-19 pandemic had increased people's and businesses' reliance on technology as never before, that figure had increased by 50 percent to $7.5 trillion.[17] All five of these companies began as startups that used venture capital funding to build massively profitable businesses. At a time when the US economy was in the throes of an unprecedented shock that threw millions of people out of work, just nine tech titans—including founders like Jeff Bezos, Mark Zuckerberg, and Elon Musk—saw their wealth skyrocket by a combined $360 billion.[18] Venture-backed startups, too, shattered funding records in both 2020 and 2021, at the same time that many Americans were experiencing an economic crisis.[19]

The increasing influence of the financial sector in the US economy has been a key driver of the rising tide of inequality in income and wealth.[20] The VC business model exemplifies this phenomenon, as VCs help startup founders turn nascent ideas into turbocharged financial assets whose skyrocketing value is largely funneled into the hands of the economic elite. One illustrative example is Uber, whose 2019 IPO pegged the company's valuation at $69 billion.[21] Although analysts and investors viewed that figure as a massive disappointment in light of prior expectations, investors still walked away with billions of dollars in profits: About 40 percent of the company's value immediately following the IPO was captured by three investment funds and the company's two cofounders.[22] When drivers protested the relationship between their poorly compensated labor and the windfall profits reaped by investors, Uber allocated $300 million in bonuses to reward 1.1 million active, longtime drivers at the time of the IPO. These bonuses for qualifying drivers who had completed at least 2,500 Uber trips averaged $273 per person. For most drivers, this was the equivalent of receiving a "tip" of four to ten cents per ride—billions for the rich and pennies for the essential workers on whom the company depends.[23]

Institutions that invest in VC funds, such as banks, insurance companies, and universities, also benefit from the rising value of tech companies. Clients of banks—including those holding individual retirement accounts—can see the worth of their portfolios swell. However, the distribution of stock market rewards is heavily skewed toward the rich. At a time when individual wealth is increasingly derived from financial assets, the wealthiest 1 percent of Americans own 38 percent of financial holdings in stocks, while the top 10 percent own 84 percent of the stock market's value.[24]

Venture capitalism is designed to further enrich the wealthiest among us—an aim it advances without regard to the social costs generated by VC-backed firms. In a "winner-take-all" tech industry with monopolistic tendencies, the startups that succeed are not necessarily those that figure out how to create a stable business model that yields sustainable growth by serving their users better than the competition. Instead, the winners are often companies that grow as quickly as possible to attract as much capital as they can.[25] Consider the example of the ride-hail startup Sidecar, which was connecting drivers with passengers prior to the emergence of both Uber and Lyft. Management scholars David B. Yoffie, Annabelle Gawer, and Michael A. Cusumano note that Sidecar executives pursued "a slow-growth strategy in order to be financially responsible" and raised far less venture capital than their rivals. The company folded in 2015 after failing to attract as many riders and drivers as its lavishly funded competitors. "Of course," Yoffie and colleagues add, "Uber and Lyft have lost billions of dollars and, even though both have now gone public, they may never generate a profit or survive as viable businesses."[26]

This and other examples raise important questions about who is being served by the business model that plunged Will's life into disarray. VC-backed firms leverage massive sums of investment capital to quickly draw in users and price competitors out of the market. As they experiment with new policies and business models, the fate of the people who have come to rely on their products must remain a secondary consideration.

The VC business model is powerful. But it is also a relatively new and historically contingent invention, fueled by policy choices enacted in the late 1970s that incentivized investors' participation. Today, a small cadre of financiers with a very particular (and arguably peculiar) strategy for making money have seized an outsized voice in determining how economic risks and rewards will be distributed.

Sociological approaches to studying technological change reveal that there is nothing inevitable about the outcomes of innovation. Although the affordances of technologies certainly influence what we do with them—after all, nobody uses Microsoft Word to browse the internet—technologies alone do not dictate whether or how we use them. Instead, innovation's effects are shaped by the social contexts in which new technologies emerge and are implemented.

IMAGINING ALTERNATIVE MODELS FOR OWNERSHIP, INNOVATION, AND WORK

Throughout this book, I have shown that those who seek to understand how social context matters for technology outcomes must attend not only to the local environments of deployment and use, but also to the broader structural and institutional forces that drive actors' incentives and motivations. Technologies, organizations, and institutions are human creations. Our current era of technological change invites us to look toward an uncertain future and to ask how we can come together to minimize the harms generated by new technologies while spreading their benefits more widely. This is not simply a question of technological design—it encompasses broader questions about how innovation is organized in our economy.

The ownership structure of venture-backed startups pushes companies to engage in relentless innovation aimed at quickly inflating the firm's perceived value. Although venture-backed startups and publicly traded corporations dominate the field, attending to the varieties of capital active in smaller niches of the tech sector can open our eyes to alternative models and politics of technological development. As a society, it's time for us to diversify our innovation portfolio and look for better ways to invest in our future. A brief survey of the platform ecosystem suggests that there are other ways to fund innovation that are likely to produce better conditions for workers and societies, while also ensuring that the bulk of the gains generated by the globe-spanning networks of people who make innovation possible are not hoarded by a small group of economic elites. Privately owned tech companies, nonprofit corporations, and platform cooperatives are among the entities that could play an important role in supporting innovation while distributing its benefits more broadly.

The online bulletin board craigslist is privately owned and has largely resisted outside investment.[27] As communication scholar Jessa Lingel argues, "Craigslist defies many of the most basic assumptions about how to be a successful tech company."[28] Founder Craig Newmark and CEO Jim Buckmaster have rarely altered the website's user interface or policies since its launch in 1995. The two have run the site with what Lingel calls a "minimal-profit politics," charging a small fee for certain (presumably wealthier) users to post listings (e.g., real estate ads or job postings in certain cities), but otherwise maintaining a conservative growth trajectory. Unlike other popular platforms founded in the years following its emergence, craigslist has refrained from constantly experimenting with its service to increase engagement, hosting ads, or harvesting and selling user information to advertisers and data brokers.

The case of craigslist demonstrates that privately owned tech companies face fewer external pressures to maximize profits and may thus be less likely to continually update their systems and implement practices that harm workers' and users' well-being. The continued existence and viability of craigslist thus indicates that it may be possible for entrepreneurs who eschew venture capital to build successful tech companies that balance the profit motive with a public-service ethos. However, the era in which craigslist first achieved popularity—which predated the tech behemoths that dominate today's internet in part by acquiring and copying competitors' products—presented a far more hospitable environment for privately owned, values-oriented companies. Sidecar's defeat at the hands of Uber and Lyft in a VC-fueled platform ecosystem suggests that if we are waiting for benevolent founders to bring about a better tech ecosystem, we could be waiting for a very long time.

Nonprofit platforms may provide another model for entrepreneurs who wish to prioritize users' well-being over the interests of investors. Amara is a nonprofit translation and video-captioning platform that launched in 2011. Its Amara On Demand service allows clients to pay workers around the world to translate and caption their content. Freed from the imperative to maximize profits, Amara pays higher wages than many for-profit digital labor platforms (experienced workers in the United States can earn $15 an hour). Amara On Demand also allows workers to communicate with each other and collaborate on projects, an improvement over the isolating working conditions offered by popular online labor platforms like Amazon's Mechanical Turk.[29]

Another alternative to the VC business model is platform cooperativism.[30] Instead of being governed by outside investors, boards of directors, and executives, cooperative businesses are collectively owned and operated by the workers who rely on them for income. One example of a platform cooperative is Up & Go, which allows customers in New York City to order house-cleaning services. Up & Go was founded with the support of a local nonprofit that helped an existing, offline cooperative business build a digital booking interface to compete with venture-funded platforms for cleaning services like Handy. Ninety-five percent of the revenue generated through Up & Go's platform is paid out to workers, almost all of whom are women who migrated to the United States from Latin America. The other 5 percent is reinvested in supporting the app. Workers' wages average $22.25 per hour, about $5 per hour above the local average.[31] Because platform cooperatives are accountable to workers rather than investors, they are more likely to innovate in ways that stabilize and increase workers' income. But they confront challenges as well: many struggle to find initial financing to launch their platforms and to attract customers in markets dominated by powerful incumbents.[32]

Each of the above models—private ownership, nonprofit organizations, and platform cooperatives—have their strengths and limitations when it comes to their potential to transform the tech sector. What they all have in common, however, is the potential to reduce entrepreneurs' dependence on external funds, and thus external control of their enterprises. Venture-backed tech companies are designed to "scale," growing as quickly as possible by incorporating a vast array of users with diverse needs and interests into the same computational system. Venture capitalists are moreover legally obligated to maximize the financial interests of limited partners in their investment funds rather than considering the needs of other stakeholders. When technologists resist "scale thinking," they are better equipped to begin to address the structural sources of inequalities: users can be treated as individuals rather than as interchangeable units, and power can be more decentralized and distributed, allowing for greater participation and mobilization.[33]

Scholars and activists are working together to build the intellectual and legal infrastructure that can help startup founders look beyond lucrative "exits" via corporate acquisitions and IPOs. Advocates argue that founders should instead consider "exiting to community" by converting their enterprises into democratically governed corporations, trusts, cooperatives, or nonprofits.[34] By promoting and investing in businesses with alternative ownership structures, consumers, workers, activists, and governments can challenge venture capital's winner-take-all model for technological innovation. In so doing, we can create ecosystems of smaller, more localized and specialized platforms that are more responsive to the people who use them and to the communities in which they are embedded.[35]

Federal agencies like the Small Business Administration, National Science Foundation, and Department of Defense—as well as numerous state governments—already provide entrepreneurs with grants and loans to support goals such as national security and economic development. These government programs use taxpayer dollars to help founders commercialize their ideas and create private wealth. Such programs could require entrepreneurs who accept government funding to commit to supporting the public good by capping prices or establishing profit sharing arrangements.[36] Publicly owned investment vehicles could also be designed to give citizens a voice in the direction of technological change.[37] Municipal governments that support tech "incubators" could become equity partners in the companies that benefit from their support so that some of the profits they generate flow back into public coffers.[38] In Quebec, labor unions have created their own venture capital funds to support workers' pensions, providing equity only to startups that can pass a "social assessment" that considers an enterprise's working conditions, employment relations, and health and safety at work.[39] Alone, none of these alternatives are likely to challenge venture capital's dominance, but the wider adoption of strategies like these can make room for new practices and ideas about funding innovation that distribute the benefits of technological change more equitably.

Societies can also support business models and institutional ecosystems outside of the VC paradigm by curbing finance capital's influence over innovation. Public policy changes enacted during the late 1970s—including rules that allowed private pension managers to include riskier investments in their portfolios and dramatic cuts in the capital gains tax rate—turbocharged the VC industry. The reversal of such policies could open space for other players to fund, and benefit from, the growth of startups. Smaller tweaks are straightforward. If legislators eliminated the "carried interest loophole" from the tax code, then the commissions VCs earn on their investments would be classified as income rather than as capital gains, which are typically taxed at a lower rate.[40] Congress could also repeal the Qualified Small Business Stock exclusion, which exempts a startup's founders, as well as its early investors and employees, from paying federal capital gains taxes on the sale of shares issued when the company was in its early stages of development.[41]

Legislation, regulations, legal actions, and antitrust enforcement aimed at bolstering labor rights and curbing the influence of the most dominant tech companies can also help other approaches to innovation thrive.[42] The Biden administration, for example, aggressively filed antitrust suits to oppose the accumulation of economic power by large, monopolistic actors in the tech sector.[43] Lawmakers can support new legislation that prevents companies from using novel technologies as an excuse to violate labor rights. These potential solutions are not aimed at curbing innovation—but they do attempt to ensure that the gains derived from innovation are more broadly shared.

At a time when the dominant narrative surrounding the future of work assumes that technology itself is the driver of change, centering the role of capital in structuring tech companies' activities helps to remind us that questions of technological design are in reality often questions of political economy—of who has power over how agendas are set and how resources are allocated, of who will take on risks and who will reap rewards. Even the most talented and well-intentioned technologists are incapable of developing systems that can bypass these social conditions. When we observe algorithms and AI systems without keeping capital firmly in view, we neglect a powerful influence on the relationship between technology and society while limiting our imagination of how it might be otherwise.

Acknowledgments

I am grateful first and foremost to the members of AllDone who shared their work lives with me. I have tried to do justice to the richness and complexity of their social world, but I know that the representations inscribed onto each page are inevitably partial truths. My hope is that, at a minimum, I have adequately conveyed the humanity of the people who appear in these pages.

I can't imagine a better environment in which to have launched this project than the Sociology Department at the University of California, Berkeley. Michael Burawoy was, and remains, a steadfast mentor who saw this work's potential long before I did. Through numerous memos and dissertation chapter drafts, Michael always seemed to know what I needed to hear to advance my writing, and, just as importantly, to convince me to believe in it. He also created a broader intellectual environment in which this work could flourish. Much of my early thinking related to this project took shape in Michael's dissertation writing group, which at various times featured Andy Chang, Herbert Docena, Fidan Elcioglu, Aya Fabros, Shannon Ikebe, Andrew Jaeger, Zachary Levenson, Thomas Peng, Josh Seim, and Shelly Steward. Conversations with Neil Fligstein and Kim Voss helped me build intellectual bridges between economic sociology and the sociology of work. Cal Morrill was a source of insight into both qualitative research methodology and organizational studies, and Leslie Salzinger helped me think about the relationship between affect and economic activity. Feedback from faculty including Claude Fischer, Marion Fourcade, Heather Haveman, and Christopher Muller helped me push the project forward, and the Center for Ethnographic Research offered both office space and intellectual community.

At the University of Pennsylvania, I was fortunate to join a cohort of spectacularly supportive junior colleagues: Regina Baker, Courtney Boen, Daniel Aldana Cohen, and Pilar Gonalons-Pons. The Wolf Humanities Center at Penn sponsored a manuscript development workshop that was adroitly anchored by Jeff Sallaz and included numerous colleagues from Penn Sociology, many of whom have provided counsel that has helped me advance this project since I arrived: Daniel Aldana Cohen, David Grazian, Jerry Jacobs, Annette Lareau, Raka Sen, Doron Shiffer-Sebba, Melissa Wilde, Guobin Yang, Zoe Zhao, and Robin Leidner, who left us too soon. Guobin also got me involved in Penn's Center on Digital Culture and Society. Jack Thornton provided feedback on a later version of the book's introductory chapter. I am especially grateful to Annette Lareau, who has provided extensive commentary on many drafts over the years. Without her generous mentorship and friendship, I would be a lesser scholar and teacher. I also thank current and former members of the Sociology Department staff for making intellectual life in our department possible, including Katee Dougherty, Julia Hawthorne, Audra Rodgers, Aline Rowans, and Marcus Wright. Elsewhere at Penn, Julia Ticona and Lindsey Cameron have provided a small but mighty community of writers on work and tech. Julia also generously organized a workshop featuring friends and luminaries including Michel Anteby, Beth Bechky, Clayton Childress, Angèle Christin, Jerry Davis, Alison Gerber, Kate Kellogg, Adam Reich, Ben Snyder, and Janet Vertesi. I am particularly grateful for the many exchanges that began before the workshop and have continued long after, and for generous and constructive reviews by Ben, Adam, Megan Tobias Neely, and an anonymous reviewer.

In addition to those listed above, this project has been enriched by conversations with many interlocutors over the years, including Steve Barley, Matt Beane, danah boyd, Jonathan Cutler, Mary Gray, Ruthanne Huising, Shreeharsh Kelkar, Karolina Mikołajewska-Zając, and Caitlin Petre. I also thank organizers of and participants in the workshops, conferences, and colloquia at which I presented parts of this work, including Data & Society's "Algorithms on the Shop Floor" workshop and the University of Chicago Ethnography Incubator. Material from this manuscript appears in *Work and Occupations* ("Working Algorithms: Software Automation and the Future of Work"), *Theory and Society* ("Making Platforms Work: Relationship Labor and the Management of Publics," with Shreeharsh Kelkar), *Communication and the Public* ("Stepping Back to Move Forward: Centering Capital in Discussions of Technology and the Future of Work"), and the *International Journal of Communication* ("Structures of Capital and Sociotechnical Change: The Case of Tech Startups and VC," with Caitlin Petre). I am grateful to the editors and anonymous reviewers for their helpful feedback.

Every author is sustained by the conviviality of friends and fellow travelers. For this I thank a cast of characters that includes Will Carroll, Rebecca Elliott, Peter Ekman, Jason Ferguson, Max Greene, Sigrid Luhr, Brian Martin, Kappy Mintie, Alex Roehrkasse, Andy Sadoway, Seth Samuels, Danya Sherman, Jon Shestakofsky, Adam Storer, Jonah Stuart Brundage, and Alan Washington, among many others. My parents, Susan Kottler and Stephen Shestakofsky, have always been in my corner.

The research featured in this book benefitted from financial support provided by the UC Berkeley Department of Sociology, the Horowitz Foundation for Social Policy, the UC Berkeley Institute for Research on Labor and Employment, and the University of Pennsylvania School of Arts and Sciences. Patti Isaacs assisted with graphics. I am tremendously grateful to Audra Wolfe, whose sharp eye helped me turn a long and meandering manuscript into something much more focused and, hopefully, enjoyable to read. I also thank Naomi Schneider at the University of California Press, whose generosity, responsiveness, and know-how have eased my anxieties and made our work together a breeze. As the book moved toward production, it was a pleasure to work with Aline Dolinh and the rest of the team at UC Press, as well as copyeditor Gary Hamel.

This book is dedicated to Isheh and Milo. I had just begun work on the manuscript when two events changed everything: first, Milo was born, and weeks later, we were locked down in a global pandemic. The ensuing months and years have tested us in ways that were previously unimaginable. What I'm most proud of is how we've come together to tackle every challenge. We've been knocked down over and over again, but each time we've pulled ourselves up we've emerged stronger than we were before. Throughout the storm, your love has sustained me. The publication of this book represents the closing of one chapter and the opening of another. I can't wait to see what's on the next page.

Methodological Appendix

GETTING IN

When I began the research described in this book during my second year of graduate school at the University of California, Berkeley, my ambition was twofold. First, by engaging in fieldwork on a weekly basis for at least three months, I would satisfy the course requirements of a seminar in participant-observation research methods. Second, I thought I might be able to turn the final paper I wrote for the class into a master's thesis over the summer.

Yet, as many researchers discover when they immerse themselves in a field site, the parameters of one's project often evolve far beyond the scope of one's initial plans. I had entered the field with an interest in the issue of overwork. Tech workers have long been known to put in long hours under pressing deadlines as they labor to launch the latest and greatest products.[1] I wanted to examine the social processes and understandings that led young people in the tech sector to work as hard as they did. I was particularly interested in how employees in their twenties integrated their work and nonwork lives in San Francisco's burgeoning tech community, which appeared to be as much a social "scene" for young workers as it was an agglomeration of workplaces.

My search for a field site was blessedly brief. I told friends and colleagues that I was looking for a startup where I could conduct research to learn about workers' experiences and attitudes. My first connection yielded a lunchtime conversation with Ted, a manager at a later-stage startup, but after we spoke, it didn't seem

241

that he was interested in trying to find a place for me at his company. My second meeting was brokered by a friend with whom Martin, one of AllDone's cofounders, had attended high school. After a brief e-mail exchange, Martin invited me to the office to discuss the possibility of conducting research at AllDone.

Before entering graduate school, I had worked for three years as a managing editor responsible for developing content at a brand-new tech startup in New York City. There, I observed the importance of projecting confidence in an industry in which it can be difficult to assess the potential of new ventures—or, for that matter, new hires. This experience informed my strategy for gaining access to a startup in the Bay Area. Rather than portraying myself as a naive student—a technique successfully employed by many fieldworkers to secure access to elite settings and elicit information from informants—I felt that my best means of gaining entry would be to convince members of the organization that I was already equipped to help AllDone achieve its business goals, even as I simultaneously pursued my research goal of examining work life and organizational culture at a startup. For this reason, I proposed that in exchange for research access, I would work for AllDone as an unpaid intern.

Fieldnotes from my first visit to the office detail my awareness that "I'm trying to engage [with staffers] as a potential colleague." I asked questions that signaled my understanding of the challenges the firm faced (e.g., "Who do you see as your primary competitors?") and I framed my prior experience as consistent with a potential role at AllDone by drawing comparisons between AllDone and the startup I had previously worked for. Although I was upfront that my primary interest was in conducting research at AllDone, I sought to avoid the perception that I was simply an academic interloper with little to offer the company.

This strategy seemed to be effective. By the end of my introductory meeting with Martin, he expressed some concern that I might find the projects he'd ask me to work on uninteresting, so I reminded him that he could feel free to assign me anything I could help with, because my personal goals were academic in nature. After our meeting, I chatted with Martin and other AllDone employees over lunch at the office. Before I left, Martin told me he would consult with the rest of the team about bringing me onboard. After they agreed to hire me as an intern, Martin introduced me to my new colleagues as "a PhD student studying startup culture." As the team in San Francisco grew and as my web of interactions extended to include members of AllDone's remote teams in the Philippines and Las Vegas, I would introduce myself with my job titles—director of customer support and operations manager—and explain that I was also a PhD student gathering data for a research project about the organization.

As my early weeks in the field passed, I began to realize that overwork was not the most salient feature of everyday life at AllDone. I had arrived just after the company announced its first round of venture capital funding, when members of the engineering team were spending most of their time deliberating about potential new hires rather than developing new product features (chapter 3). I was, however, immediately surprised, confused, and fascinated by the deluge of e-mails I received from members of AllDone Philippines welcoming me to the team.[2] The more I learned about the style of communication that prevailed among Filipino workers, the more I wanted to learn about how they contributed to AllDone and how they made sense of their position on the margins of the company. As I became increasingly involved with AllDone's remote teams, I began to shift my focus to the evolving relationship between the company's ever-changing technological systems and its human workforce.

"WE LOVE HAVING YOU HERE"

In the early days of my stint as AllDone's sole intern, I was surprised to find that executives quickly made me feel welcome, valued, and appreciated. I had been expecting to be viewed with some overt suspicion because of my primary role as a researcher, and I worried that it was taking me too long to get up to speed on the administrative systems that Martin had asked me to work with. Instead, it seemed like every time I was in the office, one of AllDone's three cofounders would tell me how happy they were to have me there and would offer praise as I executed small tasks and progressed through larger projects. On my second day in the office, Carter, AllDone's president, told me that I "fit right in." The friend who had connected me with AllDone told me that members of management had "spoke[n] highly of you" to her as well.

After just five workdays, Martin asked me if I could double my hours to take on additional projects, which would entail being paid $25 per hour as a part-time contractor. That same day, Peter, the CEO, told me "we love having you here" and said I should let him know "if you ever want to take a year off from your PhD and work full-time." Soon after I took on the part-time contractor role, Martin and Carter seemed receptive to my suggestion that I join them on their upcoming trip to the Philippines; I secured a small grant from my academic department to fund my travel and was instantly added to their itinerary. Following up on Peter's proposal, and in consultation with my advisor at Berkeley, I temporarily withdrew from my graduate program to spend a year working full-time as All-Done's director of customer support and operations manager while continuing my research activities.[3] This was a salaried position that paid $75,000 annually and also included a small stock option grant.[4]

By the time the research seminar that led me to AllDone had concluded, I was stunned by the depth of access I had achieved. I was of course pleased, but also puzzled. How had this novice ethnographer managed to ascend from an unpaid internship to middle management in just six months? And why did AllDone's leadership seem so happy to have me along for the ride?

One reason why executives may have eagerly accepted me is that my presence allowed them to delegate undesirable but consequential tasks to a subordinate who had quickly earned their trust. The first project that Martin assigned me was to build out the company's database of "request questions," or the questions that buyers were asked to answer when submitting a work request. Buyers' answers to these questions helped sellers understand the parameters of the job and submit an accurate quote to the buyer. When I arrived at AllDone, the team had not yet gotten around to writing request questions for 60 percent of the service categories that the platform covered—Martin, Carter, and Josh had abandoned this project less than halfway to its completion as other, more pressing projects arose. Data revealed that being shown request questions made buyers more likely to submit a quote, and that adding request questions to the remaining hundreds of service categories could net AllDone an additional $10,000 per month, a figure that would grow as AllDone's user base increased. It is telling that AllDone's leaders had not revived a project anticipated to generate significant additional revenue—they clearly viewed this task as tedious and time-consuming. Aside from the new office manager, I had become the only entry-level worker on the San Francisco staff who was not a software engineer or designer, making me a resource for managers who wanted to offload projects that did not require specialized technical skills.

My work performance and attitude on the job also helped solidify my relationship with ADSF leaders. Like many employees in the tech sector, I purposefully cultivated an image and identity as a "go-to guy," a reliable team player willing to "take ownership" of whatever projects I was assigned, without complaint.[5] Some of the activities I undertook early on to establish my legitimacy as a dependable, self-directed team member included: independently formulating, proposing, and executing small projects; sending Martin an unsolicited e-mail at the end of every workday summarizing my progress in relation to the company's short- and long-term goals; staying at the office until the last person was leaving, often around 9 p.m. or later (which I also felt was important for my research); responding to praise with modesty or by redirecting credit toward colleagues; and embracing "boring" but necessary work.

I was initially skeptical of my own competence because I often felt overwhelmed with new information, and it could take some time for me to pick up on how AllDone's systems worked. But I now recognize that some of my difficulties can be attributed to the fact that I received very little training—Martin typically left me to figure things out myself and ask questions when I was confused. The fact that I was able to succeed in this arrangement built managers' trust that I could execute projects without being micromanaged. I also came to understand that it is common for employees at early-stage startups—where change is endemic and workforces tend to be small and relatively unspecialized—to begin work on a project before they know what the end product will look like. In all likelihood, the fact that I was a researcher as well as an employee improved my work performance—after leaving the office, I deliberately reviewed and reflected upon the day's activities as I turned jottings into fieldnotes and analytic commentary, and I spent many of my nonwork hours thinking about the company.

Another reason AllDone executives may have accepted a researcher in their midst is that they didn't feel they had much to hide from the outside world. During my first meeting with Martin, I was surprised by how quickly he laid out the intricacies of AllDone's processes for recruiting new users, its administrative systems, and the various duties of the Filipino workforce. When I expressed that I was pleasantly surprised that he was willing to share so much information with me, Martin explained that "we're pretty open here," reflecting an ethos of transparency that I would later learn was common in Silicon Valley and among tech startups more generally.[6] Whereas I had initially assumed that AllDone would be reluctant to reveal details about how the company offshored work to the Philippines (which I imagined some observers might assume were exploitative), I found that AllDone's cofounders publicly touted their remote teams as demonstrations of their resourcefulness and of the positive impact that their venture was making around the globe.[7]

My personal identity also played a crucial role in my acceptance and advancement at AllDone. My demographic characteristics and prior experiences matched those that were valued in a notoriously exclusionary industry. In a very real sense, I "belonged" at AllDone because I was young (twenty-eight when I joined the company, matching the average age of employees in the San Francisco office), white, male, held a bachelor's degree from a highly selective college, and had previously worked as a manager at a tech startup. AllDone's executives valued prestigious academic and career credentials (for example, Ivy League degrees or prior stints at top consulting firms or major tech companies), touting them in job postings and presentations to board members and potential investors. I quickly made my way into their presentations as the employee who had "dropped out" of a PhD program at Berkeley to join AllDone, even though I had repeatedly told executives and colleagues that I planned to return to graduate school. Additionally, I did not have family care obligations that would curtail my "face time" in the office. Though many of my colleagues came from wealthier backgrounds than I did, I seemed to possess the ambiguous quality of "culture fit" that managers later told me they sought in new employees.[8] As Carter said when he shared AllDone's formal job offer, 'It's not easy to find people who are really talented and who we like working with. We like you both personally and professionally, so we wanted to find a place for you.'

Although during my time in the field I was acutely aware of my shortcomings on the job, I can now see how my employment history may have helped to prepare me for my new role in middle management. While I had no experience in customer support, I found that I was able to apply lessons from a prior job with a television network, where I had spent nearly two years clearing commercials for broadcast as part of the standards and practices department. When a commercial did not comply with the network's guidelines, I had to engage in delicate communications with angry advertising agency representatives and members of the network's sales staff—not unlike how I had to write with tact and precision when responding to e-mails from dissatisfied AllDone users. Although I did not consider my subsequent stint as a managing editor at a startup to have been particularly successful, it did provide me with experience managing the efforts (and often emotions) of others. During my time at AllDone, individuals across all three teams cited my communication and "people skills" as strengths.

Colleagues were informed of, and periodically referred to, my dual identity as a sociologist and researcher. For example, on one occasion when Martin's brother visited the AllDone office, Martin introduced me as a PhD student who was studying startups by becoming "embedded with the natives." When I was preparing to take my first trip to visit team members in Las Vegas, Brandon, a member of the marketing team, joked with Peter, the CEO, "He's gonna lead a revolt! He's gonna unionize Team Vegas!" which I assumed was a reference to my identity as a (presumably critical) sociologist rather than my new organizational role as a middle manager.

On many occasions, however, I was left with the impression that my colleagues had at least temporarily forgotten about my identity as a researcher and the research activities I had disclosed to them. After Peter announced to the team in San Francisco that I would be returning to graduate school in the fall, I participated in the following exchange at the lunch table:

> Simon [a software engineer] looks toward me and says, 'So you're going back to your PhD. What does that mean? Do you pick up where you left off?'
>
> 'Yup,' I say, 'Gotta figure out my thesis and dissertation.'
>
> Peter cuts in. 'I don't know if you guys know this, but Ben first started here because he was studying startups.' Simon raises his eyebrows as if he's surprised to hear this, even though I had told him when he joined the team.
>
> Josh [the product manager], seated to my right, says, 'Can't you get course credit if you just tell them you were "embedded" here and it was part of your research?'
>
> Peter adds with a wry smile, 'Yeah, you should see his [research] dossier!'

The way Peter delivered this line—with apparent sarcasm—immediately made me wonder if he remembered that I had initially disclosed that I would, in fact, be building a "dossier" during my time at AllDone by gathering data and recording notes about my experiences. Like other ethnographers, I found that others' interpretations of my identities as participant and observer could vary depending upon the situation.[9]

I largely avoided drawing attention to my status as a researcher, in part because I was concerned that doing so would limit my access and distance me from colleagues, and in part because I worried that my research activities would be viewed as a distraction from a demanding job. I spoke openly, if generally, about my research interests and the nature of my project when asked, but only occasionally brought up the topic myself. Although I recorded fieldnotes on my desktop computer or a laptop throughout each workday, a casual observer would have been unlikely to distinguish this action from everyday work activities. I frequently took advantage of more discreet methods of inquiry—including asking questions in informal conversations or eliciting information by making declarative statements and observing colleagues' responses—to seek people's interpretations of events and clarifications of organizational practices, and to place theory into dialogue with data.[10]

By all appearances, my colleagues treated me like any other member of the team. Prior to my first day in the office, I received a company e-mail address and was added to the intraoffice e-mail list, chat program, and social network. Even in the early days of my internship, I was included in all full-staff meetings and after-work social events. I soon developed close working relationships and friendships with members of all three work teams. I interacted frequently with leaders and team members across the organization, participating in three weekly meetings with executives and managers in the San Francisco office and holding multiple weekly calls and videoconferences with leaders from the Philippines and Las Vegas teams. I also traveled to the Philippines three times (for a total of thirty-one days), and to Las Vegas on nine occasions (with most trips lasting two or three days) to meet with local managers and workers. Additionally, I reviewed thousands of documents and e-mails during and after my tenure with the company.

ANALYTIC STRATEGY

I conducted fieldwork at AllDone between February 2012 and August 2013. During my six-month stint as an intern and then part-time contractor, I usually spent twenty to twenty-four hours in the field per week. After I took on a full-time role, forty-five to fifty hours per week was typical. When I was traveling for work with colleagues, nearly every moment of the day would become fieldwork. My research activities integrated online and offline data-gathering, as the "field" stretched across both offline and online sites and required me to attend to the associations between them.[11]

I recorded extensive jottings throughout each day that I spent in the field, usually on a work computer as events were occurring, sometimes on a mobile phone, and occasionally in a small notebook.[12] Speech that appears in double quotes was inscribed immediately as I heard it. Dialogue in single quotes was inscribed as soon as possible (usually within a few minutes) and reconstructed as best as

I was able. On my twenty-five-minute subway ride to my apartment each night I began to turn jottings into full fieldnotes and then completed them at home. Next, I reread the fieldnotes and wrote summary and analytic commentaries on the day's events. This process typically took 90 to 120 minutes, and often longer. Reviewing and analyzing each day's fieldnotes helped me identify emergent patterns in the data, link data to concepts and themes, integrate insights, and formulate questions to investigate in subsequent fieldwork. My broader analytic process was both inductive and deductive. I coded select documents in ATLAS.ti and wrote analytic memos in which I connected concepts emerging from my analytic commentaries to broader sociological themes. After my stint as a full-time employee ended, I continued to gather data by conducting informal interviews with informants across the organization and examining public sources.

After leaving the field and reviewing my fieldnotes, I identified three analytic phases, each corresponding to a roughly six-month period of my research and the company's development. Parts 1 and 2 of the book present data from the first phase of research; part 3 from the second phase; and part 4 from the third phase.[13] The construction of each analytic phase was based on my observations of major "breakpoints," when exogenous events (originating from outside of the daily activities of the firm) and shifts in organizational strategy offered new occasions for structuring the relationship between work and technology.[14]

MANAGING IN THE FIELD: POSITIONALITY, POWER, AND PRIVILEGE

I entered the field eager to "study up," or to examine the role of elites in reproducing social inequalities.[15] This strategy was appealing in part because conducting fieldwork in AllDone's San Francisco office would, I imagined, free me from the responsibility of representing the experiences of people with less social power than I possessed. However, I quickly discovered that privilege exists in relation to domination. Indeed, I would soon be thrust into a role that I never could have foreseen: that of a boss. Within months of entering the field, I found myself responsible for overseeing AllDone's customer support teams in the Philippines and Las Vegas, as well as serving as the San Francisco team's delegator-in-chief, responsible for assigning ad hoc projects to the remote teams and explaining new features in weekly product update e-mails.

Chief among the methodological issues raised by my position as a manager at AllDone is that of "reactivity," or the likelihood that, through my involvement in my field site, I was influencing or even to some extent creating the behaviors, processes, and phenomena that I observed. Following a reflexive approach to ethnographic research, rather than attempting to minimize reactivity by observing AllDone from the position of an "outsider," I used my role inside the organization to learn how people and structures responded to my presence and activities. The depth of my involvement in AllDone's operations allowed me to generate theoretical insights that likely would have been far beyond my reach had I chosen to curtail my participation. My aim is not to produce knowledge that would be statistically representative of, and thus generalizable to, a population of startup firms. Instead, I bring novel ethnographic observations to bear on prior theoretical premises concerning the relationship between capital, work, and technology. I use anomalous data to reconstruct existing theory by further elaborating social processes or the conditions under which particular phenomena may occur.[16]

Although it was inevitable that my own background and identity would filter into my work role and my relationships with colleagues, I made my best effort to limit such influences. Aware of how my presence could affect the behavior of those around me, I took a variety of practical measures to self-consciously structure my activities in the field in ways that would minimize my influence over my primary objects of analysis: namely, the character and dynamism of work, technology, and organizational cultures at AllDone. I had taken over my duties from Martin and Carter, two of AllDone's cofounders, and Josh, the product manager. Given that I had no prior experience in customer support or in managing distributed work teams, it was easy for me to either continue the policies of my predecessors or to hew closely to their agenda and instructions when planning and executing projects. Indeed, my responsibilities as a middle manager typically involved implementing plans devised by others, and I held no direct influence over the company's strategy.[17]

My relative inexperience could have had consequences for the teams I worked with. For example, someone who was already well versed in phone support operations would likely have built managerial and training infrastructure for workers in Las Vegas far more quickly than I could. At the same time, I had been an "opportunistic" hire: my job duties were carved out for me not because executives had prior plans to bring on a director of customer support and operations manager, but because they were looking for a way to keep me in the fold. As is common in early-stage startups, they were generalists, and they handed over some of their tasks to another generalist.

My status as a manager increased the risk that subordinates would think it best to parrot my interpretations of events rather than sharing their own. To mediate this risk, I aimed to solicit colleagues' sense of any given situation and what actions it called for before I offered my own opinions. For example, one day Carol called me when she was deciding whether to fire Tanya, a contractor on her team (see chapter 6). As she explained the circumstances that had led her to consider this action, Carol repeatedly asked me what I thought she should do (e.g., "What do you think?"; "Do you think I should respond?"; "Should we sleep on it?"). I replied in ways that did not betray my opinion (e.g., "What makes sense to you now?") until I felt that I fully grasped Carol's read on the situation. Only then did I tell her that I agreed with her assessment of what she should do next.[18] My intention was to provide support to Carol without closing off opportunities to learn about her perspective. It is likely that my efforts to faithfully execute the instructions of my superiors and to better understand the thinking of my subordinates not only supported my research activities, but also helped me succeed in a work role for which I did not feel entirely prepared.

In taking on the tasks that others eschewed, I found myself at the center of the contradictions that animated organizational activity. The duties my supervisors handed off to me were among those that they least enjoyed handling, either because they were monotonous or unpleasant. My presence created distance between the company's leaders and its low-wage workers and users, which at times buffered them from direct contact with the negative consequences of their actions. As director of customer support, I gained firsthand experience in the emotionally taxing work of trying to appease unhappy users, which often left me feeling anxious and drained. As operations manager, I served as an organizational broker, meticulously formulating instructions and transmitting and translating information between AllDone's disparate work teams—processes that I frequently found tedious or frustrating. And as a full-time employee of AllDone San Francisco who had received a small stock option grant, I dwelled in the gap between rhetoric and reality alongside my colleagues, confronting and helping to manage the limitations of AllDone's technological systems and the excitements and disappointments of users and employees.

Although my position as a manager and broker between AllDone's teams allowed me to see and experience a broader range of activities than did arguably any of my colleagues, it also limited my access to particular phenomena. Most notably, I was largely unable to observe the "backstage" of organizational life— what workers expressed to each other when management was not watching or listening—among the Filipino and Las Vegas-based workforces.[19] For this reason, my analyses of these teams' organizational cultures focus on the "frontstage" performances to which I was privy as a manager.

As a participant-observer, I was often faced with the challenge of balancing my roles as an employee and a researcher. As noted above, throughout my time in the field, I engaged in research activities—in particular, discreetly recording fieldnotes and informally eliciting information from colleagues—in a manner that I believed did not conflict with my member role. For instance, both Veronica and Carol (the leaders of ADP and ADLV, respectively) at times suggested that they could, if I wished, insulate me from personnel issues that arose on their teams. I repeatedly insisted that I was always available to discuss difficult matters such as these. This was consistent with both my interests as a researcher who wanted to know more about the social dynamics of the setting, and as a manager who wanted to support colleagues whom I cared about.

Occasionally, however, I became aware of opportunities to engage in research activities that seemed incongruent with my role in the organization. As a general rule, I avoided taking actions for the benefit of my research that seemed overtly inconsistent with what I thought a non-researcher in my position would do. Again, the episode in which Carol was struggling to decide whether to fire Tanya is illustrative. As her relationship with Carol was rapidly deteriorating, Tanya e-mailed me and asked if she and I could speak "in confidence" about the situation so that I could "listen to both sides" of the story, instead of only hearing Carol's perspective. I recognized that, as a researcher, I could take advantage of this situation to get more direct access to the experiences of one of AllDone's phone support agents. I wanted to learn more about how she viewed her job, her compensation, and the company.

At the same time, however, I worried that getting involved in the situation would reduce the esteem in which Carter (my supervisor) held me, because he was likely to view direct interventions in the remote teams' personnel decisions as a waste of my time and beneath my purview. (I had noticed that even when Veronica and one of her deputy managers were feuding for over a year, Carter did not directly speak with the deputy about it, but rather encouraged Veronica to adopt particular tactics to remedy the situation.) I was also wary of taking actions as a researcher that might make Carol's work more difficult. It seemed important that Carol remain in charge of personnel decisions. Her authority as a leader depended upon her ability to make these kinds of judgments; if her leadership were called into question, more and more members of AllDone Las Vegas would likely come directly to me with their requests. I shared Tanya's message with Carol, but I decided to forego the opportunity to speak with Tanya because it seemed incompatible with my organizational role.[20]

This is not to say that the conflicts between my identities as participant and observer did not bother me. I faced a variety of ethical dilemmas as a fieldworker who had unexpectedly stumbled into a position of power within an organization. I was uncomfortable with some aspects of AllDone's employment relations, including how managers in San Francisco, whether intentionally or not, often seemed unaware of the travails of workers in the Philippines and Las Vegas. I tried to use my position to improve working conditions for members of the remote teams. For example, I worked with the product team in San Francisco to ensure that contractors received notice of product changes before they were implemented so they wouldn't first learn of these changes from angry customers. I also advocated—unsuccessfully—for phone agents to be spared from the most difficult calls (chapter 5), and for them to receive a wage increase (chapter 7).[21] In practice, such activities may have in fact been consistent with my role in the organization, as it is not uncommon for middle managers to try to "protect" subordinates from corporate policies or initiatives that they believe could be damaging.[22] After I left the firm, I eagerly assisted former colleagues when I could be of use to them. For example, I wrote a letter of recommendation in support of Veronica's application for business school, and helped Jasmine advance her PhD studies by gathering articles she was unable to access and then informally advising her on her project.

Ultimately, however, by retaining my position of power, I was at least indirectly complicit in some team members' suffering. Carol's decision to fire Tanya, while likely the right choice for the organization, nevertheless had real and dramatic consequences for Tanya's life. I had no doubt that Tanya really did need her job.[23] What would it have meant for me to be accountable not only to AllDone, but also to Tanya? Should I have transcended the implicit boundaries of my role to help her? Or would additional intervention on my part have had unintended, and ultimately negative, consequences for her, other team members, or Carol? Even though my structural position in the firm insulated me from the burden of participating in personnel decisions relating to frontline staff, Carol frequently looked to me for advice, leaving me with some measure of input into the maintenance or disruption of people's livelihoods.

As a twenty-nine-year-old white man overseeing a team of mostly middle-aged women in the Las Vegas area, I felt acutely aware of my privilege. Some of AllDone's Las Vegas-based phone agents had decades of work experience and were being paid $10 per hour to speak with confused, disappointed, and often angry users. Meanwhile, I had leveraged my connections to gain access to an elite social setting where I had unintentionally stumbled into a job for which I did not feel fully qualified and for which I received a generous salary, perks, and benefits.

I felt ashamed that my position of power over contractors in the Philippines and Las Vegas at times seemed more indicative of my privilege than my abilities. I sometimes caught myself reflexively downplaying displays of inequality in an effort to minimize team members' perceptions of difference, and in so doing, to alleviate my own discomfort. For instance, I edited onboarding documents that told the story of AllDone's privileged founders to eliminate references to their Ivy League pedigree; I deleted information about AllDone San Francisco employees' salaries from a document that Carter was planning to send to Veronica (AllDone Philippines' general manager); and I was reluctant to expound on the perks available to workers in San Francisco when members of the Las Vegas team brought them up in conversation. I noted (and regretted) how my reflexive response to the discomfort caused by confronting organizational inequalities may have helped to perpetuate them by obscuring class differences.

In sum, by dint of my position in the firm—both participant and observer, manager and managed—I became implicated in the relations of domination that were present in the field site.[24] In my role as a middle manager, I created value for the company that was in part derived from the labor of low-wage workers. Although my deep immersion in the company allowed me to gain insights that would have otherwise been impossible to develop, as long as I remained in the field I would be presented with irreconcilable ethical quandaries and moral dilemmas.

Another potential criticism of my approach is that accepting payment from AllDone could have undermined the "objectivity" of my analysis. Like other workplace ethnographers, I presumed that deepening my participation in the organization would yield important firsthand knowledge of workers' experiences.[25] On a practical level, accepting payment allowed me to support myself financially during the year in which I had temporarily withdrawn from my graduate studies and therefore was not earning a stipend (though my salary from AllDone far exceeded what I would have made working as a teaching assistant at Berkeley). From an analytic perspective, receiving a small stock option grant helped me understand what it felt like to hold even a miniscule stake in a fast-growing startup, informing both my analysis of AllDone San Francisco's culture of speculative optimism (chapter 2) and of the vast inequalities in compensation between members of the San Francisco team and the remote teams in the Philippines and Las Vegas. Researchers who are personally involved in their field sites can systematically engage in a variety of mental activities to sustain a "professional distance" that is essential to generating sociological insights from data.[26] As described above, I undertook many such activities, including writing daily fieldnotes and analytic commentary, coding select documents, and writing analytic memos throughout my fieldwork.

I have frequently found myself preoccupied with another ethical concern: that some of my colleagues/research subjects might, following the publication of this book, come to feel that our friendships were purely instrumental. Many have argued that asymmetrical relationships are unavoidable in ethnographic research. Fieldworkers participate in the lives of their research subjects with an agenda and interests that others in the setting do not share. On this topic, sociologist Rachel Sherman's words resonate deeply for me: "It is hard [for an ethnographer] to separate a genuine personal interest in one's coworkers from the desire to obtain information from them. I can only say that I felt both."[27]

GETTING OUT

My relationship with AllDone had begun as an open-ended engagement. When I first met Martin, I told him I was looking for a research site where I could spend at least a semester working and gathering data. We agreed that I might stay longer if both parties decided that it would be mutually beneficial for me to continue. When I later took on a full-time position, it was with the understanding that I would return to graduate school after one year. My fieldwork appeared to have an expiration date.

However, leaving AllDone wasn't quite that simple. During the meeting in which my promotion was announced, Carter explained that I would be 'dropping out of grad school to work for AllDone full-time.' I interjected that technically I was only withdrawing from school for a year, at which point someone cried out, "That's what Bill said!" before the room burst into laughter. Bill was a software engineer who had put a computer science PhD on hold to join AllDone. He had since made it clear that he had no intention of returning to his studies. Josh, the product manager, had dropped out of a top-ranked business school to join AllDone. Others had left prestigious jobs in law and politics. And since I'd begun working at AllDone, nobody had left the San Francisco team voluntarily. It seemed to me that the prevailing impression around the office was that AllDone attracted "the best" people from a variety of professional and intellectual backgrounds, and that working for AllDone represented the logical next step in the careers of these elite young professionals.

Soon after I began working full-time, Carter suggested that if I were to make a longer-term commitment to AllDone by staying for at least two years instead of one, he would hand off all of his current managerial duties to me, putting me in charge of overseeing the entire team in the Philippines. I told him that I would consider his offer over the coming months. I was excited by how my new role had deepened my research access and imagined that yet another promotion would open new vistas for data collection and my ability to generate important insights for my academic work. But I also recognized that the longer I stayed in the field, the greater the risk that my relationships with colleagues and advisors at Berkeley—as well as my ties to the academy itself—might be weakened or severed.

I had heard cautionary tales of ethnographers who had lost touch with their role as an academic observer and became fully immersed in their role as a participant in the social worlds of those they studied.[28] Throughout my fieldwork, this danger was never far from my mind—in part because, in spite of the fact that I had entered the field with a critical perspective on startup work, I began to notice that I enjoyed working at AllDone.

From my earliest days in the field, I couldn't help but compare life in the AllDone office with my academic labor as a graduate student. As opposed to working in isolation at the library, the office's open floor plan, collective meals, and comfortable gathering spaces made some aspects of going to work feel like attending a social gathering. In contrast with the semester-long or multiyear projects that I undertook as a graduate student, I found it gratifying to begin and complete an endless series of small projects with definite endpoints. My supervisors frequently praised my work, allowing me to feel a sense of competence that had eluded me in graduate school. And, of course, there was the divergence in compensation and benefits: my salary was three times the size of my graduate student stipend (not including a stock option grant), I received three free meals five days a week, and enjoyed benefits and perks including "unlimited" vacation time, paid travel to Las Vegas and the Philippines, occasional chair massages, and more. I was acutely aware that in many respects this was about as good a job as I could ever expect to find myself in.

Eight months into my term as director of customer support and operations manager, AllDone closed its second round of venture capital funding. Carter told me that he was going to need my final decision about my future with the company so he could make plans for the operations team. Peter, AllDone's CEO, told me that 'we'll do whatever we can to keep you.' Carter followed up by asking me to name my price: what kind of compensation package could he offer to get me to stay at AllDone?

A few days later, Adam, AllDone's director of engineering, invited me to join him for a private "one-on-one"—something we had never done before. We left the office and walked to Yerba Buena Gardens, a park not far from the office. The sky was overcast when we set out, but the sun began to shine through the clouds as we sat by the base of a fountain. I watched small waves rippling in the pool below as Adam began to offer me his advice. After citing the $12.5 million in funding, Adam looked me in the eye and said, 'This is the stupidest time to leave.' He laid out the fabulous paths being 'an early guy' at AllDone would pave for my future career. I could write my own ticket, at AllDone or anywhere else. I could be a consultant and rake in a huge hourly fee! I could give talks! Adam was the most wry, sarcastic person in the office; I had rarely seen him address anyone this earnestly. I found myself sincerely confused, oddly drawn toward staying with AllDone and exploring its possibilities.

My attempt to leave the field brought me face-to-face with its seductions. I could return to graduate school—or I could make more money, receive more equity, and ride AllDone's rise into ever-greater heights of success, renown, and fortune. I could remain an analytic observer of the company, or I could fully invest in the imagined future it promoted, parlaying one lucky break into untold possibilities.

My fieldnotes from this period reflect how, like many of my colleagues, I had become gripped by the fantasies propagated by venture capitalism. I was facing what I identified at the time as an "existential crisis." My colleagues' response to my attempt to exit the field had led me to question who I was and who I wanted to be. If I surrendered my future to AllDone, anything seemed possible. After all, according to Adam, potential was oozing out of the company and affixing itself to everything and everyone associated with it. "I think about this all day, often changing my mind during the day about what I want to do," I wrote. "Academic life can be satisfying because I find the work meaningful. But AllDone can be thrilling because it's fun and it *feels good.*" If even I, a critical sociologist, could be drawn into AllDone's culture of speculative optimism, I had no doubt that venture capitalism could reshape less skeptical workers' motivations, identities, and visions of the future.

After much reflection, I decided that I would remain committed to my original vision of building a career as a sociologist. I told Carter that I would be leaving AllDone at the end of my one-year term as a full-time employee. Colleagues across the organization were supportive of my decision, though many of those with whom I'd developed the closest relationships expressed grief and sadness.

Some were puzzled. Soon after my departure was officially announced, I was sitting at the lunch table with a group of software engineers.

> Brett is talking about his recruiting network. He says everyone he knows is going to grad school.

> 'That's perfect,' Adam says. 'Start on them now. They'll be so disillusioned after a year that you can convince them to join [AllDone].' Vince glances toward me and arches an eyebrow.

> Adam turns to me with a mischievous grin. 'I heard the thing to do is to start a PhD program, drop out and join a startup, and then leave and go back to the program.'

> 'Is that what you heard?' I reply. 'Yup,' he says.

> James chimes in and asks, with a note of incredulity, "Who jumps off a rocket ship that's blasting into space?" That's a great question, I say with a sheepish smile.

> Vince says, 'Well, Ben's hoping for the soft landing of grad school.'

> Adam adds, 'Ben is going to write a dissertation that has no impact on society.' Now I'm the one raising an eyebrow. 'What? It's true!' Adam cries out. 'Nobody will read it!'

To colleagues who had committed themselves to the logic of venture capitalism, my exit was almost inconceivable. Just as the rocket ship appeared to be approaching the heights they had long fantasized about, I had chosen to jump off. Their dream and my dream were no longer aligned. I soon began to work with Carter to hire and train my replacement (see chapter 7). During my final week I visited the team in Las Vegas for a meeting and celebratory dinner, said goodbye to colleagues in the Philippines over videoconference, and went out for beers with a few coworkers in San Francisco after switching off my work computer for the last time.

Over the next couple of years I continued to receive invitations to offsite quarterly review parties and after-work events in the office, many of which I attended. Occasionally Carter would send me a text message or e-mail encouraging me to return to AllDone; I would thank him for thinking of me but explain that I was still committed to completing my PhD. I stayed in touch with former colleagues and continued to learn about the company's progress through our conversations. Many of these ties eventually faded or disappeared over time. Although academic articles that I have written about my fieldwork can be easily located online, I have yet to hear from anyone at AllDone about any reactions they might have to my research.

The only official link that remains between me and the organization is the unusual fact that, because my compensation as a full-time employee included stock options, I own a miniscule piece of the startup I studied.[29] During the company's most recent fundraise in 2021, AllDone announced that former employees would be given the opportunity to sell a significant portion of their stock options to investors. I caught up with David, a former deputy manager for AllDone Philippines, via online chat. Out of the two hundred Filipino contractors who had contributed to the company's early successes during my time with the company, he was one of five who had received a stock option grant. When I asked David how the old gang was doing, he told me, "All of us are waiting for this [stock] sale. It's a life-changer for us." By my estimate, each of the deputy managers held stock options that would be worth up to $200,000 given the company's new valuation—a massive sum in a country where the average family income is under $6,000.[30]

But when the final details of the fundraise were revealed, former employees were dismayed to learn that the deal was "oversubscribed"—because there was more stock on offer than investors wanted to buy, each person would only be permitted to sell 5 percent of his or her holdings. Meanwhile, I learned that AllDone's cofounders had arranged the deal so that they would not be subjected to this constraint—they had put themselves first in line to sell a greater proportion of their own stock, to the tune of a combined $60 million. As the tech industry headed into a downturn in late 2022, with investments in startups and IPOs sharply declining, David and his friends in the Philippines continued to wait to find out whether they would ever get their chance to cash out.

Notes

PREFACE

1. The names of the company and members of the organization have been changed to protect individuals' privacy.

2. Rosenblat (2018); Ravenelle (2019); Schor (2020).

3. Cameron (2021).

4. As Vallas and Schor (2020:286–87) note, there is an abundance of research on platform-based workers, but little on the architects of digital platforms. Kelkar (2018) and Seaver (2022) are notable exceptions.

5. Teare (2022).

INTRODUCTION

1. Grossman (2006).

2. O'Mara (2019).

3. E.g., Zuboff (2018); Silverman et al. (2022); Rosenblat (2018).

4. Harmful algorithms have been documented across many domains of social life, including health care, the criminal justice system, the delivery of government services, consumer credit scoring, and internet search (O'Neil 2016; Brayne 2017; Noble 2018; Benjamin 2019; Joyce et al. 2021). These novel systems can reproduce or amplify age-old systems of gendered and racialized domination.

Meanwhile, digital labor platforms have pioneered software that is often designed to deceive and disempower workers (Rosenblat 2018; Gray and Suri 2019). The opacity of programmers' machine-learning techniques can make it difficult to hold companies accountable for their use of dangerous and damaging software (Burrell 2016).

5. In their pursuit of success, high-flying founders have willfully broken laws, lied to investors and the public, squandered company funds on private escapades, and fostered workplaces rife with harassment and abuse. See Carreyrou (2018); Wiedeman (2020); Isaac (2019).

6. Today's dominant tech firms have adopted "platform" business models in which profits are derived from a company's role as a market intermediary connecting multiple parties, such as buyers and sellers of goods (Amazon), drivers and passengers (Uber, Lyft), or viewers and advertisers (Google, YouTube, Facebook). At the same time, platform companies extract and reap the benefits of valuable data about users and their behaviors. Platforms are subject to powerful "network effects" that exponentially increase their value to users and investors as they grow. Consequently, firms may burn through millions or even billions of dollars in investment capital as they try to outmaneuver competitors and achieve a monopolistic market position. See Langley and Leyshon (2017); Srnicek (2017); Kenney and Zysman (2019); Rahman and Thelen (2019).

7. Recent exceptions include Vertesi et al. (2020) and van Doorn and Chen (2021).

8. Although my role in the field was in many ways advantageous, it also entailed numerous limitations. See the methodological appendix for further details.

9. DiMaggio and Powell (1983).

10. I use this term to describe a model of organizational management that prescribes a distinctive set of ideologies and techniques to frame and solve organizational problems (Guillen 1994).

11. In some cases, the value of a firm's equity may appear to be completely decoupled from its economic performance: "As long as a speculator expects that other investors will remain invested in an asset because they expect its price will continue to rise, it is rational for her to also stay invested in it even when she believes it is 'fundamentally' overvalued" (Beckert 2016:146). The sudden explosion in the price of so-called "meme stocks" in early 2021—when Gamestop's stock price briefly shot up more than sixteen-fold—underscored how the value of a company's shares may rise or fall independent of corporate activity (Eavis 2021). The trade in cryptocurrencies and non-fungible tokens exhibits similar dynamics.

12. Beckert (2016:118).

13. Gompers and Lerner (2004).

14. Cutler (2018); O'Mara (2019).

15. CB Insights (2022); Griffith (2022).

16. For example, the city of San Francisco manages $20 billion to fund city workers' retirements; $1 billion of this sum is allocated to venture capital funds (Cutler 2018).

17. Mintz and Schwartz (1990); Stearns (1990).

18. Mason (2009).

19. Somerville (2020); Beltran (2020). Venture-backed companies tend to achieve IPOs at a significantly faster rate than startups that do not receive VC funding (Gompers and Lerner 2001).

20. Bussgang (2010); Shapin (2008); Cutler (2018).

21. World Bank (2021).

22. Gompers and Lerner (2004); Mason (2009); Wasserman (2017).

23. Mason (2009); Langley and Leyshon (2017); Hoffman and Yeh (2018).

24. Uber Technologies (n.d.).

25. Uber got so big that it eventually attracted investments from sovereign wealth funds and traditional Wall Street banks (Vita 2022).

26. Bort (2019).

27. Driebusch and Farrell (2018).

28. Funk (2022).

29. Many VCs have published books, articles, blog posts, and Twitter threads divulging the ins and outs of the trade (e.g. Bussgang 2010; Romans 2013). Management scholars have investigated the relationship between venture capital investments and startups' financial success (Rosenbusch, Brinckmann, and Müller 2013); gender disparities in entrepreneurs' receipt of VC funding (Greene et al. 2010); and the characteristics of successful VC firms (Gompers, Kovner, and Lerner 2009) and founders (Burton, Sørensen, and Beckman 2002), among other topics. But few have examined the experiences of the workers who populate VC-backed startups.

30. I thank Janet Vertesi for sharing this insight.

31. Vinsel and Russell (2020:10).

32. Koning, Hasan, and Chatterji (2022).

33. Kenney and Zysman (2019).

34. Vinsel and Russell (2020).

35. Neff (2012).

36. Ho (2009) shows how Wall Street investment bankers have adopted a similar outlook, justifying the dislocation of workers in the wake of corporate mergers and layoffs as collateral damage in the pursuit of more "efficient" markets.

37. Shapin (2008:309).

38. Fjermedal (1994:99).

39. Block and Keller (2009).

40. Nicholas (2019).

41. "Silicon Valley" originally referred to the Santa Clara Valley, which in the 1970s was a hub for semiconductor manufacturing south of San Francisco

(Saxenian 1994). The moniker's geographic reach has expanded to follow the spread of tech companies across the Bay Area.

42. Kenney (2000); Kenney and Zysman (2019).

43. Associated Press (2018). "Value" here refers to a company's market capitalization, or the total value of a its shares on the stock market. By early 2020, these five companies accounted for nearly 18 percent of the value of the S&P 500 Index, which tracks the performance of 500 large companies (Levy and Konish 2020). Microsoft cofounder Bill Gates has claimed that Microsoft accepted its sole VC investment not to raise money, but instead to gain access to an investor's expert advice by seating him on Microsoft's board of directors (Wilhelm 2017).

44. Osterman (1999).

45. Useem (1993).

46. Gelles (2022:23).

47. Davis (2009).

48. Neely and Carmichael (2021).

49. Davis (2009).

50. Lin and Neely (2020).

51. Useem (2019).

52. Epstein (2005:3).

53. Davis and Kim (2015).

54. Snyder (2016:70). From an investor's perspective, a tech startup is an asset first and foremost. This helps to explain why companies can take on fantastical valuations when the technologies behind them may not work very well, continually underdeliver, or even harm the lives of many of the people who use them.

55. On capitalism's "dynamic disequilibrium," see Beckert (2009).

56. Kalleberg (2011).

57. Osterman (1999); Kalleberg (2011).

58. Piketty (2014); Philippon and Reshef (2012).

59. Lin and Tomaskovic-Devey (2013). The rise of finance was intertwined with changes to the structural conditions underlying the economy that opened the doors to deindustrialization, deunionization, and the rise of employment in the service sector. See Cowie (1999) and Lichtenstein (2002) on how legal limits on union activity and the uneven geographic reach of the legal and regulatory infrastructure upon which organized labor relied left unions vulnerable to institutional change.

60. Lin and Neely (2020).

61. Neff (2012).

62. Barley (1988); Kunda (1992).

63. Here I draw on the work of sociologists who examine the cultural dimensions of economic activity. Jens Beckert (2016), in particular, emphasizes how economic actors' temporal orientation toward and imagination of the future shape their behaviors and strategies.

64. Beckert (2016).

65. Snyder (2016).

66. Hoffman and Yeh (2018); Holland (2020).

67. Burawoy (1979); Kunda (1992); Turco (2016); Vertesi (2021).

68. Irani (2015a); Ekbia and Nardi (2017); Shestakofsky (2017); Gray and Suri (2019); Roberts (2019).

69. In conceptualizing organizational drag, I draw from two intellectual lineages. First, management scholars of entrepreneurship have highlighted the nonlinear, episodic, and at times crisis-driven nature of organizational development (Greiner 1998[1972]; Bhidé 2000; Shane 2003). This research resonates with a second set of theories: the work of Marxist thinkers who emphasize how processes of capital accumulation systematically create crises that must be addressed if capitalists are to generate profits. For example, competition incentivizes capitalists to reduce production costs by decreasing wages; however, as wages drop, workers have less money to purchase those same goods. One way for capitalists to overcome this crisis is to seek out new markets. Yet the same dynamics of capitalist competition will eventually take root in new locations and reproduce similar crises. In short, capital seeks "fixes" that temporarily forestall, but do not permanently eliminate, the contradictory forces that spawn crises (Marx 1978; Harvey 1989; Silver 2003). Unlike this book, these theories typically focus on the system of capitalism as a whole rather than the challenges confronted by particular capitalist organizations.

70. Bailey and Barley (2020) emphasize the importance of developing studies that trace the entirety of the "technology timeline," from the structural forces that shape technology design, to the ways in which the uses of new technologies are influenced by local contexts, to the broader social consequences of the adoption of particular technological systems.

71. For example, sending a quote for a wedding photography job—which could ultimately yield hundreds or thousands of dollars in revenue for a seller—would cost far more than sending a quote for a job helping to edit a client's resume, for which editors typically charged between $50 and $100.

72. Hyman (2018).

73. In 2015, the *International Business Times* reported that a venture-backed company's chance of achieving a valuation of over $1 billion was .14 percent (Kenney and Zysman 2019).

74. Turco (2016) is one exception. Interview-based studies of startups may yield limited insights given that Silicon Valley technologists are prone to exaggeration.

75. See Barley and Beane (2020) on the dominant paradigm for studying work and technological change.

76. Venture-backed startups can be viewed as "exceptional cases" that "magnify relational patterns that in more mundane contexts lack visibility" (Ermakoff 2014:227). The pace of strategic shifts is typically accelerated, and processes

of technological change are often undertaken more frequently in new ventures than in established firms (Kirtley and O'Mahony 2020). Studying early-stage startups can thus afford researchers the opportunity to observe a greater number of instances in which investors' imperatives directly and indirectly shape the interplay between work and technology inside firms.

77. Some readers may wonder why AllDone succeeded, while other, similar startups have failed. Was it owing to the ways in which the company complemented computer code with human labor? Were executives more persuasive when pitching their company to investors? Did AllDone simply win the "race" and establish itself first? This book brackets such considerations. Rather than advancing a general law of startup success, my intention is to map out the dilemmas and hurdles inherent to venture capitalism by showing how one firm navigated them.

78. Echoing the economic geographer David Harvey's (2001:24) analysis of global capitalism, my use of the term *fix* is not intended to imply that the problems startups address are permanently resolved. Instead, Harvey draws on connotations of drug use, describing "a burning desire to relieve a chronic or pervasive problem." After a "fix" is achieved, "the resolution is temporary rather than permanent, since the craving soon returns."

CHAPTER 1. ORCHESTRATING CHANGE

1. Stout (2015).

2. Gompers and Lerner (2001).

3. Some startups raise an initial round of "seed" funding from VC firms, while others turn to angel investors. Like venture capitalists, angels offer entrepreneurs "equity capital," exchanging money for a stake in the firm. Unlike VCs, however, angels "tend to use investment terms and conditions that are more brief and more informal than venture capitalists," and thus they lack "many of the important screening and monitoring mechanisms" implemented by VC firms, such as holding frequent meetings with executives and reviewing regular reports on the company's progress (Gompers and Lerner 2001:10).

4. The fact that most AllDoners were able to survive for months without pay in San Francisco—which consistently ranks as one of the most expensive places to live in the United States—reflects the privilege of much of Silicon Valley's tech workforce.

5. E.g., Fried and Hisrich (1994); Hsu (2007); Hallen and Eisenhardt (2012).

6. Pfeffer and Salancik (1978).

7. Many sources peg the startup failure rate at 90 percent. According to a report tracking 1,100 US tech companies that managed to raise an initial "seed round" of VC funding between 2008 and 2010, two-thirds had either died or

become "self-sustaining" by 2018. (Such "zombie companies" fail to achieve a corporate acquisition or IPO that creates massive returns for investors.) Only 1 percent had attained a valuation of $1 billion or more (CB Insights 2018). See also Yoffie, Gawer, and Cusumano (2019).

8. Bhidé (2000); Baker and Nelson (2005); Neff and Stark (2004).

9. Wasserman (2017). Financial institutions leverage corporations' dependence on external funds to advance their own interests (Stearns 1990). Because early-stage startups typically lack meaningful sources of revenue, their dependence is likely to be particularly acute, as is investors' influence over corporate governance.

10. Carroll and Hannan (2000).

11. This model is inspired in part by general life-cycle models of organizational development (van de Ven and Poole 1995).

12. Beckert (2016).

13. Shapin (2008).

14. Beckert (2016); Langley and Leyshon (2017).

15. Srnicek (2017).

16. *Engineering* is a value-laden term. My use of the term is not intended to reify a distinction between "engineers" and "non-engineers" among members of AllDone's global workforce. As described in the following chapters, technological innovations emerging from the San Francisco office were enabled by and inextricably linked to the efforts of AllDone's remote teams in the Philippines and Las Vegas, whose activities often required them to creatively solve problems and design strategies for getting work done despite numerous constraints. In marking the San Francisco team's function as engineering work, I simply intend to emphasize its unique role in orchestrating continual experimentation in AllDone's product and organizational processes. See Irani (2019) on the acts of social recognition surrounding the word *innovation*, which are inflected by an individual's or group's social status (e.g., race, class, gender, nation), leading to the devaluation of the contributions of those who are not typically recognized as "innovators." Irani emphasizes that hierarchies of labor do not reflect "natural" allocations of skill, but are instead the result of global inequalities.

17. Dashboards and data tracking have become essential to startups' survival in the face of escalating competition and investors' expectations. See Christin (2020) and Petre (2021) on the role of dashboards in shaping journalistic practices in online newsrooms.

18. Because this blog was at one time publicly available, I have altered the phrasing of the quoted passage while attempting to preserve the meaning in order to maintain anonymity. See Shklovski and Vertesi (2013) on digital anonymization practices.

19. Spoken dialogue that appears in double quotes was inscribed in situ. Dialogue in single quotes was inscribed shortly after it occurred, reconstructed to the best of my ability.

20. These tensions between rival logics of evaluation (Stark 2009) resonate with research in domains including policing, education, and journalism, where the emergent authority of data scientists may supersede the authority of subject-matter experts (Brayne 2017; Kelkar 2018; Christin 2020).

21. Ries (2011). Research suggests that A/B testing increases the rate at which startups introduce new features. A/B testing is also associated with a higher likelihood of both massive failures and grand successes (Koning et al. 2022).

22. Vision was in these respects similar to the digital dashboards that newsrooms use to track user engagement. Building on prior studies of "work games" (Burawoy 1979), sociologist Caitlin Petre (2021) has examined how such software can be designed to capture workers' attention and motivate them to work harder.

23. Sellers could specify how many miles they were willing to travel to complete a job. Previously, AllDone would only send sellers buyer requests from within their stated range. When the system was altered to distribute requests to sellers from buyers a few miles *beyond* the travel distance they supposedly preferred, the volume of quotes submitted by sellers skyrocketed.

24. See Scott (1999) on state efforts to exact control over populations by rendering them bureaucratically legible.

25. In contrast, see Porter (1995).

26. In some workplaces, managers use metrics to rank, sort, and value employees, who may come to view metrics as a reflection of their *individual* performance or worth (Christin 2020; Petre 2021). At AllDone, however, metrics were generally viewed as an indicator of the company's progress toward *collective* goals.

27. Venture-backed companies that fail to exhibit explosive growth are unable to deliver the asset value inflation that generates returns for investors. A startup consistently making tens of millions of dollars a year would thus join the ranks of "the so-called 'living dead'" in a VC fund's portfolio" (Mason 2009:134).

28. Beckert (2016) elaborates how imagined futures underpin the dynamism of capitalist economies.

29. Meyer and Rowan (1977).

30. Packer (2013).

31. Porter (1995); Christin (2020).

CHAPTER 2. DREAMING OF THE FUTURE

1. Lounsbury and Glynn (2001).

2. Stinchcombe (1965).

3. DiMaggio and Powell (1983). The common Silicon Valley trope for describing a new startup—"It's X for Y"—demonstrates how new ventures must be simultaneously novel and yet also recognizable. For example, an on-demand dessert delivery service might be described as "Uber for ice cream."

4. Meyer and Rowan (1977).

5. Zott and Huy (2007).

6. See Beckert (2016). This is why entrepreneurs frequently stretch the truth to blur the line between lofty promises and disappointing realities. The rapid rise and fall of the blood-testing startup Theranos is one prominent example of Silicon Valley's "fake it 'til you make it" ethos (Carreyrou 2018).

7. Cockayne (2016:465).

8. Hochschild (1983); Van Maanen and Kunda (1989).

9. Neff (2012). Intel was one of the first tech companies to add stock options to employee compensation packages. Executives hoped to incentivize workers to promote the corporate interest while discouraging unionization efforts (Mallaby 2022).

10. See Mears (2020) on how managers can mobilize positive emotions for economic gain.

11. I later learned that each subsequent round of VC funding can significantly dilute the value of existing stock options. For example, imagine an employee who was granted the same allocation of stock options that I received, and whose options became fully vested after staying with the company for four years. Six funding rounds later, AllDone's valuation exceeded $3 billion. Without dilution, a $3 billion valuation would have resulted in options valued at over $3 million. But that same stock option grant was now technically valued at $800,000—undoubtedly a massive windfall if the employee were able to sell the stock, but worth about four times less in absolute terms than its value before being diluted. See the methodological appendix for details regarding the disposition of my stock options.

12. Schein (2004:17).

13. Kunda (1992); Turco (2016). For two contemporary examples, see Microsoft (https://careers.microsoft.com/us/en/culture) and Netflix (https://jobs.netflix.com/culture).

14. This statement echoes text found on a 2009 PowerPoint presentation outlining "Netflix Culture," which has been widely imitated across the tech industry. (https://www.slideshare.net/reed2001/culture-1798664/2-Netflix_CultureFreedom_Responsibility2)

15. See Thrift (2001) on the "new market culture" of the twenty-first century. Neely (2022) argues that, for women in elite workplaces, demonstrating one's "passion" for work can serve as a strategy for countering the stereotyped perception that women are primarily devoted to home and family.

16. Alfrey and Twine (2017); Mickey (2019).

17. See chapter 3 for additional details.

18. Hesmondhalgh and Baker (2015).

19. Lindtner (2020:145); see also Greene (2021).

20. See also Turco (2016).

21. Fernandez and Greenberg (2013).

22. Leighton (2020).

23. Numerous studies have documented challenges faced by women and people of color in the tech industry, where harassment, hostility, harmful stereotypes, and exclusion are commonplace (Wynn and Correll 2018; Alegria 2020). Women and ethnic minorities who experience discrimination may resort to "job-hopping" to find more egalitarian employers (Shih 2006), or downplay their femininity to avoid male employees' negative attention and assessments (Alfrey and Twine 2017). When women engineers are promoted, many are moved into business and management positions that prevent them from sharpening their technical expertise, and from which they are unlikely to ascend further into executive positions (Alegria 2019).

24. See chapter 3 for additional details regarding AllDone's hiring philosophy for filling technical roles.

25. As the company raised additional funds and continued to grow (see chapter 7), a recruiter was hired to help formalize the recruitment process. Around this time the San Francisco office began to exhibit noticeable increases in gender and racial diversity. Baron et al. (2007) find that bureaucratization can improve the representation of women in technical roles. However, Mickey (2019) argues that when startups IPO and job descriptions become more formalized, women who had previously held technical roles may be more likely to be moved into feminized and lower-status positions. See also Smith-Doerr (2004).

26. E.g., Sharone (2004); Barley and Kunda (2004).

27. Kunda (1992); Turco (2016).

28. Other tech startups evince similar practices of open communication across organizational hierarchies (Turco 2016).

29. Van Maanen and Kunda (1989); Larkey and Morrill (1995).

30. Although I entered the field as a critical sociologist, at times I, too, found myself caught up in the excitement. (See the methodological appendix.)

31. See Jasanoff and Kim (2009) on sociotechnical imaginaries.

32. Beckert (2016).

33. Alfrey and Twine (2017); Wynn and Correll (2018).

34. And yet: if not for this spatial differentiation and concomitant labor-market arbitrage, the company would not have been able to afford to hire the vast majority of its remote workforce. See chapter 3.

CHAPTER 3. WORKING ALGORITHMS

1. March (1991).

2. Tushman and O'Reilly (1996).

3. In the following chapter I detail how Filipino workers made sense of their jobs and the structure of interactions between Filipino workers and managers in San Francisco.

4. As is common among tech startups, a group of over a dozen individual investors supplied AllDone with early funding (totaling over $1 million) soon after the launch of its platform, but before the company was sufficiently developed to attract funding from a VC firm (see chapter 1).

5. Gray and Suri (2019).

6. Irani (2015a); Gillespie (2018); Gray and Suri (2019); Roberts (2019).

7. Autor (2014:136).

8. Alpaydin (2014); Autor (2015a).

9. Gillespie (2016:26).

10. I avoid the more common terms *microwork* and *crowdwork* because they typically describe tasks completed in the context of "an individualized and largely anonymous transaction" (Howcroft and Bergvall-Kåreborn 2019:24) between worker and employer. As shown in chapter 4, this description does not apply to members of AllDone Philippines. "Computation" refers to a labor process without reference to the nature of the employment relationship.

11. Koetsier (2020).

12. Gray and Suri (2019).

13. Baker and Nelson (2005:331).

14. In theory, establishing process at AllDone hewed to principles of work engineering similar to those outlined by Frederick Winslow Taylor, the prominent proponent of scientific management (Braverman 1974). In practice, however, managers at AllDone were motivated not by a drive to extract ever more labor from workers, but instead by their desire to quickly delegate tasks so that they could move on to solving new problems.

15. Alpaydin (2014:2).

16. Philippines Department of Labor and Employment (n.d.). Calculations assume an exchange rate of 42.5 pesos to one US dollar, which was the average exchange rate during the latter portion of my fieldwork (Exchangerates.org.uk n.d.a).

17. Irani (2015a); Gray and Suri (2019).

18. Workers' schedules varied according to their role. Those handling less time-sensitive operations, like verifying sellers' professional license numbers in online databases, had more control over their schedules.

19. AllDone Philippines was similar in this respect to LeadGenius, a business-to-business service that gathers and sells sales leads (Gray and Suri 2019). LeadGenius maintains an online workforce that searches the internet for the contact information of potential new customers for its clients. Instead of sourcing online workers from a relatively undifferentiated "crowd," LeadGenius interviews job candidates, asks participants to commit to working at least twenty hours per week, and structures workers into teams in which they can communicate with and learn from each other.

20. See chapter 4. An online freelancer's ties to an employer are typically severed after they complete a specified task or project (Graham, Hjorth, and Lehdonvirta 2017).

21. Irani (2015a).

22. Irani (2015a).

23. See Star and Strauss (1999) on invisible work in computational systems.

24. Irani (2015a).

25. Perrow (1999).

26. Irani (2015a).

27. Irani (2015b). Some members of AllDone San Francisco expressed ambivalence regarding the ethics of sending their "grinder" tasks to workers in the Philippines (see chapter 4).

28. AllDone's software engineers experimented not only with code, but also with labor to increase the pace of production. The nature of software work is altered when engineers have access to computational workers like members of AllDone Philippines. Developers who outsource the most tedious tasks can innovate more quickly, making their work more "creative," both symbolically and, arguably, in practice (Irani 2015b).

29. Autor (2015b:248).

30. Irani (2015b:225); Gray and Suri (2019:xxii).

CHAPTER 4. ALL IN THE FAMILY?

1. Hochschild (1983).

2. After thirty-one total days of fieldwork in the Philippines, my everyday experience working closely with ADP managers via videoconference, e-mail, and chat, and conversations with team members that continued in the months and years after I left the company, I am confident that, as in many other organizational settings, the emotional displays exhibited by Filipino workers corresponded to varying degrees with workers' inner affective states. Although sentiment and emotional expression in the workplace are deeply influenced by organizational expectations, they are of course not exclusively determined by employer dictates (Kunda 1992). Both employees and managers abide by feeling rules that can blur the "authenticity" of sentiment (Hochschild 1983). Even when participants are aware that they are engaging in "deep acting" and "role embracement," the emotions that they experience may be no less "real" than those experienced in other social settings (Goffman 1959; Van Maanen and Kunda 1989). The meanings that members derive from participating in organizational cultures are not fixed, and can vary from situation to situation (Larkey and Morrill 1995). Still, it remains difficult for me to draw definitive conclusions about the inner lives of AllDone's Filipino contractors, given how my access to workers'

internal affective states was constrained by my elevated position as an American manager in the corporate hierarchy. My inability to understand conversations among workers conducted in Tagalog or regional dialects further limited my comprehension of the "backstage" of organizational life (Goffman 1959). In short, in many instances I was only able to observe acts of impression management in public encounters—what Scott (1985) calls the "partial transcript" of interactions between members of dominant and dominated groups.

3. For a contrasting approach, see Barsade and O'Neill (2014:551), who theorize and explicitly measure how organizational cultures that promote "feelings of affection, compassion, caring, and tenderness for others" can affect work outcomes.

4. Constable (2003). Similarly, communication scholar Nancy Baym (2015:20) makes a case for the complexity of affective life as it pertains to employment relations: "We do not have to understand relationships in labor as inherently either genuine or alienating, empowering or oppressive. They are all of these and more, often at the same time."

5. In the postwar era, it was common for large firms to offer an implicit guarantee of job security in exchange for workers' loyalty (Osterman 1999). To stave off unionization, technology companies like IBM and Digital actively promoted "strong" workplace cultures as a mechanism of social control (O'Reilly 1989; Kunda 1992). By fostering shared norms and values, managers hoped to encourage behaviors that would support organizational goals while bolstering employees' identification with and commitment to the firm.

6. Although managerial ideologies emphasizing the value of corporate community and commitment have declined (Kunda and Ailon-Souday 2006), they are not altogether absent from elite workplaces where instability and uncertainty are the norm. Neely (2022) documents how hedge fund workers build "family-like" ties. They often use the rhetoric of family to justify homophily, and leverage close bonds with others when looking for a new job or starting a new venture.

7. West (1997).

8. ADP's five top managers remained independent contractors, but they were eventually awarded stock option grants. Even though she led a team of two hundred people and had started working for AllDone three years before I did, the general manager's grant was the same size as mine: at the time her stock options were issued, they would have been worth $1 million if the company were to achieve a $1 billion valuation, though as explained in chapter 2 the value of stock options is diluted with each subsequent round of VC funding. The four deputy managers' grants were a quarter of that size.

9. Chan, Selden, and Ngai (2020).

10. Irani (2015a); Gray and Suri (2019).

11. For a similar perspective drawn from a study of another industry, see Sallaz (2019) on the mutual attraction and attachment between American companies and Filipino call center workers.

12. Cook et al. (2009).

13. Friends and family members would indeed become a significant source of new recruits for AllDone Philippines.

14. For decades, the American electronics industry has relied on the repetitive, low-cost labor of South Asian women in semiconductor manufacturing (Grossman 1979; McKay 2006). Managers' decisions about where to locate production were often based on the assumption that women in the Global South possess "nimble" fingers and "docile" dispositions (Salzinger 2003). Today, management consultants typically identify the Philippines and India as the best sites for American companies seeking to offshore knowledge work. Due to differences in the structure of each country's labor market institutions and gender relations, managers are increasingly locating jobs that do not require advanced technical skills (e.g., call center and data processing work) in the Philippines (Sallaz 2019).

15. Sallaz (2019); Newcomer and Dotan (2014); Shestakofsky (2015).

16. Graham et al. (2017).

17. Graham et al. (2017).

18. During the U.S. occupation of the Philippines (1898–1946) and beyond, American influence empowered political elites who have failed to adequately advance the public interest. The United States permitted the nation's landed elite to monopolize influence in the national legislature in exchange for their support of colonial rule. After independence, the U.S. continued to prop up corrupt regimes that would serve American interests. The Philippines has maintained low rates of foreign investment and high poverty in comparison to other developing South Asian nations while establishing few social welfare institutions to provide nonmarket income to the great number of people in dire economic need. These issues are compounded by demographics. The nation's fertility rate—an average of four children per woman—is far higher than those of other industrializing countries in Southeast Asia. Consequently, the pool of available workers has expanded to levels the economy can scarcely sustain while burdening eldest daughters, who are traditionally considered "breadwinners" in Filipino society, with the obligation to provide both material support and care to large extended families (Sallaz 2019).

19. Philippine Statistics Authority (2013).

20. During the first half of the twentieth century, when the Philippines was under U.S. colonial rule, the nation became a source of cheap labor for American firms owing to Filipinos' status as U.S. nationals. Today, state-run training programs prepare workers with skills that are deemed to be in demand on the world market. English instruction is included in all primary and secondary schools in the Philippines, and postsecondary instruction is almost exclusively in English (Rodriguez 2010; Sallaz 2019).

21. Rodriguez (2010); Sallaz (2019).

22. Sallaz (2019).

23. Sallaz (2019).

24. Sociologist Alinaya Fabros' (2016) study of outsourced call-center work in the Philippines document these and many other sources of stress, anxiety, and burnout.

25. Braverman (1974); Fabros (2016).

26. Many also valued the opportunity to refer friends and family members for new positions as the team expanded. (Workers received referral bonuses of twenty dollars, equivalent to over a day's pay for the typical contractor.)

27. Sallaz (2019). See Parreñas (2015) on the importance of fulfilling consanguineal responsibilities in Filipino culture. Many members of ADP used their wages to support others. For example, Veronica paid to remodel her family's home and bought new equipment for her father's business; Ross said that he distributed 75 percent of his income to relatives, supporting his entire extended family; and Jasmine sponsored meals, school supplies, and clothes for six impoverished children in a neighboring town so they could attend school.

28. For those accustomed to working in the outsourcing sector or holding multiple jobs to make ends meet, it did not seem unusual to wake up in the middle of the night to log on during peak US hours or to nap during the day. Filipino call center workers commonly valorize working the night shift, noting that this affords them the flexibility to engage in care work and run errands during daylight hours (Sallaz 2019).

29. It is important to note that this form of economic empowerment perpetuates an unequal gendered division of labor (Graham et al. 2017; Sallaz 2019).

30. The voice industry became so central to Manila's economy that by 2011, 40 percent of the city's office space was devoted to call centers (ABS-CBN News 2011).

31. Burawoy (1979).

32. D'Cruz and Noronha (2016); Sallaz (2019).

33. Involuntary dismissal of new recruits who had failed to log the expected number of hours or repeatedly exhibited unsatisfactory performance was more common.

34. Kunda (1992:7).

35. Prior research supports the notion that ADP's style of expressive communication could serve important practical functions for the organization. Including non-work content in e-mails and communicating enthusiasm can foster trust and commitment in virtual work teams (Jarvenpaa and Leidner 1999). A study of workers in a long-term health care facility found that a workplace "culture of companionate love" based on warmth, connection, and affection was associated with increased employee satisfaction and decreased burnout (Barsade and O'Neill 2014). Additionally, in a survey study of Filipino workers, Restubog and Bordia (2006:579–80) found that employees who held stronger "family-oriented feelings" in the workplace were more likely to align their behavior with organizational goals.

36. Rafael (2000); Go (2008).

37. Scott (1972:92).

38. Franco (2014:12); see also Restubog and Bordia (2006).

39. Bernadas and Flores (2014); Swidler and Watkins (2017).

40. Rodriguez (2010); Swidler and Watkins (2017).

41. Rodriguez (2010).

42. Rafael (2000); Go (2008).

43. Google (2004).

44. In contrast, San Francisco-based employees convened for quarterly parties, but each of these events was preceded by an afternoon-long meeting spent discussing the business. Team members representing each division dissected metrics, presented information about past performance and future goals, answered questions, and debated corporate strategy.

45. Bourdieu (1977:191).

46. This sentiment was shared by others in the San Francisco office. After a software engineer named Brett assigned an information-processing procedure to members of AllDone Philippines, he remarked to me, "We could have done it ourselves, but it was a really annoying task. I felt bad making them do it."

47. Leighton (2020).

48. In San Francisco, Carter told me that he was acutely aware of how his interaction style changed when communicating with team members in the Philippines. "I feel it every day," he explained during one meeting. "I'll be sending an e-mail [to members of AllDone Philippines] with smiley faces and all caps—and then I'll look over at an e-mail to San Francisco and be like—*woah*," he marveled, beaming and opening his eyes wide. The two modes of expression, he seemed to be indicating, were completely different.

49. Swidler and Watkins (2017:208).

50. Hoang (2015).

51. Carter's use of the word "unfathomable" in this context was likely not a reference to some objective standard of wealth, but rather to ADP managers' own expectations of the earnings they could achieve while working in the Philippines.

52. During our visits to the Philippines, I repeatedly saw Carter drape an arm over Veronica's shoulder in a manner that seemed similar to how one romantic partner might touch the other.

53. This sentiment was echoed by other team members; the phrase "AllDone changed my life!" was even included in ADP team member Jasmine's e-mail signature.

54. Other common testimonials featured favorable comparisons between ADSF managers and prior bosses. Some workers told ADSF managers that in Philippine companies, employment relations were typically more overtly hierarchical and despotic than at AllDone. Others told managers that members of ADSF treated them with more politeness and respect than Filipino bosses they'd

had in the past. One team leader claimed that in eight years of working at a call center, his boss had never personally thanked him for his efforts.

55. AllDone paid for Filipino contractors' travel to subsequent gatherings.

56. Constable (2003).

57. As management scholar Rosabeth Moss Kanter (1983:203) explains, strong organizational cultures can offer workers "a high" that "may be the closest to an experience of 'community' or total commitment for many workers, a dramatic, exciting, and almost communal process brought to the corporation."

58. Whenever new recruits joined ADSF, they received a firsthand glimpse into ADP's culture of familial love. Members of ADP were informed each time a new employee was hired in San Francisco. The new employee's inbox would quickly be flooded with cheerful, emoticon-laden messages welcoming them to the team.

59. Go (2008).

60. At least two contractors got jobs at a startup founded by a friend of an All-Done employee.

61. Gray and Suri (2019).

62. Kellogg et al. (2020).

63. Cerulo (2006); Petriglieri, Ashford, and Wrzesniewski (2019). See also Neely (2022) on how hedge fund workers manage uncertainty in part by cultivating family-like ties.

CHAPTER 5. WORKING THE PHONES

1. Although the majority of the women who worked for AllDone Philippines were in their twenties or early thirties, many were in their late thirties and forties. The fact that a large proportion of Filipina contractors were mothers likely contributed to Carter's impression that much of the workforce was "middle-aged."

2. Irani (2015b).

3. Srnicek (2017).

4. E.g., Zuboff (1988); Lee et al. (2015).

5. For example, Uber claims that its algorithms simply reflect market forces, but in fact Uber's software engineers design their algorithms to manipulate supply and demand, maximizing profits at the expense of drivers (Rosenblat 2018).

6. E.g., Rosenblat (2018); Ravenelle (2019).

7. Researchers have devoted a great deal of attention to the *impersonal* and *procedural* methods platform companies use to manage their relationships with participants. These include the algorithmic management of user activity (Lee et al. 2015; Rosenblat 2018), the content moderation processes employed by social media platforms (Roberts 2019), and the rating and review systems that help

users navigate the risk and uncertainty posed by transaction partners (Cook et al. 2009). However, such studies consistently overlook interpersonal interactions between agents of the software company and its participants (Shestakofsky and Kelkar 2020).

8. Bandelj (2015:242). Economic sociologists reject views of economic action positing that exchange partners are "rational actors with clear goals and stable preferences intent on maximizing utility" (Bandelj 2015:243). Instead, the aims and desires of exchange partners can change as they engage with one another. The concept of relational work emphasizes the emotional dimensions of exchange, drawing our attention to the processes of negotiation and meaning-making through which economic actors work things out.

9. AllDone Las Vegas' relational work is an example of what social scientists of technology have called articulation work—practices that support "the smooth interaction of parts within complex sociotechnical wholes, adjusting and calibrating each to each" (Jackson 2014: 223).

10. Kirtley and O'Mahony (2023).

11. See also Fabros (2016).

12. Hochschild (1983).

13. Stovel and Shaw (2012).

14. Bandelj (2009); Beckert (2006).

15. Hochschild (1983); Korczynski (2003).

16. Cook et al. (2009).

17. Greiner (1998 [1972]).

18. Female call center workers may be more likely to suffer the abuse of male customers (Korczynski 2003). See also Hochschild (1983) and Leidner (1993).

19. Goffman (1952).

20. Carreyrou (2018).

CHAPTER 6. BEARING THE BURDENS OF CHANGE

1. Hoffman and Yeh (2018:198, Part IV).

2. Viewed through the lens of absolute economic difference, workers in Las Vegas did indeed enjoy a higher standard of living than their Filipino counterparts, as would most Americans.

3. AllDone's cost savings were derived from paying for neither full-time employees' benefits and employment taxes, nor the fees that outsourcing companies charge clients to hire and manage their subcontracted phone support teams.

4. I was subsequently able to spend company funds on buying her a new PC.

5. Identifying information has been removed.

6. Leidner (1993).

7. AllDone does not appear to be unique in failing to offer its phone agents the training and coaching they would need to deliver high-quality service. See, for example, Sallaz's (2015) observations of an outsourced call center in the American Southwest where the vendor limited its managerial resources to cut costs.

8. Just listening to recordings of team members' more difficult calls with users made me feel nauseous.

9. I suspect that workers preferred replying to voicemails over taking live, inbound calls for two reasons. First, responding to a voicemail gave them time to assess a customer's issue and plan their intervention before the conversation began. Second, responding to a voicemail gave them a chance to steel themselves for conflict rather than feeling ambushed.

10. Leidner (1993).

11. Carol once told me, 'If I had a billion dollars, I'd give $250 million to All-Done so it can do everything it wants to do.'

12. Carol's first visit to the ADSF office also highlighted the incompatibility of ADLV's and ADSF's cultural practices, as well as ADLV's concordance with ADP's. When Carol arrived, she walked around the office and hugged every team member. For most if not all ADSF staffers, this was the first time they had been hugged by a colleague in the office. That set the tone for Carol's visit—she did not fit in. She was twice the age of many ADSF employees, and most in male-dominated ADSF spoke a different "language": more business-oriented, less touchy-feely. During her visit to the Philippines, however, Carol's "love and hugs" style matched many Filipino workers' modes of emotional expression.

13. Constable (2003).

14. As Rao and Neely (2019) argue, expressing one's "passion" for work can also be understood as a way of demonstrating one's commitment in an unstable and uncertain employment landscape.

15. See also Hodson (2001).

16. See Leidner (1993) and Lopez (2010) on how customers can serve as both antagonists and allies of service workers vis-à-vis management.

17. Sallaz (2015).

18. 'People will always complain when they pay,' Adam stated confidently to a handful of members of the product team who were assembled around a conference room table.

> 'Don't listen. Sellers' NPS ["net promoter score," drawn from a survey that measures a user's willingness to recommend AllDone to others] is bad, but quote rates are constant. So it may look like [the] Vietnam [War] if you listen to what sellers say. Maybe it's not going to be positive. But they need business so badly that they'll deal with the fact that they think the product is terrible. We can always get better, but we shouldn't think there's a systemic problem with sellers getting rolled out of our system.'

> The group is nodding along in agreement with Adam when Michel, a recent product design hire, chimes in: 'When I first got here, I thought everyone loved AllDone.

Now I know everyone hates AllDone—but that's OK!' he exclaims as the room bursts out in laughter.

Software developers were instructed not to worry about what sellers *said* about AllDone. Adam was more concerned with what sellers were *doing*, or whether they continued to pay AllDone to use the platform.

19. One morning during the transition to the new payment model, Josh, ADSF's product manager, stopped by my desk and asked me for "a sense of what's going on in the *real world* of AllDone"—phrasing that acknowledged the difference between the numbers the product team followed religiously and the on-the-ground realities of sellers' emotional reactions to the change.

20. Keeping subordinates better informed could result in better information flow up the chain of command. But because this would defeat the purpose of delegation, subordinates are often intentionally deprived of organizational knowledge. ADLV contractors' structural position allowed workers to understand potential new sources of value, but not to communicate process improvements to ADSF engineers and convince them to follow through on making desired changes (cf. Leonardi and Bailey 2017).

21. I would later discover that the word "spreadsheet" had become a running gag for the group—team members would start laughing and rolling their eyes at the mention of the word.

22. Silva (2012).

23. In spite of the difficulties faced by phone support agents, only one of ADLV's contractors voluntarily left AllDone during the year I spent working with the team. As other scholars of digital labor have pointed out, many low-wage workers consider online jobs to be preferable to the in-person alternatives available in their local labor markets, in part because they find it easier to structure their work around other obligations including housework, care work, and additional jobs (Gray and Suri 2019). Many members of ADLV spoke of working from home as an employment "benefit" offered by AllDone, and they enjoyed the relative predictability of their schedules and lack of supervision, particularly compared to other low-wage service jobs (see Reich and Bearman [2018] on retail work).

24. This is similar to Turco's (2012) observation that employees may use symbolic resources propagated by management against managerial interests. See also Scott (1985) on conflict within hegemony. My response to this incident is further detailed in the methodological appendix.

CHAPTER 7. GROWING PAINS

1. Goldfarb, Kirsch, and Miller (2007); Park and Tzabbar (2016); Greiner (1998[1972]); Bhidé (2000); Shane (2003).

2. Hellmann and Puri (2002); Davila et al. (2003).

3. Baron, Hannan, and Burton (2001); Stark (2009); DeSantola and Gulati (2017); Christin (2020).

4. AllDone is not the only startup that has surreptitiously altered its procedures to augment the experiences of an important set of users. Companies developing autonomous vehicles sent prospective venture capital investors for test rides on so-called "'golden routes' . . . on which their cars could reliably drive without encountering major problems" (Conger 2021). Reporter Mike Isaac (2019) revealed a technological tool that Uber used to evade regulation: users who were potentially affiliated with law enforcement or city agencies were secretly flagged and served a fake version of the app that prevented them from being matched with drivers.

5. This form of automation was powered by machine-learning algorithms that were "trained" by the vast dataset created by workers' past operations. The vetting algorithm determined which types of buyer requests were most likely to be rejected by human screeners, and the matching algorithm learned which types of requests, in which locations, were most likely to be matched with particular types of sellers. The software algorithms took over an increasing percentage of each task as developers continued to tune them.

6. Even as AllDone raised five additional rounds of venture capital funding amounting to nearly $700 million in the years since my departure from the field—eventually achieving a valuation of over $3 billion—the company continued to rely on its offsite teams.

7. As Peter once explained to Brett (a new software engineering recruit at the time) and me during an all-staff party at a local bar, the company's strategy for finding technical talent was different: "Hiring for marketing has been opportunistic; engineering only wants the best." See chapter 3 for additional details on technical recruiting.

8. The cofounders spent weeks courting Brandon before he signed on with AllDone, giving him the opportunity to participate in defining his own role. Meanwhile, the sole marketing specialist who had been brought on at this time— an MBA with prior experience in business and finance—was let go after just a few months after her search engine marketing projects failed to make a sizable dent in user acquisition metrics.

9. See the methodological appendix for a discussion of how my employment history may have influenced my job performance at AllDone, as well as additional details on how I was perceived by AllDone's leaders.

10. After my departure from the field, I found myself in a similar position to "Old Doug," the "indulgent" foreman who appears in sociologist Alvin Gouldner's (1954) ethnography of a gypsum plant. Old Doug was replaced by a manager who evoked dissatisfaction and distrust among employees as he attempted to rationalize operations on the shop floor, leading employees to speak wistfully of their former manager.

11. Sociologists will note familiar echoes of Max Weber's (2001) theory of the "iron cage" of bureaucracy.

12. Sociologist Ashley Mears (2020) describes how framing employment relations as friendship can help employers secure profits while obscuring inequalities. Employers can perform relational work to generate commitment among workers rooted in the misrecognition that work is primarily about friendship, community, and fun rather than a relationship of exploitation. Here I suggest that, as the organization grew, ADP employees' ties with managers began to feel more like wage-labor relationships and less like friendships than they had previously (see chapter 4). This speaks to the impermanence of the work cultures that emerge in startups' early stages (Baron et al. 2001).

13. I paid for this research trip with an academic grant; it was neither funded nor organized by AllDone.

14. Years later, AllDone did eventually open an office in Manila.

15. Carol was now on salary and received benefits, and three longer-tenured team members took on additional tasks and made an extra dollar or two per hour over the $10 base wage.

16. My attentiveness may have been in part related to the fact that I was eager to learn from them in my dual role as a researcher.

17. According to guidelines provided by the Internal Revenue Service (2017), "an expectation that the [employment] relationship will continue indefinitely," "a regular wage amount" for hourly work, "training a worker on how to do the job," instructions on when to work, and "evaluation systems to measure the details of work" are all indications that a worker should be classified as an employee. Perhaps because they assumed that "online" workers are qualitatively different from employees who work in an office, ADLV team members may have been largely unaware that their status as independent contractors could be called into question.

18. This dynamic also appears in Gouldner's (1954) succession story.

19. The implication that AllDone's phone agents had moved to Las Vegas to party does not accord with reality. When I worked with the team, most contractors seemed to have little disposable income and appeared to spend most of their free time in their homes. As far as I could tell, the problems in their lives were largely rooted in financial distress or romantic relationships.

20. In her next job (also providing customer support as a member of a work-from-home team for a tech company), Carol also would report working twelve-hour days with no overtime pay, and this time with no benefits.

21. Neff (2012).

22. In the years following Google's IPO, a thousand current and former employees saw the value of their stock exceed $5 million. The ranks of the Google rich famously included the massage therapist whom the founders had hired in 1999 (O'Mara 2019).

23. Startup workers' internalization of financial institutions' priorities echoes anthropologist Karen Ho's (2009) observations of Wall Street investment bankers.

24. Similar dynamics of raised expectations and dashed hopes can be found in other settings where marginal actors maintain proximity to economic elites. See, for instance, Ashley Mears's (2020) research on the stunted dreams of night-life promoters who believe they can parlay their connections with elite club owners and clients into great wealth. Very few are able to do so.

25. Berlant (2011).

CONCLUSION: REORGANIZING INNOVATION

1. Newcomer (2017).

2. Ravenelle (2019); Schor (2020).

3. Fligstein and Goldstein (2022).

4. e.g., Marx (1978); Noble (1984).

5. Delfanti and Frey (2021); Kantor and Sundaram (2022).

6. Lee (2018)

7. Existing research suggests that the ascendance of financial logics within the firm has homogeneous effects on work and employment, making jobs more demanding, flexible, and precarious (Osterman 1999; Ho 2009; Kalleberg 2011; Snyder 2016; Kelly and Moen 2020). The case of AllDone, however, demonstrates how financial logics may have varied effects on work not only across firms with different ownership structures (e.g., publicly traded corporations vs. venture-backed startups), but also *within* firms.

8. These conclusions pertaining to the unequal distribution of the pressures associated with organizational adaptability may not be unique to the tech sector. For example, workers in a variety of low-wage logistics occupations manage the frictions associated with delivering goods to customers "just in time." However, long-haul truck drivers who are paid per mile driven are more vulnerable to un-anticipated contingencies than loading dock employees and clerks who are paid by the hour (Snyder 2016).

9. Sociologist Gina Neff (2012) uses the term *venture labor* to describe how workers have increasingly come to embrace the risk and instability that have become characteristic of jobs in the tech industry and across the economy more broadly.

10. For a recent example, see Mallaby (2022).

11. Noble (2018); Benjamin (2019); Joyce et al. (2021).

12. Deloitte (2021).

13. RateMyInvestor & DiversityVC (2019).

14. Clark (2018). Many argue that diversifying the ranks of startup founders will result in the production of less harmful technologies. Yet the case of Elizabeth Holmes—the founder of the blood-testing startup Theranos, who inflated the company's valuation by lying about the capabilities of its technology and was

later convicted on four counts of criminal fraud—suggests that, regardless of their individual identities, entrepreneurs face enormous pressure to comply with the logic of venture capitalism.

15. Alegria (2020).

16. Google (2021). These figures only apply to Google's full-time employees; the company also employs a "shadow workforce" of temporary workers and contractors around the globe that exceeds the size of the workforce on the books (Wakabayashi 2019).

17. Wall Street Journal (2021).

18. Tayeb (2021).

19. CB Insights (2022).

20. Lin and Tomaskovic-Devey (2013); Lin and Neely (2020).

21. Isaac, de la Merced, and Sorokin (2019).

22. Bort (2019).

23. Lekach (2019). Active drivers received bonuses based on the number of lifetime trips they had completed for Uber: $100 for 2,500 trips, $500 for 5,000 trips, $1,000 for 10,000 trips, and $10,000 for 20,000 trips.

24. Gebeloff (2021).

25. Kenney and Zysman (2019).

26. Yoffie et al. (2019).

27. In 2004, eBay (a publicly traded company that runs an online auction site) purchased a 28.4 percent stake in craigslist. After eBay launched its own classified site in 2007, craigslist's leaders removed eBay's members from its board of directors. Following a prolonged and contentious legal battle, eBay sold back its stake in craigslist (Lingel 2020).

28. Lingel (2020:159).

29. Gray and Suri (2019).

30. Scholz and Schneider (2016).

31. Thompson (2019).

32. Schor (2020).

33. Hanna and Park (2020).

34. Alleyne et al. (2020).

35. For example, the city of Seoul banned Uber and set up seed funds to promote local startups (Schor 2020:172).

36. Block (2008).

37. McCarthy (2022).

38. Zukin (2020).

39. Wright (2010:226).

40. O'Mara (2019); Manjoo (2022).

41. Viswanathan (2023).

42. Rahman and Thelen (2019).

43. McCabe (2022).

METHODOLOGICAL APPENDIX

1. Cooper (2000); Sharone (2004).

2. See Timmermans and Tavory (2012) on how surprising data can drive ethnographic analysis.

3. See chapter 5 for additional details on my transition to a full-time role. During the first four months of my tenure as an employee, I returned to the Berkeley campus once a week to audit a graduate seminar in Qualitative and Observational Field Methods. On those days I arrived at the office around 1 p.m.

4. My salary was roughly equivalent to the median household income in San Francisco from 2012 to 2013, which was nearly 50 percent greater than the nationwide figure of $51,371 (Federal Reserve Bank of St. Louis, n.d.).

5. Cooper (2000); see also O'Mahoney and Bechky (2006) on "differentiating competence."

6. Saxenian (1994); Turco (2016). I later discovered that AllDone's leaders occasionally met with executives from rival companies for informal conversations.

7. Unlike leaders at some other tech companies (Irani 2015b), executives did not seem concerned that investors would value AllDone less if they were aware that the company relied on human labor to support its software systems. See chapter 3.

8. Rivera (2015).

9. Lofland et al. (2005).

10. Snow, Zurcher, and Sjoberg (1982).

11. Sade-Beck (2004).

12. Emerson, Fretz, and Shaw (2011).

13. The first phase of research spanned February to July 2012; the second phase lasted from August 2012 to February 2013; and the third phase includes March 2013 to August 2013, as well as many events that occurred after I left the research site.

14. Barley (1986).

15. Nader (1972).

16. Burawoy (1998); Anteby (2013).

17. Gjerde and Alvesson (2020).

18. In waiting to offer my opinions to subordinates, I was not replicating some "neutral" or "natural" state of the social setting. If Carter had still been overseeing the Las Vegas team, he may have approached the interaction differently.

19. After I left AllDone, however, some former colleagues shared their criticisms of the company with me more openly (chapter 7). The opinions they voiced did not call my prior conclusions into question.

20. I faced a similar dilemma when Tanya had invited me to join the team's online chat system months earlier. I told Tanya that I would be happy to join the group, but then Carol advised me not to, suggesting that 'they just want to

complain directly to you and go around me.' In light of Carol's warning, I decided to forego this opportunity to connect with contractors.

21. Similarly, in her ethnographic study of a Wall Street investment bank, anthropologist Karen Ho (2009) describes writing a report advocating that the company limit layoffs of back-office workers and finding that top managers ignored her recommendations.

22. Gjerde and Alvesson (2020).

23. See chapter 6 for additional details of this episode and Tanya's reaction to being fired.

24. Burawoy (1998).

25. E.g., Burawoy (1979); Sherman (2007).

26. Anteby (2013).

27. Sherman (2007:284).

28. O'Reilly (2009).

29. At the time of this writing, my AllDone equity is worth $200,000 on paper, though there have been few opportunities for former employees to liquidate their assets and realize any actual monetary gain, as explained below.

30. Based on a 2018 survey (Philippine Statistics Authority 2020) and average exchange rate in 2018 of 52.662 Philippine pesos to one US dollar (Exchangerates .org.uk n.d.b.).

References

ABS-CBN News. 2011. "PH Is Best Outsourcing Destination in Asia: CBRE." November 9. https://news.abs-cbn.com/business/11/09/11/ph-best -outsourcing-destination-asia-cbre.

Alegria, Sharla. 2019. "Gendered Labor and Token Processes in Tech Work." *Gender & Society* 33(5):722–45.

———. 2020. "What Do We Mean by Broadening Participation? Race, Inequality, and Diversity in Tech Work." *Sociology Compass* 14(6).

Alfrey, Lauren, and France Winddance Twine. 2017. "Gender-Fluid Geek Girls: Negotiating Inequality Regimes in the Tech Industry." *Gender & Society* 31(1):28–50.

Alleyne, Malene, Camille Canon, Amelia Evans, Yichen Feng, Nathan Schneider, and Mara Zepeda. 2020. "Exit to Community: A Primer." Media Design Lab, University of Colorado. https://www.colorado.edu/lab/medlab /sites/default/files/attached-files/exittocommunityprimer-book.pdf.

Alpaydin, Ethem. 2014. *Introduction to Machine Learning.* 3rd ed. Cambridge, MA: MIT Press.

Anteby, Michel. 2013. "Relaxing the Taboo on Telling Our Own Stories: Upholding Professional Distance *and* Personal Involvement." *Organization Science* 24(4):1277–90.

Associated Press. 2018. "Apple, Amazon, Facebook, Alphabet, and Microsoft Are Collectively Worth More Than the Entire Economy of the United Kingdom." *Inc.*, April 27. https://www.inc.com/associated-press

/mindblowing-facts-tech-industry-money-amazon-apple-microsoft-facebook
-alphabet.html.

Autor, David. 2014. "Polanyi's Paradox and the Shape of Employment Growth."
National Bureau of Economic Research Working Paper No. 20485.

———. 2015a. "Why Are There Still So Many Jobs? The History and Future of
Workplace Automation." *Journal of Economic Perspectives* 29(3):3–30.

———. 2015b. "Paradox of Abundance: Automation Anxiety Returns." Pp. 237–
60 in *Performance and Progress: Essays on Capitalism, Business, and
Society*, edited by Subramanian Rangan. New York: Oxford University
Press.

Bailey, Diane E., and Stephen R. Barley. 2020. "Beyond Design and Use: How
Scholars Should Study Intelligent Technologies." *Information and Organization* 30(2):1–12.

Baker, Ted, and Reed E. Nelson. 2005. "Creating Something from Nothing:
Resource Construction through Entrepreneurial Bricolage." *Administrative
Science Quarterly* 50(3):329–66.

Bandelj, Nina. 2009. "Emotions in Economic Action and Interaction." *Theory
and Society* 38:347–66.

———. 2015. "Thinking about Social Relations in Economy as Relational Work."
Pp. 227–51 in *Re-Imagining Economic Sociology*, Patrik Aspers and Nigel
Dodd, eds. New York: Oxford University Press.

Barley, Stephen R. 1986. "Technology as an Occasion for Structuring: Evidence
from Observations of CT Scanners and the Social Order of Radiology
Departments. *Administrative Science Quarterly* 31(1):78–108.

———. 1988. "Technology, Power, and the Social Organization of Work: Towards
a Pragmatic Theory of Skilling and Deskilling." *Research in the Sociology of
Organizations* 6:33–80.

Barley, Stephen R., and Matthew I. Beane. 2020. "How Should We Study
Intelligent Technologies' Implications for Work and Employment?"
Pp. 69–115 in *Work and Technological Change* by Stephen R. Barley. New
York: Oxford University Press.

Barley, Stephen R., and Gideon Kunda. 2004. *Gurus, Hired Guns, and Warm
Bodies: Itinerant Experts in a Knowledge Economy.* Princeton, NJ:
Princeton University Press.

Baron, James N., Michael T. Hannan, and M. Diane Burton. 2001. "Labor
Pains: Change in Organizational Models and Employee Turnover in Young,
High-Tech Firms." *American Journal of Sociology* 106(4):960–1012.

Baron, James N., Michael T. Hannan, Greta Hsu, and Özgecan Koçak. 2007. "In
the Company of Women: Gender Inequality and the Logic of Bureaucracy in
Start-Up Firms." *Work and Occupations* 34(1):35–66.

Barsade, Sigal G., and Olivia A. O'Neill. 2014. "What's Love Got to Do with It?
A Longitudinal Study of the Culture of Companionate Love and Employee

and Client Outcomes in a Long-Term Care Setting." *Administrative Science Quarterly* 59(4):551–98.

Baym, Nancy. 2015. "Connect With Your Audience! The Relational Labor of Connection." *The Communication Review* 18(1):14–22.

Beckert, Jens. 2006. "Trust and Markets." Pp. 318–31 in *Handbook of Trust Research*, edited by Reinhard Bachmann and Akbar Zaheer. Northampton, MA: Edward Elgar Publishing.

———. 2009. "The Social Order of Markets." *Theory and Society* 38(3):245–69.

———. 2016. *Imagined Futures: Fictional Expectations and Capitalist Dynamics*. Cambridge, MA: Harvard University Press.

Beltran, Luisa. 2020. "Sequoia Capital Scores Big Wins with Airbnb, DoorDash IPOs." *Barron's*, December 11. https://www.barrons.com/articles/sequoia -capital-scores-big-wins-with-airbnb-doordash-ipos–51607701706.

Benjamin, Ruha. 2019. *Race After Technology: Abolitionist Tools for the New Jim Code*. Polity: New York.

Berlant, Lauren. 2011. *Cruel Optimism*. Durham, NC: Duke University Press.

Bernadas, Jan, and Jaime Manuel Q. Flores. 2014. "Communication in Filipino Organizations." Pp. 179–193 in *Understanding the Filipino Worker and Organization*, edited by Ma. Regina M. Hechanova, Mendiola Teng-Calleja, and Vanessa C. Villaluz. Manila: Ateneo de Manila University Press.

Bhidé, Amar V. 2000. *The Origin and Evolution of New Businesses*. Oxford: New York.

Block, Fred. 2008. "Swimming against the Current: The Rise of a Hidden Developmental State in the United States." *Politics & Society* 36(2):169–206.

Block, Fred, and Matthew R. Keller. 2009. "Where Do Innovations Come From? Transformations in the US Economy, 1970–2006. *Socio-Economic Review* 7(3):459–83.

Bort, Julie. 2019. "Here's Who's Getting Rich on Uber's Massive IPO." *Business Insider*, May 10. https://www.businessinsider.com/uber-ipo-here-is-who-is -getting-rich–2019-4#softbank–93-billion–1.

Bourdieu, Pierre. 1977. *Outline of a Theory of Practice*. New York: Cambridge University Press.

Braverman, Harry. 1974. *Labor and Monopoly Capital: The Degradation of Work in the Twentieth Century*. New York: Monthly Review Press.

Brayne, Sarah. 2017. "Big Data Surveillance: The Case of Policing." *American Sociological Review* 82(5):977–1008.

Burawoy, Michael. 1979. *Manufacturing Consent: Changes in the Labor Process under Monopoly Capitalism*. Chicago: University of Chicago Press.

———. 1998. "The Extended Case Method." *Sociological Theory* 16(1):4–33.

Burrell, Jenna. 2016. "How the Machine 'Thinks': Understanding Opacity in Machine Learning Algorithms." *Big Data & Society* 3(1):1–12.

Burton, M. Diane, Jesper B. Sørensen, and Christine M. Beckman. 2002. "Coming from Good Stock: Career Histories and New Venture Formation." *Research in the Sociology of Organizations* 19:229–62.

Bussgang, Jeffrey. 2010. *Mastering the VC Game: A Venture Capital Insider Reveals How to Get from Start-up to IPO on Your Terms.* New York: Portfolio.

Cameron, Lindsey D. 2021. "'Making Out' While Driving: Relational and Efficiency Games in the Gig Economy." *Organization Science* 33(1):231–52.

Carreyrou, John. 2018. *Bad Blood: Secrets and Lies in a Silicon Valley Startup.* London: Picador.

Carroll, Glenn R., and Michael T. Hannan. 2000. "Why Corporate Demography Matters: Policy Implications of Organizational Diversity." *California Management Review* 42(3):148–63.

CB Insights. 2018. "Venture Capital Funnel Shows Odds of Becoming a Unicorn Are About 1%." September 6. https://www.cbinsights.com/research/venture -capital-funnel–2/.

———. 2022. "State of Venture 2021 Report." January 12. https://www.cbinsights .com/research/report/venture-trends–2021/.

Cerulo, Karen A. 2006. *Never Saw It Coming: Cultural Challenges to Envision- ing the Worst.* Chicago: University of Chicago Press.

Chan, Jenny, Mark Selden, and Pun Ngai. 2020. *Dying for an iPhone: Apple, Foxconn, and the Lives of China's Workers.* London: Pluto Press.

Christin, Angèle. 2020. *Metrics at Work: Journalism and the Contested Meaning of Algorithms.* Princeton, NJ: Princeton University Press.

Clark, Kate. 2018. "Female Founders Have Brought in Just 2.2% of US VC This Year (Yes, Again)." *TechCrunch*, November 4. https://techcrunch.com/2018/11 /04/female-founders-have-brought-in-just–2–2-of-us-vc-this-year-yes-again/.

Cockayne, Daniel G. 2016. "Entrepreneurial Affect: Attachment to Work Practice in San Francisco's Digital Media Sector." *Environment and Planning D: Society and Space* 34(3):456–73.

Conger, Kate. 2021. "Uber Survived the Spying Scandal. Some Careers Didn't." *New York Times*, November 28. https://www.nytimes.com/2021/12/06 /technology/uber-spying-allegations.html.

Constable, Nicole. 2003. *Romance on a Global Stage: Pen Pals, Virtual Ethnog- raphy, and "Mail Order" Marriages.* Berkeley: University of California Press.

Cook, Karen, Coye Cheshire, Alexandra Gerbasi, and Brandy Aven. 2009. "Assessing Trustworthiness in Providers." Pp. 189–214 in *eTrust: Forming Relationships in the Online World,* edited by Karen Cook, Chris Snijders, Vincent Buskens, and Coye Cheshire. New York: Russell Sage Foundation.

Cooper, Marianne. 2000. "Being the 'Go-To Guy': Fatherhood, Masculinity, and the Organization of Work in Silicon Valley." *Qualitative Sociology* 23: 379–405.

Cowie, Jefferson. 1999. *Capital Moves: RCA's Seventy-Year Quest for Cheap Labor.* New York: The New Press.

Cutler, Kim-Mai. 2018. "The Unicorn Hunters." *Logic*, April 1. https://logicmag
    .io/scale/the-unicorn-hunters/.

Davila, Antonio, George Foster, and Mahendra Gupta. 2003. "Venture Capital
    Financing and the Growth of Startup Firms." *Journal of Business Venturing*
    18(6):689–708.

Davis, Gerald F. 2009. *Managed by the Markets: How Finance Re-Shaped
    America*. New York: Oxford University Press.

Davis, Gerald F., and Suntae Kim. 2015. "Financialization of the Economy."
    Annual Review of Sociology 41:203–21.

D'Cruz, Premilla, and Ernesto Noronha. 2016. "Positives Outweighing Nega-
    tives: The Experiences of Indian Crowdsourced Workers." *Work Organisa-
    tion, Labour & Globalisation* 10(1):44–63.

Delfanti, Alessandro, and Bronwyn Frey. 2021. "Humanly Extended Automa-
    tion or the Future of Work Seen through Amazon Patents." *Science, Technol-
    ogy, & Human Values* 46(3):655–82.

Deloitte. 2021. "VC Human Capital Survey." March. https://www2.deloitte.com
    /content/dam/Deloitte/us/Documents/audit/vc-human-capital-survey
    -march–2021.pdf.

DeSantola, Alicia, and Ranjay Gulati. 2017. "Scaling: Organizing and Growth in
    Entreprenurial Ventures." *Academy of Management Annals* 11(2):640–68.

DiMaggio, Paul J., and Walter W. Powell. 1983. "The Iron Cage Revisited:
    Institutional Isomorphism and Collective Rationality in Organizational
    Fields." *American Sociological Review* 48(2):147–60.

Driebusch, Corrie, and Maureen Farrell. 2018. "IPO Market Has Never Been
    This Forgiving to Money-Losing Firms." *Wall Street Journal*, October 1,
    2018.

Eavis, Peter. 2021. "What Is GameStop, the Company, Really Worth? Does It
    Matter?" *New York Times*, February 1. https://www.nytimes.com/2021/02/01
    /business/gamestop-how-much-worth.html.

Ekbia, Hamid R., and Bonnie A. Nardi. 2017. *Heteromation and Other Stories of
    Computing and Capitalism*. Cambridge, MA: MIT Press.

Emerson, Robert M., Rachel I. Fretz, and Linda L. Shaw. 2011. *Writing Ethno-
    graphic Fieldnotes*. 2nd ed. Chicago: University of Chicago Press.

Epstein, Gerald A, ed. 2005. *Financialization and the World Economy*.
    Cheltenham, UK: Edward Elgar Publishing.

Ermakoff, Ivan. 2014. "Exceptional Cases: Epistemic Contributions and
    Normative Expectations." *European Journal of Sociology* 55(2):223–43.

Exchangerates.org.uk. n.d.a. "US Dollar to Philippine Peso Spot Exchange
    Rates for 2013." Accessed June 15, 2021. https://www.exchangerates.org.uk
    /USD-PHP-spot-exchange-rates-history–2013.html.

——. n.d.b. "US Dollar to Philippine Peso Spot Exchange Rates for 2018."
    Accessed January 16, 2023. https://www.exchangerates.org.uk/USD-PHP
    -spot-exchange-rates-history–2018.html.

Fabros, Alinaya. 2016. *Outsourceable Selves: An Ethnography of Call Center Work in a Global Economy of Signs and Selves.* Manila: Ateneo de Manila University Press.

Federal Reserve Bank of St. Louis. n.d. "Estimate of Median Household Income for San Francisco County/City, CA." Accessed March 22, 2021. https://fred .stlouisfed.org/series/MHICA06075A052NCEN.

Fernandez, Roberto M., and Jason Greenberg. 2013. "Race, Network Hiring, and Statistical Discrimination." *Research in the Sociology of Work* 24:81–102.

Fjermedal, Grant, 1984. *Magic Bullets.* New York: Macmillan.

Fligstein, Neil, and Adam Goldstein. 2022. "The Legacy of Shareholder Value Capitalism." *Annual Review of Sociology* 48:193–211.

Franco, Edna P. 2014. "Political, Economic, Environmental, and Cultural Influences on Organizational Behavior." Pp. 1–19 in *Understanding the Filipino Worker and Organization*, edited by Ma. Regina M. Hechanova, Mendiola Teng-Calleja, and Vanessa C. Villaluz. Manila: Ateneo de Manila University Press.

Fried, Vance H., and Robert D. Hisrich. 1994. "Toward a Model of Venture Capital Investment Decision Making." *Financial Management* 23(3):28–37.

Funk, Jeffrey L. 2022. "The 'Unproductive Bubble'": Unprofitable Startups, Slow Growth in Digital Technologies, and Little Commercialization of New Science." *National Development*, May 16. https://nationaldev.org/the -unproductive-bubble-unprofitable-startups-slow-growth-in-digital -technologies-and-little-bc5d508ab624.

Gebeloff, Robert. 2021. "Who Owns Stocks? Explaining the Rise in Inequality during the Pandemic." *New York Times*, January 26. https://www.nytimes .com/2021/01/26/upshot/stocks-pandemic-inequality.html.

Gelles, David. 2022. *The Man Who Broke Capitalism: How Jack Welch Gutted the Heartland and Crushed the Soul of Corporate America—and How to Undo His Legacy.* New York: Simon & Schuster.

Gillespie, Tarleton. 2016. "Algorithm." Pp. 18–30 in *Digital Keywords: A Vocabulary of Information Society and Culture*, edited by Benjamin Peters. Princeton, NJ: Princeton University Press.

———. 2018. *Custodians of the Internet: Platforms, Content Moderation, and the Hidden Decisions that Shape Social Media.* New Haven, CT: Yale University Press.

Gjerde, Susann, and Mats Alvesson. 2020. "Sandwiched: Exploring Role and Identity of Middle Managers in the Genuine Middle." *Human Relations* 73(1):124–51.

Go, Julian. 2008. *American Empire and the Politics of Meaning: Elite Political Cultures in the Philippines and Puerto Rico during U.S. Colonialism.* Durham, NC: Duke University Press.

Goffman, Erving. 1952. "On Cooling the Mark Out: Some Aspects of Adaptation to Failure." *Psychiatry* 15(4):451–63.

———. 1959. *The Presentation of Self in Everyday Life*. New York: Doubleday.

Goldfarb, Brent, David Kirsch, and David A. Miller. 2007. "Was There Too Little Entry during the Dot Com Era?" *Journal of Financial Economics* 86(1):100–144.

Gompers, Paul, Anna Kovner, and Josh Lerner. 2009. "Specialization and Success: Evidence from Venture Capital." *Journal of Economics & Management Strategy* 18(3):817–44.

Gompers, Paul, and Josh Lerner. 2001. *The Money of Invention: How Venture Capital Creates New Wealth*. Cambridge, MA: Harvard Business School Press.

———. 2004. *The Venture Capital Cycle*. 2nd ed. Cambridge, MA: MIT Press.

Google. 2004. "Form S–1 Registration Statement under the Securities Act of 1993." Accessed September 23, 2013. https://www.sec.gov/Archives/edgar/data/1288776/000119312504073639/ds1.htm.

———. 2021. "Google Diversity Annual Report 2020." Accessed May 4, 2021. https://kstatic.googleusercontent.com/files/25badfc6b6d1b33f3b87372ff7545d79261520d821e6ee9a82c4ab2de42a01216be2156bc5a60ae3337ffe7176d90b8b2b3000891ac6e516a650ecebf0e3f866.

Gouldner, Alvin. 1954. *Patterns of Industrial Bureaucracy*. Glencoe, IL: Free Press.

Graham, Mark, Isis Hjorth, and Vili Lehdonvirta. 2017. "Digital Labour and Development: Impacts of Global Digital Labour Platforms and the Gig Economy on Worker Livelihoods." *Transfer* 23(2):135–62.

Gray, Mary, and Siddharth Suri. 2019. *Ghost Work: How to Stop Silicon Valley from Building a New Global Underclass*. Boston: Houghton Mifflin Harcourt.

Greene, Daniel. 2021. *The Promise of Access: Technology, Inequality, and the Political Economy of Hope*. Cambridge, MA: MIT Press.

Greene, Patricia, Candida G. Brush, Myra M. Hart, and Patrick Saparito. 2010. "Patterns of Venture Capital Funding: Is Gender a Factor?" *Venture Capital* 3(1):63–83.

Greiner, Larry E. 1998[1972]. "Evolution and Revolution as Organizations Grow." *Harvard Business Review* May–June 1998.

Griffith, Erin. 2022. "'It's All Just Wild': Tech Start-Ups Reach a New Peak of Froth." *New York Times*, January 19. https://www.nytimes.com/2022/01/19/technology/tech-startup-funding.html.

Grossman, Lev. 2006. "You—Yes, You—Are *TIME*'s Person of the Year." *Time*, December 25. https://content.time.com/time/magazine/article/0,9171,1570810,00.html.

Grossman, Rachel. 1979–1980. "Women's Place in the Integrated Circuit." *New England Free Press* 4:48–55.

Guillen, Mauro. 1994. *Models of Management: Work, Authority, and Organization in a Comparative Perspective*. Chicago: University of Chicago Press.

Hallen, Benjamin L., and Kathleen M. Eisenhardt. 2012. "Catalyzing Strategies and Efficient Tie Formation: How Entrepreneurial Firms Obtain Investment Ties." *Academy of Management Journal* 55(1):35–70.

Hanna, Alex, and Tina M. Park. "Against Scale: Provocations and Resistances to Scale Thinking." *arXiv preprint:2010.08850.*

Harvey, David. 1989. *The Condition of Postmodernity: An Enquiry into the Origins of Cultural Change.* Hoboken, NJ: Wiley-Blackwell.

———. 2001. "Globalization and the 'Spatial Fix.'" *Geographische Revue* 3(2):23–30.

Hellmann, Thomas, and Manju Puri. 2002. "Venture Capital and the Professionalization of Start-Up Firms: Empirical Evidence." *Journal of Finance* 58(1):169–97.

Hesmondhalgh, David, and Sarah Baker. 2015. "Sex, Gender and Work Segregation in the Cultural Industries." *The Sociological Review* 63(S1):23–36.

Ho, Karen. 2009. *Liquidated: An Ethnography of Wall Street.* Durham, NC: Duke University Press.

Hoang, Kimberly Kay. 2015. *Dealing in Desire: Asian Ascendancy, Western Decline, and the Hidden Currencies of Global Sex Work.* Oakland: University of California Press.

Hochschild, Arlie. 1983. *The Managed Heart: Commercialization of Human Feeling.* Berkeley: University of California Press.

Hodson, Randy. 2001. *Dignity at Work.* New York: Cambridge University Press.

Hoffman, Reid, and Chris Yeh. 2018. *Blitzscaling: The Lightning-Fast Path to Building Massively Valuable Businesses.* New York: Currency.

Holland, Domm (@domm). 2020. "In startups, if you take your foot off the pedal, the default mode is reverse, not neutral." Twitter, June 21, 2020, 10:32. https://twitter.com/domm/status/1274711734826217473.

Howcroft, Debra, and Birgitta Bergvall-Kåreborn. 2019. "A Typology of Crowdwork Platforms." *Work, Employment and Society* 33(1):21–38.

Hsu, David H. 2007. "Experienced Entrepreneurial Founders, Organizational Capital, and Venture Capital Funding." *Research Policy* 36(5):722–41.

Hyman, Louis. 2018. *Temp: The Real Story of What Happened to Your Salary, Benefits, and Job Security.* New York: Penguin.

Internal Revenue Service. 2017. "Understanding Employee vs. Contractor Designation." July 20. https://www.irs.gov/newsroom/understanding -employee-vs-contractor-designation.

Irani, Lilly. 2015a. "The Cultural Work of Microwork." *New Media & Society* 17(5):720—39.

———. 2015b. "Difference and Dependence among Digital Workers: The Case of Amazon Mechanical Turk." *The South Atlantic Quarterly* 114(1):225–34.

———. 2019. *Chasing Innovation: Making Entrepreneurial Citizens in Modern India.* Princeton, NJ: Princeton University Press.

Isaac, Mike. 2019. *Super Pumped: The Battle for Uber.* New York: W.W. Norton & Company.

Isaac, Mike, Michael J. de la Merced, and Andrew Ross Sorokin. 2019. "How the Promise of a $120 Billion Uber I.P.O. Evaporated." *New York Times*, May 15. https://www.nytimes.com/2019/05/15/technology/uber-ipo-price.html.

Jackson, Steven. 2014. "Rethinking Repair." Pp. 221–40 in *Media Technologies: Essays on Communication, Materiality, and Society*, edited by Tarleton Gillespie, Pablo J. Boczkowski, and Kirsten A. Foot. Cambridge, MA: MIT Press.

Jarvenpaa, Sirkaa L., and Dorothy E. Leidner. 1999. "Communication and Trust in Global Virtual Teams." *Organization Science.* 10(6):791–815.

Jasanoff, Sheila, and Sang-Hyun Kim. 2009. "Containing the Atom: Sociotechnical Imaginaries and Nuclear Power in the United States and South Korea." *Minerva* 47:119-46.

Joyce, Kelly, Laurel Smith-Doerr, Sharla Alegria, Susan Bell, Taylor Cruz, Steve G. Hoffman, Safiya Umoja Noble, and Benjamin Shestakofsky. 2021. "Toward a Sociology of Artificial Intelligence: A Call for Research on Inequalities and Structural Change." *Socius* 7:1–11.

Kalleberg, Arne L. 2011. *Good Jobs, Bad Jobs: The Rise of Polarized and Precarious Employment Systems in the United States, 1970s–2000s.* New York: Russell Sage Foundation.

Kanter, Rosabeth Moss. 1983. *The Change Masters: Innovation and Entrepreneurship in the American Corporation.* New York: Simon & Schuster.

Kantor, Jodi, and Arya Sundaram. 2022. "The Rise of the Worker Productivity Score." *New York Times*, August 14. https://www.nytimes.com/interactive/2022/08/14/business/worker-productivity-tracking.html.

Kelkar, Shreeharsh. 2018. "Engineering a Platform: The Construction of Interfaces, Users, Organizational Roles, and the Division of Labor." *New Media & Society* 20(7):2629–46.

Kellogg, Katherine C., Melissa A. Valentine, and Angèle Christin. 2020. "Algorithms at Work: The New Contested Terrain of Control." *Academy of Management Annals* 14(1):366–410.

Kelly, Erin, and Phyllis Moen. 2020. *Overload: How Good Jobs Went Bad and What We Can Do about It.* Princeton, NJ. Princeton University Press.

Kenney, Martin, ed. 2000. *Understanding Silicon Valley: The Anatomy of an Entrepreneurial Region.* Stanford, CA: Stanford University Press.

Kenney, Martin, and John Zysman. 2019. "Unicorns, Cheshire Cats, and the New Dilemmas of Entrepreneurial Finance." *Venture Capital* 21(1):35–50.

Kirtley, Jaqueline, and Siobhan O'Mahony. 2020. "What Is a Pivot? Explaining When and How Entrepreneurial Firms Decide to Make Strategic Changes and Pivot." *Strategic Management Journal* 44(1):197–230.

Koetsier, John. 2020. "Report: Facebook Makes 300,000 Content Moderation Mistakes Every Day." *Forbes*, June 9. https://www.forbes.com/sites /johnkoetsier/2020/06/09/300000-facebook-content-moderation-mistakes -daily-report-says/?sh=592f163954do.

Koning, Rembrand, Sharique Hasan, and Aaron Chatterji. 2022. "Experimentation and Start-up Performance: Evidence from A/B Testing." *Management Science* 68(9):6434–53.

Korczynski, Marek. 2003. "Communities of Coping: Collective Emotional Labour in Service Work." *Organization* 10(1): 55–79.

Kunda, Gideon. 1992. *Engineering Culture: Control and Commitment in a High-Tech Corporation*. Philadelphia: Temple University Press.

Kunda, Gideon, and Galit Ailon-Souday. 2006. "Managers, Markets, and Ideologies: Design and Devotion Revisited." Pp. 200–219 in *The Oxford Handbook of Work and Organization*, edited by Stephen Ackroyd, Rosemary Batt, Paul Thompson, and Pamela S. Tolbert. New York: Oxford University Press.

Langley, Paul, and Andrew Leyshon. 2017. "Platform Capitalism: The Intermediation and Capitalisation of Digital Economic Circulation." *Finance and Society* 3(1):11–31.

Larkey, Linda, and Calvin Morrill. 1995. "Organizational Commitment as Symbolic Process." *Western Journal of Communications* 59(3):193–213.

Lee, Ching Kwan. 2018. *The Specter of Global China: Politics, Labor, and Foreign Investment in Africa*. Chicago: University of Chicago Press.

Lee, Min Kyung, Daniel Kusbit, Evan Metsky, and Laura Dabbish. 2015. "Working with Machines: The Impact of Algorithmic and Data-Driven Management on Human Workers." *Proceedings of the 33rd Annual ACM Conference on Human Factors in Computing Systems*:1603–12.

Leidner, Robin. 1993. *Fast Food, Fast Talk: Service Work and the Routinization of Everyday Life*. Berkeley: University of California Press.

Leighton, Mary. 2020. "Mythos of Meritocracy, Friendship, and Fun Work: Class and Gender in North American Academic Communities." *American Anthropologist* 122(3):444–58.

Lekach, Sasha. 2019. "Uber Beats Lyft with IPO Payout to Drivers." *Mashable*, April 11. https://mashable.com/article/uber-ipo-driver-cash-reward-stock -program.

Leonardi, Paul, and Diane Bailey. 2017. "Recognizing and Selling Good Ideas: Network Articulation and the Making of an Offshore Innovation Hub." *Academy of Management Discoveries* 3(2):116–44.

Levy, Ari, and Lorie Konish. 2020. "The Five Biggest Tech Companies Now Make Up 17.5% of the S&P 500—Here's How to Protect Yourself." CNBC, January 28. https://www.cnbc.com/2020/01/28/sp-500-dominated-by-apple -microsoft-alphabet-amazon-facebook.html.

Lichtenstein, Nelson. 2002. *State of the Union: A Century of American Labor.* Princeton, NJ: Princeton University Press.

Lin, Ken-Hou, and Megan Tobias Neely. 2020. *Divested: Inequality in the Age of Finance.* New York: Oxford University Press.

Lin, Ken-Hou, and Donald Tomaskovic-Devey. 2013. "Financialization and U.S. Income Inequality, 1970–2008." *American Journal of Sociology* 118(5):1284–329.

Lindtner, Silvia M. 2020. *Prototype Nation: China and the Contested Promise of Innovation.* Princeton, NJ: Princeton University Press.

Lingel, Jessa. 2020. *An Internet for the People: The Politics and Promise of Craigslist.* Princeton, NJ: Princeton University Press.

Lofland, John, David A. Snow, Leon Anderson, and Lyn H. Lofland. 2005. *Analyzing Social Settings: A Guide to Qualitative Observation and Analysis.* 4th edition. Belmont, CA: Thomson Wadsworth.

Lopez, Steven Henry. 2010. "Workers, Managers, and Customers: Triangles of Power in Work Communities." *Work and Occupations* 37(3):251–71.

Lounsbury, Michael, and Mary Ann Glynn. 2001. "Cultural Entrepreneurship: Stories, Legitimacy, and the Acquisition of Resources." *Strategic Management Journal* 22: 545–64.

Mallaby, Sebastian. 2022. *The Power Law: Venture Capital and the Making of the New Future.* New York: Penguin.

Manjoo, Farhad. 2022. "Private Equity Doesn't Want You to Read This." *New York Times*, August 4. https://www.nytimes.com/2022/08/04/opinion/private-equity-lays-waste.html.

March, James G. 1991. "Exploration and Exploitation in Organizational Learning." *Organization Science* 2(1):71–87.

Marx, Karl. 1978. *The Marx-Engels Reader*, edited by Robert C. Tucker. New York: W.W. Norton & Company.

Mason, Colin. 2009. "Venture Capital." Pp. 131–37 in *International Encyclopedia of Human Geography*, edited by Rob Kitchin and Nigel Thrift. Amsterdam: Elsevier.

McCabe, David. 2022. "Why Losing to Meta in Court May Still Be a Win for Regulators." *New York Times*, December 7. https://www.nytimes.com/2022/12/07/technology/meta-vr-antitrust-ftc.html.

McCarthy, Michael A. 2022. "A World Where Finance Is Democratic." *Noema*, April 12. https://www.noemamag.com/a-world-where-finance-is-democratic/.

McKay, Steven C. 2006. *Satanic Mills or Silicon Islands? The Politics of High-Tech Production in the Philippines.* Ithaca, NY: Cornell University Press.

Mears, Ashley. 2020. *Very Important People: Status and Beauty in the Global Party Circuit.* Princeton, NJ: Princeton University Press.

Meyer, John W., and Brian Rowan. 1977. "Institutionalized Organizations: Formal Structure as Myth and Ceremony." *American Journal of Sociology* 83:340–63.

Mickey, Ethel L. 2019. "When Gendered Logics Collide: Going Public and Restructuring in a High-Tech Organization." *Gender & Society* 33(4):509–33.

Mintz, Beth, and Michael Schwartz. 1990. "Capital Flows and the Process of Financial Hegemony." Pp. 203–26 in *Structures of Capital: The Social Organization of the Economy*, edited by Sharon Zukin and Paul DiMaggio. New York: Cambridge University Press.

Nader, Laura. 1972. "Up the Anthropologist—Perspectives Gained from Studying Up." Pp. 294–311 in *Reinventing Anthropology*, edited by Dell Hymes. New York: Pantheon.

Neely, Megan Tobias. 2022. *Hedged Out: Inequality and Insecurity on Wall Street*. Oakland: University of California Press.

Neely, Megan Tobias, and Donna Carmichael. 2021. "Profiting on Crisis: How Predatory Financial Investors Have Worsened Inequality in the Coronavirus Crisis." *American Behavioral Scientist* 65(12):1649–70.

Neff, Gina. 2012. *Venture Labor: Work and the Burden of Risk in Innovative Industries*. Cambridge, MA: MIT Press.

Neff, Gina, and David Stark. 2004. "Permanently Beta: Responsive Organization in the Internet Era." Pp. 173–188 in *Society Online: The Internet in Context*, edited by Philip N. Howard and Steve Jones. Thousand Oaks, CA: SAGE.

Newcomer, Eric. 2017. "In Video, Uber CEO Argues with Driver over Falling Fares." *Bloomberg*, February 28. https://www.bloomberg.com/news/articles/2017-02-28/in-video-uber-ceo-argues-with-driver-over-falling-fares.

Newcomer, Eric P., and Tom Dotan. 2014. "Startups Look to Philippines for Low-Tech Help." *The Information*, August 6. https://www.theinformation.com/articles/Startups-Look-to-Philippines-for-Low-Tech-Help.

Nicholas, Tom. 2019. *VC: An American History*. Cambridge, MA: Harvard University Press.

Noble, David F. 1984. *Forces of Production: A Social History of Industrial Automation*. New York: Oxford University Press.

Noble, Safiya Umoja. 2018. *Algorithms of Oppression: How Search Engines Reinforce Racism*. New York: New York University Press.

O'Mahony, Siobhan, and Beth A. Bechky. 2006. "Stretchwork: Managing the Career Progression Paradox in External Labor Markets." *The Academy of Management Journal* 49(5):918–41.

O'Mara, Margaret. 2019. *The Code: Silicon Valley and the Remaking of America*. New York: Penguin.

O'Neil, Cathy. 2016. *Weapons of Math Destruction: How Big Data Increases Inequality and Threatens Democracy*. New York: Broadway Books.

O'Reilly, Charles A. 1989. "Corporations, Culture, and Commitment: Motivation and Social Control in Organizations." *California Management Review* 31(4):9–25.

O'Reilly, Karen. 2009. *Key Concepts in Ethnography*. Thousand Oaks, CA: SAGE Publishing.

Osterman, Paul. 1999. *Securing Prosperity: The American Labor Market: How It Has Changed and What to Do about It*. Princeton, NJ: Princeton University Press.

Packer, George. 2013. "Change the World." *New Yorker*, May 20. https://www.newyorker.com/magazine/2013/05/27/change-the-world.

Park, Haemin Dennis, and Daniel Tzabbar. 2016. "Venture Capital, CEOs' Sources of Power, and Innovation Novelty at Different Life Stages of a New Venture." *Organization Science* 27(2):336–53.

Parreñas, Rhacel Salazar. 2015. *Servants of Globalization: Migration and Domestic Work*. 2nd ed. Stanford, CA: Stanford University Press.

Perrow, Charles. 1999. "Organizing to Reduce the Vulnerabilities of Complexity." *Journal of Contingencies and Crisis Management* 7(3):150–55.

Petre, Caitlin. 2021. *All the News That's Fit to Click: How Metrics Are Transforming the Work of Journalists*. Princeton, NJ: Princeton University Press.

Petriglieri, Gianpiero, Susan J. Ashford, and Amy Wrzesniewski. 2019. "Agony and Ecstasy in the Gig Economy: Cultivating Holding Environments for Precarious and Personalized Work Identities." *Administrative Science Quarterly* 64(1):124–70.

Pfeffer, Jeffrey, and Gerald Salancik. 1978. *The External Control of Organizations: A Resource Dependence Perspective*. New York: Harper & Row.

Philippines Department of Labor and Employment. n.d. "Summary of Daily Minimum Wage Rates per Wage Order, by Region Non-Agriculture (1989–Present)." Accessed June 15, 2021. https://nwpc.dole.gov.ph/stats/summary-of-daily-minimum-wage-rates-per-wage-order-by-region-non-agriculture–1989-present/.

Philippine Statistics Authority. 2013. "2012 Annual Labor and Employment Status." Accessed March 18, 2018. https://psa.gov.ph/content/2012-annual-labor-and-employment-status-annual-estimates–2012.

———. 2020. "2018 Family Income and Expenditure Survey." Accessed January 16, 2023. https://psa.gov.ph/sites/default/files/FIES%202018%20Final%20Report.pdf.

Philippon, Thomas, and Ariell Reshef. 2012. "Wages and Human Capital in the U.S. Finance Industry: 1909–2006." *Quarterly Journal of Economics* 127(4):1551–609.

Piketty, Thomas. 2014. *Capital in the Twenty-First Century*. Cambridge, MA: Harvard University Press.

Porter, Theodore M. 1995. *Trust in Numbers: The Pursuit of Objectivity in Science and Public Life*. Princeton, NJ: Princeton University Press.

Rafael, Vicente L. 2000. *White Love and Other Events in Filipino History*. Durham, NC: Duke University Press.

Rahman, K. Sabeel, and Kathleen Thelen. 2019. "The Rise of the Platform Business Model and the Transformation of Twenty-First-Century Capitalism." *Politics & Society* 47(2):177–204.

Rao, Aliya Hamid, and Megan Tobias Neely. 2019. "What's Love Got to Do with It? Passion and Inequality in White-Collar Work." *Sociology Compass* 13(12):1–14.

RateMyInvestor & Diversity VC. 2019. "Diversity in U.S. Startups." Accessed May 4, 2021. https://ratemyinvestor.com/DiversityVCReport_Final.pdf.

Ravenelle, Alexandra J. 2019. *Hustle and Gig: Struggling and Surviving in the Sharing Economy*. Oakland: University of California Press.

Reich, Adam, and Peter Bearman. 2018. *Working for Respect: Community and Conflict at Walmart*. New York: Columbia University Press.

Restubog, Simon Lloyd D., and Prashant Bordia. 2006. "Workplace Familism and Psychological Contract Breach in the Philippines." *Applied Psychology: An International Review* 55(4):563–85.

Ries, Eric. 2011. *The Lean Startup*. New York: Crown Business.

Rivera, Lauren A. 2015. *Pedigree: How Elite Students Get Elite Jobs*. Princeton, NJ: Princeton University Press.

Roberts, Sarah T. 2019. *Behind the Screen: Content Moderation in the Shadows of Social Media*. New Haven, CT: Yale University Press.

Rodriguez, Robyn. 2010. *Migrants for Export: How the Philippine State Brokers Labor to the World*. Minneapolis: University of Minnesota Press.

Romans, Andrew. 2013. *The Entrepreneurial Bible to Venture Capital: Inside Secrets from the Leaders in the Startup Game*. New York: McGraw Hill.

Rosenblat, Alex. 2018. *Uberland: How Algorithms Are Rewriting the Rules of Work*. Oakland: University of California Press.

Rosenbusch, Nina, Jan Brinckmann, and Verena Müller. 2013. "Does Acquiring Venture Capital Pay Off for the Funded Firms? A Meta-Analysis on the Relationship between Venture Capital Investment and Funded Firm Financial Performance." *Journal of Business Venturing* 28(3):335–53.

Sade-Beck, Liav. 2004. "Internet Ethnography: Online and Offline." *International Journal of Qualitative Methods* 3(2):45–51.

Sallaz, Jeffrey J. 2015. "Permanent Pedagogy: How Post-Fordist Firms Generate Effort but Not Consent." *Work and Occupations* 42(1):3–34.

———. 2019. *Lives on the Line: How the Philippines Became the World's Call Center Capital*. New York: Oxford University Press.

Salzinger, Leslie. 2003. *Genders in Production: Making Workers in Mexico's Global Factories*. Berkeley: University of California Press.

Saxenian, AnnaLee. 1994. *Regional Advantage: Culture and Competition in Silicon Valley and Route 128*. Cambridge, MA: Harvard University Press.

Schein, Edgar H. 2004. *Organizational Culture and Leadership*. 3rd edition. San Francisco: Jossey-Bass.

Scholz, Trebor, and Nathan Schneider, eds. 2016. *Ours to Hack and to Own: The Rise of Platform Cooperativism, a New Vision for the Future of Work and a Fairer Internet*. New York: OR Books.

Schor, Juliet B. 2020. *After the Gig: How the Sharing Economy Got Hijacked and How to Win It Back*. Oakland: University of California Press.

Scott, James C. 1972. "Patron-Client Politics and Political Change in Southeast Asia." *American Political Science Review* 66(1):91–113.

———. 1985. *Weapons of the Weak: Everyday Forms of Peasant Resistance*. New Haven, CT: Yale University Press.

———. 1999. *Seeing Like a State: How Certain Schemes to Improve the Human Condition Have Failed*. New Haven, CT: Yale University Press.

Seaver, Nick. 2022. *Computing Taste: Algorithms and the Makers of Music Recommendation*. Chicago: University of Chicago Press.

Shane, Scott A. 2003. *A General Theory of Entrepreneurship: The Individual-Opportunity Nexus*. Northampton, MA: Edward Elgar.

Shapin, Steven. 2008. *The Scientific Life: A Moral History of a Late Modern Vocation*. Chicago: University of Chicago Press.

Sharone, Ofer. 2004. "Engineering Overwork: Bell-Curve Management at a High-Tech Firm." Pp. 191–218 in *Fighting for Time: Shifting Boundaries of Work and Social Life*, edited by Cynthia Fuchs Epstein and Arne L. Kalleberg. New York: Russell Sage Foundation.

Sherman, Rachel. 2007. *Class Acts: Service and Inequality in Luxury Hotels*. Berkeley, CA: University of California Press.

Shestakofsky, Benjamin. 2015. "More Machinery, Less Labor? Jobs and Technological Change in the 19th and 21st Centuries." *Berkeley Journal of Sociology* 59:86–90.

———. 2017. "Working Algorithms: Software Automation and the Future of Work." *Work and Occupations* 44(4):376–423.

Shestakofsky, Benjamin, and Shreeharsh Kelkar. 2020. "Making Platforms Work: Relationship Labor and the Management of Publics." *Theory and Society* 49:863–96.

Shih, Johanna. 2006. "Circumventing Discrimination: Gender and Ethnic Strategies in Silicon Valley." *Gender & Society* 20(2):177–206.

Shklovski, Irina, and Janet Vertesi. 2013. "Un-Googling" Publications: The Ethics and Problems of Anonymization." *CHI 2013 Extended Abstracts*: 2169–78.

Silva, Jennifer. 2012. "Constructing Adulthood in an Age of Uncertainty." *American Sociological Review* 77(4):505–22.

Silver, Beverly J. 2003. *Forces of Labor: Workers' Movements and Globalization Since 1870*. New York: Cambridge University Press.

Silverman, Craig, Craig Timberg, Jeff Kao, and Jeremy B. Merrill. 2022. "Facebook Hosted Surge of Misinformation and Insurrection Threats in Months Leading Up to Jan. 6 Attack, Records Show." *ProPublica*, January 4. https://www.propublica.org/article/facebook-hosted-surge-of -misinformation-and-insurrection-threats-in-months-leading-up-to -jan-6-attack-records-show.

Smith-Doerr, Laurel. 2004. "Flexibility and Fairness: Effects of the Network Form of Organization on Gender Equity in Life Science Careers." *Sociological Perspectives* 47(1):25–54.

Snow, David, Louis Zurcher, and Gideon Sjoberg. "Interviewing by Comment: An Adjunct to the Direct Question." *Qualitative Sociology* 5(4):285–311

Snyder, Benjamin. 2016. *The Disrupted Workplace: Time and the Moral Order of Flexible Capitalism*. New York: Oxford University Press.

Somerville, Heather. 2020. "Tech IPO Bonanza Yields Riches for Venture-Capital Firms." *Wall Street Journal*, December 11. https://www.wsj.com /articles/tech-ipo-bonanza-yields-riches-for-venture-capital-firms-1160 7714745.

Srnicek, Nick. 2017. *Platform Capitalism*. Malden, MA: Polity.

Star, Susan Leigh, and Anselm Straus. 1999. "Layers of Silence, Arenas of Voice: The Ecology of Visible and Invisible Work." *Computer Supported Cooperative Work* 8(1):9–30.

Stark, David. 2009. *The Sense of Dissonance: Accounts of Worth in Economic Life*. Princeton, NJ: Princeton University Press.

Stearns, Linda Brewster. 1990. "Capital Market Effects on External Control of Corporations." Pp. 175–202 in *Structures of Capital: The Social Organization of the Economy*, edited by Sharon Zukin and Paul DiMaggio. New York: Cambridge University Press.

Stinchcombe, Arthur L. 1965. "Social Structure and Organizations." Pp. 142–193 in *Handbook of Organizations*, edited by James March. New York: Rand McNally.

Stout, Hilary. 2015. "Amazon, Google and More Are Drawn to Home Services Market." *New York Times*, April 12. https://www.nytimes.com/2019/10/08 /technology/silicon-valley-startup-profit.html.

Stovel, Katherine, and Lynette Shaw. 2012. "Brokerage." *Annual Review of Sociology* 38:139–58.

Swidler, Ann, and Susan Cotts Watkins. 2017. *A Fraught Embrace: The Romance and Reality of AIDS Altruism in Africa*. Princeton, NJ: Princeton University Press.

Tayeb, Zahra. 2021. "Mark Zuckerberg, Jeff Bezos, Elon Musk, and Other Billionaires Reportedly Made More Than $360 Billion during the

Pandemic." *Business Insider*, March 13. https://www.businessinsider.com/tech-billionaires-zuckerberg-bezos-musk-360-billion-covid-19-pandemic-2021-3.

Teare, Gené. 2022. "Global Venture Funding and Unicorn Creation in 2021 Shattered All Records." *Crunchbase News*, January 5. https://news.crunchbase.com/news/global-vc-funding-unicorns-2021-monthly-recap/.

Thompson, Clive. 2019. "When Workers Control the Code." *Wired*, April 22. https://www.wired.com/story/when-workers-control-gig-economy/

Thrift, Nigel. 2001. "'It's the Romance, Not the Finance, That Makes the Business Worth Pursuing': Disclosing a New Market Culture." *Economy and Society* 30(4):412–32.

Timmermans, Stefan, and Iddo Tavory. 2012. "Theory Construction in Qualitative Research: From Grounded Theory to Abductive Analysis." *Sociological Theory* 30(3):167–86.

Turco, Catherine J. 2012. "Difficult Decoupling: Employee Resistance to the Commercialization of Personal Settings." *American Journal of Sociology* 118(2):380–419.

———. 2016. *The Conversational Firm: Rethinking Bureaucracy in the Age of Social Media*. New York: Columbia University Press.

Tushman, Michael L., and Charles A. O'Reilly III. 1996. "Ambidextrous Organizations: Managing Evolutionary and Revolutionary Change." *California Management Review* 38(4):8–30.

Uber Technologies, n.d. "The History of Uber." Accessed January 13, 2022. https://www.uber.com/newsroom/history/.

Useem, Michael. 1993. *Executive Defense: Shareholder Power and Corporate Reorganization*. Cambridge, MA: Harvard University Press.

Useem, Jerry. 2019. "The Stock-Buyback Swindle." *Atlantic*, August 2019. https://www.theatlantic.com/magazine/archive/2019/08/the-stock-buyback-swindle/592774/.

Vallas, Steven, and Juliet B. Schor. 2020. "What Do Platforms Do? Understanding the Gig Economy." *Annual Review of Sociology* 46:273–294.

van de Ven, Andrew H., and Marshall Scott Poole. 1995. "Explaining Development and Change in Organizations." *Academy of Management Review* 20(3):510–40.

van Doorn, Niels, and Julie Yujie Chan. 2021. "Odds Stacked against Workers: Datafied Gamification on Chinese and American Food Delivery Platforms." *Socio-Economic Review* 19(4):1345–67.

Van Maanen, John, and Gideon Kunda. 1989. "Real Feelings: Emotional Expression and Organizational Culture." *Research in Organizational Behavior* 11:43–103.

Vertesi, Janet. 2021. *Shaping Science: Organizations, Decisions, and Culture on NASA's Teams*. Chicago: University of Chicago Press.

Vertesi, Janet A., Adam Goldstein, Diana Enriquez, and Larry Liu. 2020. "Pre-Automation: Insourcing and Automating the Gig Economy." *Sociologica* 14(3):167–93.

Vinsel, Lee, and Andrew L. Russell. 2020. *The Innovation Delusion: How Our Obsession with the New Has Disrupted the Work That Matters Most*. New York: Currency.

Viswanathan, Manoj. 2023. "Money for Nothing: The Qualified Small Business Stock Capital Gains Exclusion Is a Giveaway to Wealthy Investors, Startup Founders, and Their Employees." Washington Center for Equitable Growth, June. https://equitablegrowth.org/wp-content/uploads/2023/06/060823-QSBS-ib.pdf.

Vita, Stephen. 2022. "The Companies That Are Funding Uber and Lyft." *Investopedia*, September 15, 2022. https://www.investopedia.com/articles/markets/011516/companies-are-funding-uber-and-lyft.asp.

Wakabayashi, Daisuke. 2019. "Google's Shadow Work Force: Temps Who Outnumber Full-Time Employees." *New York Times*, May 28. https://www.nytimes.com/2019/05/28/technology/google-temp-workers.html.

Wall Street Journal. 2021. "How Big Tech Got Even Bigger." February 6. https://www.wsj.com/articles/how-big-tech-got-even-bigger-11612587632.

Wasserman, Noam. 2017. "The Throne vs. the Kingdom: Founder Control and Value Creation in Startups." *Strategic Management Journal* 38(2):255–77.

Weber, Max. 2001. *The Protestant Ethic and the Spirit of Capitalism*. New York: Routledge.

West, Lois A. 1997. *Militant Labor in the Philippines*. Philadelphia: Temple University Press.

Wiedeman, Reeves. 2020. *Billion Dollar Loser: The Epic Rise and Spectacular Fall of Adam Neumann and WeWork*. Boston: Little, Brown and Company.

Wilhelm, Alex. 2017. "A Look Back in IPO: Microsoft, the Software Success." *TechCrunch*, August 8, 2017. https://techcrunch.com/2017/08/08/a-look-back-in-ipo-microsoft-the-software-success/.

World Bank. 2021. "GDP Growth (Annual %)—United States." Accessed July 30, 2021. https://data.worldbank.org/indicator/NY.GDP.MKTP.KD.ZG?locations=US.

Wright, Erik Olin. 2010. *Envisioning Real Utopias*. New York: Verso.

Wynn, Alison T., and Shelley J. Correll. 2018. "Puncturing the Pipeline: Do Technology Companies Alienate Women in Recruiting Sessions?" *Social Studies of Science* 48(1):149–64.

Yoffie, David B., Annabelle Gawer, and Michael A. Cusumano. 2019. "A Study of More Than 250 Platforms Reveals Why Most Fail." *Harvard Business Review*, May 29, 2019. https://hbr.org/2019/05/a-study-of-more-than-250-platforms-reveals-why-most-fail.

Zott, Christoph, and Quy Nguyen Huy. 2007. "How Entrepreneurs Use Symbolic Management to Acquire Resources." *Administrative Science Quarterly* 52(1):70–105.

Zuboff, Shoshana. 1988. *In the Age of the Smart Machine: The Future of Work and Power.* New York: Basic Books.

———. 2018. *The Age of Surveillance Capitalism: The Fight for a Human Future at the New Frontier of Power.* New York: PublicAffairs.

Zukin, Sharon. 2020. *The Innovation Complex: Cities, Tech, and the New Economy.* New York: Oxford University Press.

Index

Founded in 1893,
UNIVERSITY OF CALIFORNIA PRESS
publishes bold, progressive books and journals
on topics in the arts, humanities, social sciences,
and natural sciences—with a focus on social
justice issues—that inspire thought and action
among readers worldwide.

The UC PRESS FOUNDATION
raises funds to uphold the press's vital role
as an independent, nonprofit publisher, and
receives philanthropic support from a wide
range of individuals and institutions—and from
committed readers like you. To learn more, visit
ucpress.edu/supportus.

Milton Keynes UK
Ingram Content Group UK Ltd.
UKHW010701190624
444195UK00003BB/36